Contents

D1823740

Introduction

Who is the course for?

World Club 1 is the first of a series of four levels for secondary school students. The syllabuses for all four levels have been carefully worked out to develop and extend students' English. At the same time it has a lot of revision and recycling in each level, enabling students to consolidate what they have learnt.

General principles

1 Themes and Tasks

For young learners, motivation and interest are crucial factors in the learning process. *World Club* is based around themes which have been chosen for their interest and relevance to this age group. Themes have not been dictated by language.

Each theme-based module builds up to a final oral and written activity or project, enabling students to carry out extensive real world communication, which is enriched by both the thematic and linguistic input that they have received throughout the module.

There are three main thematic elements in *World Club*. Students can use English to find out about the world; they can develop their imagination and have fun in English; and they can relate English to their own lives and environments.

2 Bridge from primary

As the first in a secondary course book series, a conscious effort has been made to integrate primary and secondary approaches to language learning. This is reflected in the organisation of the book, in the treatment of language and in skills development.

This "bridge" approach can be seen in language. Key grammar areas that students will have seen at primary are revised systematically in a more explicit and conscious way in the first part of the book. This will enable students to build a firm grammatical base for future years without having to start from the beginning whenever they go into a new cycle.

At the same time, themes link in with primary approaches and develop towards a more secondary feel. The first part of the book deals with topics that are immediately related to students' own lives: Families; Cartoons; Hobbies; Parties. The second half of the book contains broader thematic elements related to the wider world: Planet Earth; Villages; The Wild West; Travel.

3 Fun and variety

It is very important for lower secondary students to enjoy learning English and there is a large fun element in *World Club*. Such activities include a wide variety of games, such as guessing games, grammar games and memory games. There are also songs, quizzes, puzzles and stories, as well as plenty of opportunities for students to be creative and to use their own imagination.

Variety is also essential for maintaining interest. Therefore, within each module, the broad theme has three different topic focuses. Also, there is a wide variety of activity types throughout the course, and no fixed lesson format.

4 Practicality and flexibility

World Club is a course which is highly user-friendly and achievable in real classroom conditions, including the following:

- achievable objectives-clearly outlined in the editorial project
- clear and systematic vocabulary presentation
- plenty of material in the Student's Book, Activity Book and Teacher's Resource File to deal with diversity
- clear, motivating and workable lessons
- communicative activities at the end of each module that are achievable and which build students' confidence
- thorough consolidation lessons at the end of each unit with lexical and grammatical references
- plenty of revision and extension material in the Students' Book, the Activity Book and the Teacher's Resource File
- a special *Language Work-out* feature in the Teacher's Resource File providing extra practice
- a complete and up-to-date assessment programme giving the teacher total support in the difficult area of assessment
- a mini-dictionary in the Student's Book
- a *Teacher's HELP* in this introduction which gives practical suggestions about using the material

These features give teachers the support that they need to use the material in the classroom. The modular nature of the course plus all of the extra material provided also means that the course is extremely flexible and can easily be adapted to widely differing classroom conditions.

WORLD CLUB

1

TEACHER'S RESOURCE FILE

Michael Harris   David Mower
Mady Musiol

Longman

Pearson Education Limited,
Edinburgh Gate
Harlow
Essex CM20 2JE
England
and Associated Companies throughout the World.

www.longman-elt.com

First published 2000
Third impression 2001

Set in 12pt Footlight Light and Eurocrat

Printed in Spain by Graficas Estella

ISBN 0582 34982 6

Illustrated by Amy, Bernabeu, Enrique Bernabeu, Fernando Cano, Victor Diaz, Robin Edmonds, Fernando Gómez, Phil Healey, Alberto de Hoyos, Adriana Juárez, Chris Pavely and Chris Simpson.

Acknowledgements

The authors and publishers would like to thank Val Emslie for writing additional materials for World Club 1.

We are also very grateful to the following people and institutions for their contribution:
Mónica Marinakis and her team from AACI; Marta Moure and Liliana Luna from Asoc. Ex-Alumnas del Prof. en Lenguas Vivas J.R.F; Nora Gervasio, Patricia Ugo, Gabriela Atrio y alumnos del Colegio Monseñor Dillon.

We are grateful to the following for permission to reproduce copyright material:
© Jobete Music/Stone Diamond/EMI Songs España, S.L. for the lyrics to 'Dancing in the Street' (Ivy Jo Hunter, William Stevenson and Marvin Gaye); © 1969 Tro Essex Music Ltd., Tro Essex Músic España S.L. for the lyrics to 'Space Oddity' by David Bowie; Pearson Education for the adapted song 'Billy the Kid' from Pathway 4 Teacher's Guide by Nicolas Hawke and Donald Dallas © Longman Group UK Ltd (1985).

Photo Acknowledgements

We are grateful to the following for permission to reproduce copyright photographs:
AGE for pages:12 (bottom left), 60 (right) & 77 (bottom). Britain on view for pages: 4 (a), 58 & 60 (left). Chus del Águila for page 8 (right). Columbia for page 67 (bottom). G. Boden for pages: 5 (top right) & 91. Image Bank for pages: 4(h), 28 (right), & 32 (right). Incolor for pages: 6, 8 (background), 12 (top left & right), 13, 32 (left), 47 (background), 57 & 77 (middle). Javier Jaime for page 5. Longman Photographic Unit for pages: 4 (g), 27, 28 (left) & 62. Ronald Grant Archive for page 67 (top). Stock Market for page 77 (top). Superstock for page 42 (top). Telegraph Colour Library for page 52 (top left). Tony Stone for pages: 10, 52 (bottom left) & 52 (right). Zardoya for pages: 4 (c, b), 7 (left), 8 (left), 27 (bottom right), 37 & 77 (middle middle).

5 Skills

Throughout the course, half of the lessons are skills-based, with fluency the primary goal. The four skills are developed systematically in the following ways:

Speaking

Students are encouraged to develop this skill through activities where they can communicate freely and develop fluency in English. Effective communication, rather than accuracy, is the goal and students are given plenty of help and guidance. At this level, there is a particular emphasis on giving and asking about personal information, with personalisation activities and surveys as well as some basic role-play situations. Particular attention is also paid to the use of classroom language by students. Guessing games, memory games, describe and draw activities and quizzes are also common.

Finally, each module builds up to an oral activity giving students opportunities to participate in more extensive (but still guided) communication. These exercises are carefully staged and allow students to use the language they have acquired throughout the module.

Pronunciation is dealt with systematically and in this level more complex areas are looked at such as sentence stress and intonation. There is also a contrastive element and pronunciation boxes deal with the particular problems of learners of English.

Listening

Texts in the first level of the series are closely graded and controlled. Students are gradually introduced to the extensive listening activities that are common in the series: gist listening and listening for specific information. Monologues, dialogues and radio programmes are the most frequently used text types. Stories, songs and quizzes can also be found in the *Fluency* lesson of each module.

Reading

In the same way, reading texts are closely graded and new lexical input is carefully controlled. However, realistic text types are provided throughout: cartoons; letters; stories; non-fiction. Extensive tasks are given priority, with plenty of practice in prediction, skimming and scanning for specific information. Work on vocabulary not only aims to prepare students for texts but for dealing with new vocabulary they find in them. In this they are helped by the mini-dictionary.

Writing

Activities at this level are very carefully guided and students are not expected to produce long pieces of writing. Specific sub-skills such as linking, punctuation and spelling are systematically developed in the Student's Book and the Activity Book. The written activities or projects at the end of each module introduce students to process writing (brainstorming, planning, drafting and editing their own work). These tasks also give students a chance to write more freely and imaginatively, using the language they have acquired throughout the module.

Writing tasks also provide the ideal springboard for project work – see *Teacher's HELP 41* for practical advice about project work.

6 Grammar

The modular structure of the material and the approach to grammar in *Worldwide* enable constant recycling and revision to take place at the same time as a gradual focus on new key language. The first level begins by going over structures which students will have seen at primary before moving any further. Then, throughout the material there is constant recycling of structures studied in the level and in previous levels.

There is also a contrastive element in the approach to grammar. There is a particular emphasis on common problem grammar areas and editing of common mistakes is a systematic language practice activity.

There are two *Language Focus* lessons in each module. Target input is controlled and graded, with new language items previewed, presented and practised. Presentation of new items is varied, but throughout students are encouraged to work out rules for themselves, to be aware of basic grammatical terms and to use them appropriately. The input of grammatical terminology is carefully controlled at this level, so that learners gradually build up their knowledge of the language.

There are plenty of both spoken and written practice activities to follow up the language presented. In addition, the speaking and writing activities in skills lessons provide ample opportunities for using this language communicatively. There is also plenty of further guided practice in the Activity Book, the *Consolidation* lesson and the *Language Workout* in the Teacher's Resource File.

The *Test Yourself* feature at the end of each module in the Activity Book gives students the chance to monitor their own learning of key structures presented in the module. Students can also use the *Grammar Reference* at the end of each unit in the Student's Book to check on target structures in the book.

Introduction

Finally, in the *Grammar File* in the Activity Book students can keep their own, active record of grammatical structures and rules as they go along. At the same time, they can use the file to relate new structures to the grammar of their own language.

7 Vocabulary

Learners are given considerable help to deal with lexical input in this course. The *Keyword* boxes in the lead-in to each module activate or introduce the key vocabulary centred around the module theme. *Keyword* boxes in lessons then present important vocabulary, either to help students deal with listening and reading texts or to help them in speaking and writing activities. Students often do matching activities using pictures, definitions or synonyms to work out the meaning of words themselves.

This key vocabulary is then practised in the Activity Book and in the *Consolidation* lesson at the end of each module. Finally, a *Keyword Check* in the *Module Check* at the end of each module gives students a checklist of important lexical items looked at.

Functional language is also looked at lexically unless there are structural problems, in which case it is included in *Language Focus* (for example, physical description). Useful phrases and expressions are practised in the Activity Book and listed in the *Keyword Check*.

Lexical features are focused on systematically in the course, in the Activity Book or in the *Consolidation* lesson. These include activities on lexical sets, collocation, compound nouns, spelling, synonyms and antonyms.

Learner training activities also develop students' capacity for storing and learning new lexis independently. Throughout the course students are encouraged to use vocabulary books, not only for storage of words and expressions, but for revising, checking and learning vocabulary.

The mini-dictionary provides another useful resource for students dealing with lexis themselves.

8 Learner training

Students of this age group are long-term learners and learner training is crucial. In this course they have opportunities to reflect on their learning and assess their own progress.

The first three lessons of this level (*Learning to Learn*), prepare students for using the material, to deal with vocabulary and finally focus on classroom language –

both receptive and productive. This "zero" module is then followed up by other similar activities that develop study skills – in particular the ability to deal with new language.

At the start of each module students are given a very clear idea of the objectives of the module, in terms of language and skills. Then, the *Module Check* enables learners to think about what they have learnt, in terms of grammar and vocabulary. Activities suggested in the Teacher's Book also give them a chance to reflect on how they have dealt with aspects of communication in the four skills.

The *Test Yourself* in the Activity Book enables students to test the vocabulary and grammar that they have learnt throughout the module.

The *Mini-dictionary* is also a useful tool for learners to be used independently, when reading texts and doing grammar exercises.

All of these different activities help students to become more active and autonomous and to take responsibility for their own learning.

9 Dealing with diversity

This course caters for diversity amongst students in a number of ways. Firstly, the variety of topics in the course means that all students can find something that they are interested in. In addition, equal opportunities are offered to students with different learning styles, drawing on non-linguistic skills such as knowledge about other subjects, an ability to draw, competence in logical thinking and puzzles, etc. Pair and groupwork encourages students of different abilities to work together and learn from each other in these activities.

Reading and listening tasks are often graded – allowing weaker students to answer some questions and stronger students to be stretched.

The *World Club Magazine* is an important resource for students who finish earlier than others. In each coursebook lesson students are directed to material at the back of the book, which closely corresponds to the lesson in terms of both language and topic. The magazine contains a wide variety of optional activities such as reading, writing, quizzes, word games and puzzles.

There are also reinforcement and extension activities both in the Activity Book and the Teacher's Resource File. The former activities are suitable for students who fall into one of the following categories:

• Students with particular difficulty in acquiring linguistic concepts. *Reinforcement* or *revision*

4

activities aim to bring these students up to the general level of the course.

- Students with different levels in specific areas who need further practice to bring them up to the level of the class.
- Students with learning disabilities who are not able to reach the level of the rest of the class. Exercises which require non-linguistic skills such as puzzles, questionnaires, underlining and drawing give these students fun activities which cover language at a basic level.

The *Extension* activities are designed to be motivating and fun for fast learners who tend to finish early. In the Activity Book, extension activities include reading stories, puzzles, and games. The more able students can do these while the teacher helps weaker students with *Reinforcement* activities.

Finally, the self-assessment in *World Club (Module Check)* encourages students to see their own progress in individual terms and has a particular emphasis on attitudes towards learning.

10 Introducing Social and Moral Values

Moral and Social Development

Students are encouraged to actively participate in classroom activities and respect the opinions of others (for example, to be courteous, to use the polite forms of language, to wait their turn). In addition, other aspects are also dealt with consistently in each module, for example, respect and tolerance within family relationships (Families), meeting people at parties (Parties), politeness when meeting people you do not know (Planet Earth) and awareness of the importance of communities (Villages).

Peace Studies

Students are encouraged to be tolerant and respectful of fellow students in their daily relationships and co-operative in group and pairwork. Students will also look at tolerance and respect for people from different cultures and their customs (Families, Parties, Planet Earth, Villages), the effects of war on peaceful communities (The Wild West), and the cultural diversity and distinct national identities within Britain (Villages).

Health and Sex Education

World Club 1 gives plenty of opportunities to develop awareness of the importance of a healthy lifestyle with active free time activities (Hobbies, Villages). Students are also made aware of the main functions of the parts of the body and a healthy attitude to the opposite sex is promoted.

Non-sexism

Teachers should ensure that both sexes participate actively in all the activities. Care has been taken to avoid sexual stereotypes in *World Club*, and the illustrations and examples can be used to develop this theme. Topics looked at include: family relationships and the role of both mother and father (Families), equality of men and women in terms of employment (Villages) and the active role of women in history (The Wild West).

Protection of the Environment

Attitudes of respect and curiosity towards nature and the protection of animals are encouraged. The following topics reinforce the main objective: life in rural communities (Families, Villages), animals and animal families around the world (Families), the planet – flora, fauna, climate, and protection of the environment (Planet Earth).

Consumer Education

Attitudes of analysis and control are developed towards consumer items, as well as an emphasis on the need to consume goods and services according to our needs, thus avoiding unnecessary expenditure. Students are also encouraged to develop a critical attitude towards the way leisure time is used (Hobbies).

Road Safety

Students learn about different kinds of transport and the importance of safety on the roads (Travel) and are encouraged to respect fellow travellers and pedestrians.

11 Sociocultural Elements

There is a systematic development of students' awareness of target English-speaking cultures as well of other cultures around the world. Particular emphasis is given to making students aware of how people live together (Families, Villages), their customs and festivals (Parties) and their history (The Wild West, Travel).

There is also an important emphasis given to helping students deal with cultural differences in communication. At this level, particular importance is given to politeness in oral English, both in classroom language and social occasions (Parties, Planet Earth).

12 Formative assessment

A detailed system of continual assessment is provided, enabling teacher and students to monitor progress throughout the course. Suggestions are made for informal assessment and assessment tasks are provided which test both skills and language input. Both kinds of assessment are then linked in with the systematic self-assessment in the course (see the *Assessment* section).

Organisation of the course

What does the course consist of?

- Students' Book
- Teacher's Resource File (including assessment tasks)
- Cassettes
- Activity Book

How is the Students' Book organised?

There is an introductory module and eight other modules, each based around a theme.

The introductory module has three short lessons which familiarise students with tasks and activities used in the book and contain a sizeable learner training element.

The other modules have the following structure:

- lead-in page (introducing the topic and key vocabulary)
- three lessons – one of which is skills-based and two of which include explicit language focuses and controlled practice
- a *Fluency* lesson including oral and written activities and extra listening
- a *Consolidation* lesson with extra language practice
- a *Module Check* including a *Grammar Reference* summarizing the new structures and a *Keyword Check* with the important words from the module

The *World Club Magazine* is at the end of the Students' Book. Numbers in the magazine correspond directly to the number of lessons in the book.

How are lessons organised?

Each lesson provides at least enough material for an average classroom period of about fifty minutes and some will take up to two classroom periods. Here are the regular symbols used:

	Speaking activities
	Writing activities
	Listening activities using the cassette
	Learner training activities
	Activities which focus on key vocabulary

Lesson formats

Skills-based lessons have no fixed format of activities and the skills are integrated. However, there is a balance between receptive skills, where students are exposed to authentic language input, and productive skills, where students often have the opportunity to use language that has appeared in previous *Language Focus* lessons, with fluency the main objective.

Language Focus lessons follow a basic pattern of providing context, presentation and practice. Warmers and skills activities start off the lessons to provide a context for target language. These are followed by the *Language Focus* boxes which focus on new language items and where students work out or complete rules.

Fluency lessons usually start with a written task, followed by a speaking activity, plus the optional listening activity (normally a song or quiz). *Consolidation* lessons consist of grammar practice activities, vocabulary practice exercises and pronunciation activities.

The final page of each module includes the *Module Check* with a *Grammar Reference* – a clear summary of the new grammar – plus the *Keyword Check* – a systematised record of the most important vocabulary from the module.

What is on the cassettes?

All the listening texts and pronunciation exercises from the Students' Book are on the cassettes and are signalled by the cassette symbol. The transcripts of the listening texts are in the Teacher's Resource File.

How is the Activity Book organised?

The Activity Book provides further practice of the new language introduced and developed in the Students' Book, recycles language that students have studied at earlier levels of the course, and gives further skills development. In addition, there are learner training activities and an important fun element.

Each lesson in the Activity Book corresponds to one in the Students' Book and there are specific references in the teacher's notes for each lesson to back-up activities in the Activity Book. The activities are as follows:

Language practice

After each *Language Focus* lesson there are exercises in the corresponding lesson of the Activity Book, giving further practice. There are also further *Language Practice* exercises in the following Skills lessons, especially when the new structure presents difficulties of form or usage. Practice activities generally concentrate on the most difficult aspects of new language from a contrastive point of view.

Vocabulary

These activities focus on and practise key vocabulary from the Students' Book lessons (lexical sets and lexical features such as wordbuilding).

Spelling

Linked with vocabulary activities are spots which systematically focus on problem spelling areas.

Revision

The Activity Book also recycles very basic language that students should have studied at primary but need to revise. Target language is outlined in a box and is followed by practice activities.

Extension

The extension activities are linked with Activity Book lessons in the same way as the *World Club Magazine* is linked with Students' Book lessons. Activities include writing, reading and fun activities such as games and puzzles. This material is for those students who need stretching and who do not need to do basic revision.

Punctuation

Linked to the writing activities in the final tasks are activities that focus systematically on elements of punctuation (for example, use of commas, capital letters, etc.).

How is the Teacher's Resource File organised?

The teacher's notes are organised in the following way:

Module objectives

A list of objectives at the beginning of each module. The *Moral and Social Values* to be developed in the lesson are also indicated.

Background

These are notes giving supplementary information about the topic of the lesson and explaining references made in texts as well as providing sociocultural information where necessary.

Activities

At the beginning of each activity the aim and type of activity is stated clearly (for example, Reading/Individual).

Reinforcement and extension activities

At the end of each lesson there is always either a Reinforcement or Extension activity which gives additional practice or extends the theme of the lesson.

How does assessment work?

An integrated system of continual assessment is provided which monitors progress over the academic year. Assessment tasks are related directly to the themes and test both language input and skills.

Teachers are given permission to photocopy them, and only these, for use in the class.

For productive skills, detailed assessment criteria are provided, which will help to increase the reliability of assessment. Each suggested assessment task takes approximately twenty minutes.

Teacher's Help

50 Practical ideas for using *World Club.*

Starting off

1 Prioritise when planning. Make a list of three or four absolute priorities. If you are short of time, leave out activities not related to them.

2 Contribute to topic content yourself. Read through a module and choose topic areas you are particularly interested in. Think of input that you could add to the module.

3 Don't be afraid to cut. Adapt the material to your own students and don't feel that you have to finish every lesson in the book. Key language is continually revised and extended.

4 Start each lesson with a warmer. The Lead-in page serves as an introduction to the topic and generates interest and enthusiasm.

Classroom management

5 Establish the right environment. Decorate the room with posters of Britain and other English-speaking countries. Put up material produced by students, so that students feel proud of what they have done and put up posters with useful classroom language.

6 Work on classroom language. The *Learning to Learn* module has work on classroom language. Write key examples and put them up on the walls. Check and practice classroom language using activities like the Simple Simon game.

Dealing with diversity

7 Encourage an individual view of progress. Use an initial diagnostic self-assessment and the *Module Checks* to make students aware that their progress and their positive attitudes to learning are as important as their final level.

8 Make students aware of their strengths. Intelligence is multiple and everyone has strengths and weaknesses. Make it clear to students that you value more than just their linguistic ability.

9 Focus on achievement. Focus on what students have been able to achieve rather than the mistakes they make, especially with weaker students.

10 Use the reinforcement and extension material. There is a large amount of material aimed at helping teachers to deal with diversity which can be used either in class or for homework.

11 Use classroom readers. Classroom readers enable students to work at their own level and at their own pace. Create a space of 15 or 20 minutes every week and go around and help them and talk about what they are reading. When they have finished, get students to report on what they have read.

12 Use groupwork. In groupwork students can work together doing as much as they can.

Grammar

13 Start by finding out what they know. At the beginning of the course ask learners to write down as much as they can about themselves and their lives. This will give you a good idea of their knowledge of structures. At primary level many students will have used structures without focusing on them in terms of grammatical structure. This course enables students to start building up a systematic and explicit understanding of English grammar.

14 Remember that learning is not a tidy process. Do not feel that you cannot move on simply because students continue to make mistakes. Mistakes are part of the learning process.

15 Don't explain everything. Focus on meaning in reading texts and make students aware that they do not have to be familiar with all the language to understand the general meaning of the text.

16 Let them work it out. Rather than start off by trying to explain grammar points to students, use the find-the-rule activities which get students to work things out for themselves. If students still have problems your explanations can help them out.

Vocabulary

17 Vocabulary learning is individual. Learners need to decide what words are important for them. The key to this approach is the vocabulary books which students establish at the start of the course and complete during the year.

18 Include functions. Unless there are particular problems of form, treat functional language lexically. Get students to include a space in their vocabulary book for useful expressions related to each theme.

19 Monitor vocabulary books. Your assessment should take into account the organisation of lexis, how easy it is to find your way around the book, what information is given, whether examples provide a context for words and how much is included.

20 Activate thematic vocabulary. A good way of doing this is by writing up a vocabulary network on the board and getting students to add as many words as possible.

21 Get students to use the mini-dictionary. The mini-dictionary is an essential tool for learner independence. Learners can use it when doing keyword activities in the lead-in or in module lessons and to help them with keywords in reading texts.

22 Use keyword boxes to build confidence. Keyword boxes aim to help and guide students. They either revise or present key vocabulary related to the topic of the lesson at the beginning or focus on key lexis and lexical features from reading texts.

23 Use practice activities to systematise vocabulary. The practice activities in the Activity Book and the *Consolidation* lesson focus on lexical features which can help students see patterns and help them boost their own vocabulary.

Pronunciation

24 "Troubleshoot" difficult sounds. The pronunciation syllabus in *World Club* focuses on sounds that are difficult for learners. These are looked at in the Pronunciation section in the *Consolidation* lesson.

25 Choral drilling. It allows students to practice sounds, words or longer sentences without any problems they have being apparent to others.

Speaking

26 Build confidence. The key is to make students realise that participation and effort are the most important thing. They must also be aware that this does not necessarily mean talking in front of the class. Shy students can participate successfully in pair and groupwork.

27 Use students' L1 selectively. There are occasions when the use of students' L1 in the class can be beneficial, to relate grammar points to students' own language or to discuss learning problems.

28 Don't correct during speaking activities. Errors which do not interfere with communication should be tolerated. It is useful to go round the class during an oral activity listing inaccuracies, then go over some of them with the whole class afterwards.

29 Monitor groupwork. Managing groupwork can be difficult. Make sure that pairs and groups are working and ensure mixed ability pairs.

30 Give marks for oral performance. Unless you assess oral performance, students will feel it is a waste of time. See the assessment section on page 95.

Listening

31 Build confidence through strategies. A particularly important strategy is the tolerance of ambiguity. Reduce panic by getting students to think about what they have understood and not worry so much about what they have not understood.

32 Do as much practice as possible. Students only improve their listening through practice. Listening is also vital for general language acquisition.

33 Focus on task achievement. Activities are carefully graded so that even when a text is difficult, students can successfully complete the task even when they do not understand every word.

34 Assess listening. Even though students are often afraid of listening tests, these are vital to make students aware of the importance of listening and also to monitor their progress.

Reading

35 Develop awareness of how we read. After reading a text get students to evaluate texts and activities in terms of interest and difficulty as well as commenting on how students dealt with vocabulary.

36 Build up interest before reading. See the ideas for pre-reading activities in the Teacher's Notes and those in the coursebook. Students do not only sometimes need help with key vocabulary, they also need to be motivated to read.

37 Get students to focus on gist. In extensive reading activities students do not have to understand every word of the text, they only need to work out the general idea or to extract specific information. As for listening, tasks are carefully graded so that they are always within students' reach. In this way they gain confidence in dealing with texts.

38 Don't go through all the new words in a text. It can sometimes be tempting to go through all the new vocabulary in a reading text. In the long run this is not helpful as it makes students believe that they need to know all the words to understand a text. The keyword activities after texts focus on lexical sets or important lexical features and should provide plenty of contextualised vocabulary work.

Writing

39 Give students time to work in class. Doing work on final written tasks in class is very useful to help students with problems and to ensure that they go through the different stages in the process.

40 Make sure tasks/projects are read. It is important for other students to read final tasks so that students see them as more than mere products to be handed in to the teacher and marked.

41 Do project work. All of the final writing tasks can be extended into full-scale project work which is motivating and fun for students. Here are some ideas:

Families: Students could do a project about their own extended family, including photos or drawings and a family tree with a couple of sentences about each person.

Cartoons: In groups, students could produce a comic with short cartoon strips. Alternatively, they could use an existing cartoon strip and write their own version by sticking papers over the words.

Hobbies: Students could make a poster about their own/their group's hobbies, or do a presentation to the class.

Parties: Students could actually hold a party, bringing in soft drinks, music, etc. and speaking in English.

Planet Earth: In groups, you could extend the activity to inventing an alien planet poster – different students responsible for describing the planet, drawing a map, describing daily life, etc.

Villages: In groups, they could produce a 'tourist brochure' where their descriptions could include more detailed information about the places, the local festivals, how to get their, etc.

The Wild West: Students could make a series of posters with texts and pictures. Assign different descriptions to each group: an indian village, a settler's home, a biography of a famous person, a typical western story

Travel: the story can be extended and students can add pictures and maps to it.

Learner training

42 See learner training as a long-term investment. The aim is for students to develop the motivation and the skills to become independent and active learners. Only by carrying out systematic learner training over a period of months will you see a substantial growth in students' ability to work independently.

43 Establish the basics in the first two weeks. In addition to preparing students for dealing with communication, the zero module aims to provide students with the basics for working on their own.

44 Give students plenty of time to organise vocabulary books. Vocabulary books are one of the keys to independence. Give students time to actually organise their notebooks, either by topic or alphabetically and give them hints about how many pages to leave for each letter or to leave a few blank pages to list useful expressions, etc.

45 Make students aware of module objectives. When starting off a module, focus on the list of module objectives and get students to choose two or three that are priorities for them.

46 Spend time in class discussing the Module Check. As well as getting students to reflect on their own learning the diary can give you useful feedback about the lessons and the material.

47 Link self-assessment with your assessment. At the end of term get students to do a final self-assessment to compare it with yours, and if you have time, discuss the two with students individually.

The Activity Book

48 Go through homework as quickly as possible. Exercises in the Activity Book can be set for homework and these can be gone through the following day in the class. One way of making this quicker and more learner-centred is by photocopying answers from the teacher's notes and getting students to check their own work.

49 Use the Activity Book to help cater for diversity. You will find that certain students finish much more quickly than others: they can then be asked to do extension tasks in the Activity Book while the slower students catch up.

The Teacher's Notes

50 Add your own ideas and material to this file. These notes are an ideal place to build up a bank of your own materials related to this course. Add in worksheets that you have done, pictures, tests, etc.

WORLD CLUB

1

STUDENTS' BOOK

Michael Harris   **David Mower**

Longman

CONTENTS MAP

Module	Page	Vocabulary	Grammar	Skills
Planet Earth 5	47	actions; parts of the body; the weather	the present continuous – all forms	**Reading:** a tourist brochure **Listening:** a tourist guide; a quiz; a song **Speaking:** talk about our planet **Writing:** invent an alien
Villages 6	57	places and buildings; adjectives; jobs; free time activities	*there is / are*; *some* and *any*	**Reading:** tourist information; letters **Listening:** dialogues; a quiz about Britain **Speaking:** talk about your area; a shopping role-play **Writing:** invent a village
The Wild West 7	67	rooms; furniture; weapons; animals; verb	the past simple tense (regular verbs) – affirmative and negative	**Reading:** Native Americans; *The Little House*; Billy the Kid **Listening:** a story; a song **Speaking:** talk about life in the Wild West; talk about your own life **Writing:** a short biography
Travel 8	77	transport; countries; the weather; verbs; adjectives	the past simple tense – questions; irregular verbs	**Reading:** explorers; airships **Listening:** a story **Speaking:** tell a story **Writing:** an adventure story

Learning to learn

A Welcome

a

Match the modules with the pictures.
Use the mini-dictionary on pages 98-105.

Example: 1 b

1 Families	5 Planet Earth
2 Cartoons	6 Villages
3 Hobbies	7 The Wild West
4 Parties	8 Travel

b
QUIZ

• Find these items in the book.

Example: 1 page 42

1   A photo of a carnival.

2   Lesson 22: Gulliver's Travels.

3   Lesson 3: Animal Families.

4   A photo of a model ship.

5   A picture of Asterix.

6   A comic story.

c
Write a quiz like the one in exercise b.

d
In pairs, do your quiz.

Example: A: A picture of a shop.

B: Here, on page 62.

A: Yes, correct!

Learning to Learn

Objectives

This module introduces students to the course. They are also introduced to some important aspects of language learning and encouraged to develop independent study habits.

Contents

Language Aims

Functions:

- Revising vocabulary and structures from previous courses
- Asking the meaning, pronunciation and spelling of words in English
- Revising the alphabet

Target language:

- *I'm sorry, I don't understand.*
- *Can you spell that, please?*
- *What's ... in our language?*
- *What's ... in English?*

Vocabulary:

families, cartoons, hobbies, parties, planet Earth, villages, The Wild West, travel, pen, ruler, bag, rubber, pencil, dictionary, students' book, activity book, piece of paper, notebook, chalk, blackboard, animals, elephant, lion, tiger, jaguar, kangaroo

Pronunciation:

- Saying the alphabet

Activity types

- Matching words and pictures
- Skimming and scanning a text to find information
- Writing and doing a quiz in pairs
- Playing a guessing game in pairs
- Ordering words alphabetically
- Organising words in the vocabulary book
- Listening to instructions and putting them in order
- Using the dictionary as an aid to learner autonomy

Attitudes to learning

- Showing interest in getting to know one's classmates better
- Understanding the importance of developing learner autonomy and good study habits

Moral and Social Values

- Peace Studies

Encouraging students to be tolerant and respectful of fellow students in their daily relationships (Lesson C: *a*, *b* and *d*)

A

a Vocabulary/Individual

- Write the names of the modules on the board and elicit the meaning.
- Explain *title*, *picture* and *module* and look at the mini-dictionary with them.

Answers: 2f; 3g; 4d; 5e; 6a; 7h; 8c

b Reading/Individual

- Elicit or explain the meaning of the word *quiz* and *photo*.
- Ask students to find the different items in their books. They can work in pairs if you wish.

Answers:
2 page 78; 3 page 12; 4 page 28; 5 page 17; 6 page 18

c Writing/Individual

- Write an example on the board (a picture of a house) and help them with any vocabulary they may need.
- Give them time to write four things (or more for the quicker students).

d Speaking/Pairs

- Divide the class into pairs. Partners ask each other questions and check answers in the book.
- You can include a game element by dividing the class into teams and awarding points.

Activity Book Key

A 2 page 9; 3 page 75; 4 page 10; 5 page 64; 6 page 56

B 1 page 13; 2 page 32; 3 page 39; 4 page 8; 5 page 18; 6 page 26

C 2 d; 3 e; 4 a; 5 c

D cartoons, families, hobbies, parties, planet earth, travel, villages, wild west

Teacher's notes

a Keywords/Individual

- Say the words while you point to each picture in turn.
- Remind them to use the mini-dictionary if they need help with the vocabulary.

Answers:

bag 1; rubber 3; pencil 7; dictionary 10; Students' Book 4; Activity Book 5; ruler 6; sheet of paper 9; notebook 2

b Speaking/Pairs

- Put some of the classroom objects in a bag and say: *Guess the things in the bag.*
- When students call out a correct item, take it out of the bag.
- Divide the class into pairs. Students put a few objects in their bags and their partners guess what they are.

c Cassette/Whole class

- Play the tape and ask students to repeat the letters chorally. Say the alphabet yourself more and more quickly and see if students can follow you.
- Say letters and point to individual students who must take it from there and say the next few letters until you signal them to stop.

TAPESCRIPT:

Module O, Lesson B, Exercise c. Listen to the alphabet and repeat the letters.

A, B, C, D, E, F, G, H, I, J, K, L, M, N, O, P, Q, R, S, T, U, V, W, X, Y, Z.

d Keywords/Individual

- Focus students' attention on the differences between the English alphabet and their own. Write both systems on the board graphically in parallel lines. How many letters are there in each? What letters exist in one but not in the other?
- Ask students to order the words alphabetically in their notebooks. They can work in pairs if you wish. Check the exercise orally.

Answers:

alligator, cat, dog, eight, elephant, five, jaguar, kangaroo, lion, nine, one, six, three, zebra

e Keywords/Individual

- Ask students to look at the extracts from a vocabulary book. Explain that they are going to organise their own vocabulary books along the same lines, both alphabetically and by topic-based networks.
- Tell them to divide the first two thirds of their notebooks alphabetically. Go through the letters with the whole class and decide how many pages to leave for each letter.
- Then tell students to put another section at the back, titled *topics*. Have them do a network with words related to the classroom. Do it on the board at the same time.
- Finally, students write some of the important new vocabulary from the first two lessons in their vocabulary books. Remind them to include a translation and an example sentence. Tell them that you will collect and mark these books several times during the year.

Reinforcement activity

Quiz: Vocabulary/Groups

- Divide the students into four or five groups. Tell them that if they get a question right they get 2 points. If they don't know the answer, the next group has a chance of answering and gets 2 points and 2 bonus points (4). If they can't answer, the following group tries for 6 points. Give bonus points up to 10 points.
- For questions, you can have students spell words, give the English for words in their mother tongue or vice-versa, or give example sentences with words you say.

Activity Book Key

B Numbers: two, four, thirteen, nineteen, twenty; **Animals:** cat, crocodile, elephant, penguin, tiger; **Classroom objects:** blackboard, chalk, pencil, rubber, ruler

C 1 good; 2 small; 3 hot; 4 easy; 5 wet; 6 tall/long

B Words

a  KEYWORDS

Match the words with the pictures. Use the mini-dictionary on pages 98-105.

Example: pen 8

> pen bag rubber pencil dictionary
> students' book activity book ruler
> piece of paper notebook

b

In pairs, put some things in your bag. Guess your partner's things.

Example: A: A pen?
    B: No.

c

PRONUNCIATION

Listen to the alphabet and repeat the letters.

d KEYWORDS

Put the words in alphabetical order. Then test your partner's spelling.

Example: A: Spell 'alligator'.
    B: a-l-l-i-g-a-t-o-r.

> lion six alligator one eight kangaroo zebra
> dog five elephant cat three nine jaguar

e

Organise words in your vocabulary book alphabetically like this:

> **K: Kangaroo**
> Kangaroos are from Australia.

Or by topics like this:

> **animals**
> lion tiger jaguar elephant kangaroo

C Classroom Language

a

Listen. Copy and complete.

please spell understand speak please you

1 I'm sorry, I don't ...

2 Can you ... more slowly, ...?

3 Can ... repeat that, ...?

4 Can you ... that, please?

Listen again and repeat.

b

In pairs, one person says words fast and the other writes them.

Example: A: A piece of paper.

B: I'm sorry, I don't understand. Can you speak more slowly, please?

A: A... piece... of... paper...

B: Can you spell *piece*, please?

A: P-i-e-c-e.

B: Thanks.

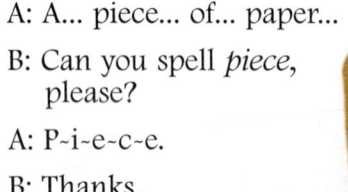

c

Listen and put the instructions in the order you hear them.

Example: 1 D

A Listen to the story and answer the questions.

B Read the story again. True or false?

C  Think of an animal. In pairs, ask questions about your partner's animal. Guess what it is.

D Language Focus
Copy and complete the table.

E  Look at the photo and write sentences about the people.

F 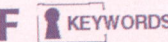 KEYWORDS
Match the words in the box with the photos.

d

In pairs, give your partner a vocabulary test.

Example: A: What's ... in our language?

B: —.

A: Yes, right.

B: What's ... in English?

A: I don't know. Tiger?

B: No, wrong!

a Cassette/Individual

- Go over the words in the box. Students copy the sentences plus blanks in their notebooks.
- Play the tape. Students listen and complete the sentences. Make sure students understand what each expression means.

Answers:

1 understand; 2 speak, please; 3 you, please; 4 spell

TAPESCRIPT:

Module 0, Lesson C, Exercise a. Listen. Copy and complete. One.

TEACHER: Now, in pairs, ask and answer questions about your family.

STUDENT: I'm sorry, I don't understand.

TEACHER: Now, in pairs, ask and answer questions about your family.

NARRATOR: **Two.**

TEACHER: Read the story again and answer these questions.

STUDENT: Can you speak more slowly, please?

TEACHER: Read the story again and answer these questions.

NARRATOR: **Three.**

TEACHER: Write five sentences about your family.

STUDENT: Can you repeat that, please?

TEACHER: Write five sentences about your family.

NARRATOR: **Four.**

TEACHER: Number one, elephant.

STUDENT: Can you spell that, please?

TEACHER: Yes, E ...L...E...P...H...A...N...T.

STUDENT: Thank you.

b Pairs/Speaking

- Divide the class into pairs. Students take turns saying words fast while their partners try to write them down. Partners use the expressions in exercise **a** to ask for clarification.

c Cassette/Individual

- Explain that to do the task it is only necessary to understand the key words.
- Play the tape and correct orally.

Answers:

2E; 3F; 4A; 5B; 6C

TAPESCRIPT:

Module 0, Lesson C, Exercise c. Listen and put the instructions in the order you hear them. One.

TEACHER: OK, now Language Focus. In your notebooks, copy and complete the table. For example, affirmative: "I am from California."

NARRATOR: **Two.**

TEACHER: Now writing. Look at the photo and write sentences about the people.

NARRATOR: **Three.**

TEACHER: Now vocabulary. Match the words in the box with the photos.

NARRATOR: **Four.**

TEACHER: OK, now listening. Listen to the story and answer the questions.

NARRATOR: **Five.**

TEACHER: Next, reading. Read the story again. True or false? Use the mini dictionary to help you.

NARRATOR: **Six.**

TEACHER: Now, speaking. Think of an animal. Now in pairs. That's it... In pairs. Ask questions about your partner's animal. Guess what it is.

d Speaking/Pairs

- Focus on the example. Then ask the same questions related to the students' own language.
- Ask them several more questions about classroom objects. Then ask them to write down five English words and five words in their own language on a piece of paper. (They must know the meaning of all the words!)
- Students test each other about the vocabulary they have written down.

Reinforcement activity

"Hangman": Vocabulary/Groups

- Students play Hangman in groups.

Activity Book Key

A 2 speak; 3 language; 4 know; 5 answer; 6 sorry; 7 repeat

B 2 speaking; 3 writing; 4 listening; 5 reading; 6 vocabulary

C 1 c; 2 f; 3 a; 4 e; 5 b

D 2 table; 3 story; 4 questions; 5 photo; 6 partner

1 Families

Objectives

Read about a Nepalese family; talk about one's family; do quizzes on animals and families; write a description of an invented family.

Contents

Language Aims

Functions:

- Naming the different members of the family and describing them
- Describing states and conditions
- Indicating position
- Talking about personality
- Saying where one comes from and one's age
- Linking sentences with the conjunction *and*
- Asking and answering *yes/no* and *wh-* questions
- Reviewing the colours
- Using classroom language

Target language:

- *This is my uncle and this is my brother.*
- *My parents are called Oscar and Silvia.*
- *His parents are farmers in the village. They aren't rich.*
- *Magda is with me in the photo. I'm on the right.*
- *I'm very sociable and Magda is quiet.*
- *My dad is from Alicante.*
- *Jabu is twelve years old.*
- *Are penguins from the Arctic? Yes, they are.*
- *Where are tigers from? Asia.*
- *Copy and complete the table.*

Vocabulary:

Families: *aunt, brother, daughter, father, granddaughter, grandfather, grandmother, grandson, mother, nephew, niece, parents, sister, son, uncle*
Adjectives: *bad, big, cold, different, fantastic, favourite, good, identical, modern, quiet, rich, similar, small, sociable, sporty, strange*
Sports: *basketball, badminton, cycling, football, swimming, tennis*
School subjects: *art, English, geography, history, maths, science*
Jobs: *doctor, engineer, farmer, teacher*
Animals: *elephant, kangaroo, lion, panther, parrot, penguin, tiger*
Colours: *black, blue, brown, green, grey, orange, pink, purple, red, white, yellow*

Pronunciation:

- Using rising intonation in *yes/no* questions
- Using falling intonation in *wh-* questions
- Pronouncing the contractions of the verb *be* in the present simple

Activity types

- Identifying the members of a fictional family and drawing a family tree
- Skimming and scanning texts
- Completing tables with specific information from the texts
- Writing personal information about oneself
- Doing the activities in the *World Club Magazine*
- Comparing words in English with similar ones in L1
- Punctuating with capital letters and full stops
- Doing a quiz in pairs and deciding which sentences are false
- Classifying animals
- Matching questions and answers
- Writing questions for specific answers
- Playing guessing games in pairs
- Inventing and describing a strange family
- Asking and answering questions about the family in groups
- Listening to a quiz
- Ordering words to make sentences
- Correcting grammatical errors in sentences
- Playing Bingo to review the alphabet
- Completing the *Module Check*
- Organising the new vocabulary in a notebook
- Carrying out self-evaluation tasks

Attitudes to learning

- Showing interest in learning about cultures that are different from one's own
- Showing respect for classmates' personal circumstances
- Understanding the importance of developing learner autonomy and good study habits
- Displaying confidence in one's ability to communicate successfully in English

Moral and Social Values

- Peace Studies
Encouraging students to accept and understand social and cultural differences worldwide (Lesson 1: *A*; Lesson 2: *B*).
- Moral and Social Development
Helping students develop attitudes of respect and tolerance towards the family and the community (Lesson 1: *E*; Lesson 2: *G* and *H*).

Families

Lead-in

MODULE OBJECTIVES

IN THIS MODULE YOU WILL ...

...d   about a Nepalese family and twin sisters.
...sten   to an animal quiz and a family quiz.
...lk   about yourself and your family.
...ractise the verb *to be* and questions.
...Vrite   a description of an invented family.

Gómez

Fester

...randma

Morticia

Wednesday

Pugsley

a 🔑 KEYWORDS

...ook at the Addams Family. Match the
...words in the box with the names. Use the
...mini-dictionary on pages 98-105.

mother/son   husband/wife   father/daughter
brother/sister   grandmother/grandson
uncle/nephew   uncle/niece

Example: 1 husband/wife

1 Gómez/Morticia
2 Pugsley/Wednesday
3 Gómez/Wednesday
4 Grandma/Pugsley
5 Fester/Wednesday
6 Morticia/Pugsley
7 Fester/Pugsley

b 🗨️

Imagine you are Pugsley or Wednesday.
Test your partner.

Example: A: Fester and me.
B: Uncle and niece.
A: Yes, right.

1

1 A Nepalese Family

A village family

Jabu and his family are from a village in the Himalayas in Nepal. Jabu is thirteen years old. His sister is called Pomzi and she's four years old. His brother Norbu is two years old. His father is called Kepu and his mother Cheuki. His grandmother is called Bajai and she lives with the family.

His parents are farmers in the village and they aren't rich. Their house is small and it isn't very modern, but it's warm in the winter. Jabu is a pupil in the village school and he helps his mother and father on the farm. His favourite sport is badminton and he plays it with his friends in the village. They're very good players!

A

Look at the pictures and read the text. Who are the people?

Example: 1 Norbu

B

Read the text again. Copy and complete the information.

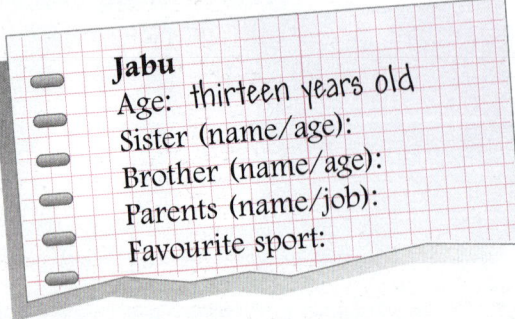

Jabu
Age: thirteen years old
Sister (name/age):
Brother (name/age):
Parents (name/job):
Favourite sport:

Module Objectives

Read and explain the module objectives to your students and make sure that they understand them.

Topic focus

- Family life is a very sensitive area for many students, especially those whose parents may be dead, divorced, in jail, etc. Never force students to discuss or answer questions about their families if they show the least unwillingness to do so.

a Keywords/Individual

- Ask students to look at the photo and say if they recognise the family. Explain the vocabulary in the Keywords box by drawing a family tree on the board.
- Check orally with the whole class.

Answers:

2 brother/sister; 3 father/daughter; 4 grandmother/grandson; 5 uncle/niece; 6 mother/son; 7 uncle/nephew

b Speaking/Pairs

- Partners pretend they are Pugsley or Wednesday and test one another on their respective family relationships.

Topic focus

- Ask students if they know where Nepal is (in Asia, north of India and Bangladesh), if they think most people live in cities or in villages (in villages) and if they think most people are rich or poor (poor).

A Reading/Individual

- Ask students to read the first paragraph of the text quickly and name the people in the photos.

Answers:

1 Norbu; 2 Cheuki; 3 Pomzi; 4 Jabu

B Reading/Individual

- Ask students to copy the table and headings in their notebooks.
- Ask them to read the text again and complete the table. While they are doing this, draw the headings on the board yourself.
- Have one or two volunteers come to the board and complete the table with the help of the other students.

Answers:

Sister: Pomzi, four; Brother: Norbu, two; Parents: Kepu, Cheuki; farmers; Favourite sport: badminton

Language Focus: *To be*

C Writing/Individual

- If you wish, go over the verb *to be* orally first.
- Students look at the two tables and complete them.
- Correct on the board with the whole class.

Answers:

2 is; 3 are not; 4 isn't

D Writing/Individual

- Ask students to copy and complete the sentences in their notebooks.
- Correct orally, with individual students reading out their sentences.

Answers:

2 are; 3 is; 4 are; 5 is; 6 is; 7 am; 8 are; 9 is; 10 are

E Writing/Speaking/Individual/ Groups

- Look at the ideas in the example with the whole class. Ask students to write down personal information about themselves on a piece of paper.

- Once they have done this, divide the class into groups. The papers are shuffled and handed out again. One student reads the sentences and the others must guess who is being described.

Extra Time!

- Students turn to *World Club Magazine* and do Activity 1 on page 88.

Answers:

grandfather / husband / favourite / daughter

F Dictionary work

- With the whole class find the mini-dictionary at the end of the book.

- Begin the activity together, making sure that students understand what to do. Then let them continue on their own.

- Check orally, writing words on the board and refering to the mini-dictionary where necessary.

Answers:

1 favourite friend modern village warm winter
2 paper parents partner pen pencil pupil
3 school sentence small spell sport swim

Extension activity

Cities and countries:
Vocabulary/Whole class

- Give students a few minutes to come up with as many countries as they can in Asia, and then quiz their classmates on the names of the capitals, the local currency and eventually, the languages spoken there.

- If they seem especially interested in the topic, encourage them to do some additional research and prepare a wall chart with the information.

Activity Book Key

A 1 are; 2 is; 3 isn't; 4 am, is; 5 aren't; 6 aren't; 7 is; 8 aren't

B 1 am, is, are, Sarah
2 am, is, is, is, Debbie
3 am, is, George
4 is, is, is, Robert

C 2 a; 3 e; 4 b; 5 f; 6 d

D 2 fifty-eight; 3 thirty-four; 4 thirty-three; 5 eight; 6 eleven

F 2 Your name is Susana Sánchez and you are from Spain.
3 Her name is Francoise Flaubert and she is from France.
4 His name is Carl Carlson and he is from the UK.
5 My name is Alicia Álvarez and I am from Argentina.

G 3 daughter; 4 eight; 5 twelve; 6 parents; 7 nephew; 8 fifteen

Extension Activity Key

1F; 2T; 3F; 4F; 5T

Language Focus: *To be*

C

Copy and complete the tables.

Example: 1 are

AFFIRMATIVE		
I	am ('m)	
you / we / they	¹ ... ('re)	from Nepal.
he / she / it	² ... ('s)	

NEGATIVE		
I	am not ('m not)	
you / we / they	³ ... (aren't)	rich.
he / she / it	is not (⁴ ...)	

D

Copy and complete the sentences about Jabu.

Example: 1 am

1 I ... thirteen years old.

2 We ... from Nepal.

3 My family ... from a village.

4 My parents ... farmers.

5 My house ... very modern.

6 My favourite sport ... football.

7 I ... from Britain.

8 My parents ... teachers.

9 My house ... very warm in winter.

10 We ... from Spain.

E

WHO IS IT?

• Complete this personal information on a piece of paper.

> I'm from ...
> My parents are called ...
> My birthday is in ... (month)
> My favourite sport is ...
> My favourite film is ...

• In groups, mix up the pieces of paper. One student reads the sentences and the others guess who it is.

F  DICTIONARY SKILLS

Put these words in alphabetical order. Then check your answers in the mini-dictionary.

1 warm modern village winter friend favourite

2 pen pencil paper partner parents pupil

3 school sport swim spell small sentence

> **EXTRA TIME**

Look at World Club magazine on page 88. Do activity 1.

2 Twins

A   KEYWORDS

Which words in the box are similar in your language? Use the mini-dictionary.

> identical similar different
> sporty fantastic sociable quiet
> favourite good small strange

B

Read about these identical twins. Copy and complete the family tree.

Danuta (12)

C

Read the text again. Copy and complete the table.

	Danuta	Magda
Personality	sociable	quiet
Age		
Favourite group/singer		
Favourite sport		
Favourite subjects		

Dear Alice,

My name is Danuta and I'm twelve years old. I am from San Diego in California. Magda is with me in the photo – she is my twin sister. I'm on the right! It's very strange – Magda and I are identical twins, but we're very different. We're both very sporty, but I'm very sociable and Magda is quiet.

Our favourite sport is basketball and we are in the school team. My favourite group is The Prodig— they're fantastic! Magda likes Janet Jackson. favourite subjects at school are geography and science. Magda prefers English and history.

Our parents are from Poland. My dad is calle Stan. He's forty-two. My mum is called Ewa she's thirty-nine. She's a doctor at a hospital San Diego.

Write to me soon.

Love,

Danuta

Topic focus

- If you have any twins in the class, ask them questions in their own language about what it means to be a twin. Encourage other students to ask questions too.

A Keywords/Individual

- Ask students to look at the words in the box and say which ones are similar in their own language.
- You can extend this activity by having them say other words they have learned in the first lessons or remember from before.

B Reading/Individual

- Students read the text in order to complete the family tree of identical twins Magda and Danuta. Remind them to use the mini-dictionary if necessary.
- Correct by sketching the tree on the board and asking a student to fill in the information.

Answers:

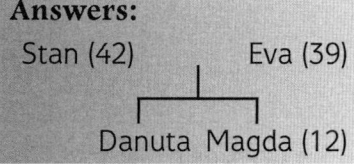

Stan (42)   Eva (39)

Danuta Magda (12)

C Reading/Individual

- Ask students to read the text again and copy and complete the table in their notebooks.
- Correct the exercise by having a student complete this table on the board while the rest of the class check the information to see if it is correct.

Answers:

Age: Danuta: twelve/Magda: twelve;
Favourite group/singer: Danuta: The Prodigy/Magda: Janet Jackson; **Favourite sports:** Danuta and Magda: basketball;
Favourite subjects: Danuta: geography and science/Magda: English and history

D Learn to Learn/Whole class

- Draw two columns on the board and write the headings *You can guess* and *You can't guess*.
- Students look at the text again and list the words they are able to guess the meaning of

because they are similar in their own language, and the ones that they can't guess.

- Once the lists are long enough, have them write the words from the 2nd column in their vocabulary books and look up the meanings in their mini-dictionary.

E Writing/Individual

- Read the example with the whole class. Explain the use of the conjunction *and* if necessary.
- Students complete the exercise in their notebooks.
- Check orally with the whole class.

Answers:

2 I am sociable and I am sporty. 3 My dad is called David and he's from Alicante. 4 My mum is called Rosa and she's from Lugo.
5 She is quiet and she is strange.

F Writing/Individual

- First review the use of capital letters and full stops with the whole class.
- Give students a few examples and then ask them to copy the letter in their notebooks and make all the necessary corrections.
- Correct the exercise on the board by having different students come up and write a sentence. The rest of the class says whether it is right or wrong.

Answers:

I'm thirteen years old and I'm from London. I'm very sporty. My favourite sport is tennis and I'm a good player. My favourite group is Pearl Jam. My favourite school subject is art. I'm not a very good pupil! Write to me soon. Daniel

G Writing/Individual

- Students rewrite the letter in exercise F with details about themselves. They can use the words in the Keywords box if necessary. Tell them to include one piece of false information.

H Reading/Speaking/Pairs

- Divide students into pairs. Read the example with the whole class.
- Tell students that they must guess the false information given in their partners' letters.
- Ask volunteers to read out their letters to their classmates to see if they can find the false information.

Extra Time!

- Students turn to *World Club Magazine* and do Activity 2 on page 88.

Answers:

1 Paris; 2 France; 3 teacher; 4 mother; 5 sister; 6 basketball; 7 science; 8 maths; 9 blue; 10 yellow

Reinforcement activity

Sounds/vocabulary: Learning to learn/Individual

- Select one or two sounds students are having special difficulty with (for example /b/ and /v/). Ask them to go through their vocabulary books and find several examples of each.
- Students then stand up one by one and say their words. The rest of the class must try to correct them if the pronunciation is wrong.
- Repeat this activity frequently. Once students get used to it, it should not take more than 10 minutes, and it is a good way to end a class.

Activity Book Key

A 2 am; 3 am; 4 am; 5 are; 6 aren't; 7 is; 8 is; 9 is; 10 isn't; 11 are; 12 is; 13 am

B tennis, history, geography, science, mathematics, swimming, cycling

C 2 different; 3 fantastic; 4 strange; 5 favourite; 6 sociable

D 1 My name is Jabu. I am twelve.

2 He is from a village. He is from Nepal.

3 His house is small. It isn't very modern.

4 Jabu is a student. He helps on the farm.

E 1 My name is Jabu and I am twelve.

2 He is from Nepal and he is from a village.

3 His house is small and it isn't very modern.

4 Jabu is a student and he helps on the farm.

Extension Activity Key

1 similar; 2 sporty; 3 good; 4 different; 5 sociable; 6 quiet; 7 good; 8 bad

D

List words from the text.

1 you can guess – they are similar in your language.

2 you can't guess – use the mini-dictionary.

E

Join these sentences with *and*.

Example: 1 My favourite sport is football and I'm a good player.

1 My favourite sport is football. I'm a good player.

2 I am sociable. I am sporty.

3 My dad is called David. He's from Alicante.

4 My mum is called Rosa. She's from Lugo.

5 She is quiet. She is strange.

F

Punctuate the letter using capital letters and full stops.

Example: Dear Carlos,

Hi! My name's Daniel...

Dear carlos,
hi! my name's daniel i'm thirteen years old and i'm from london i'm very sporty my favourite sport is tennis and i'm a good player my favourite group is pearl jam my favourite school subject is art i'm not a very good pupil!
write to me soon
Daniel

G

Re-write the letter in exercise F about yourself. Include one false piece of information.

Sports: basketball tennis   football cycling
swimming

School subjects: maths English history
science geography

H

In pairs, read your letters and guess the false information.

Example: A: Your favourite subject isn't maths!

B: No, it isn't. My favourite subject is art.

Did you know?

Every year, thousands of twins have a party in Twinsburg, Ohio, in the U.S.A – a town started by twins.

EXTRA TIME

**Look at World Club magazine on page 88.
Do activity 2.**

3 Animal Families

A  KEYWORDS

What colours are the animals?

Example: Elephants are grey.

blue orange **Yellow**

grey

red black

green white

brown **purple**

pink

B  KEYWORDS

Which animals are *mammals*? Which are *birds*? Which are *cats*?

Example: Polar bears are mammals.

C

ANIMAL QUIZ

• Listen and guess the animals from exercise A.

Example: 1 tiger

Language Focus: Questions

D

Look at the word order in these examples:

YES/NO QUESTIONS		
Is	it	a tiger?
Are	they	from Africa?

ANSWERS
Yes, it is.
No, they aren't.

WH- QUESTIONS		
Where	is	it from?
What	are	your favourite animals?

ANSWERS
Asia.
Cats.

Listen to part 1 of the quiz again and match these questions and answers.

1 Where is it from?
2 Is it big?
3 What colour is it?
4 Is it a lion?

a No, it isn't.
b Yes, it is.
c Asia.
d Yellow and black.

A Keywords/Individual

- Ask students to look at the photos and say what colours the animals are. They may do this in pairs if you wish. Check with the whole class.

Answers:

Polar bears are white; lions are orange (or brown or yellow); parrots are green, blue and orange; tigers are orange, black and white

B Keywords/Whole class

- Draw three columns on the board and write the following headings: *Mammals / Birds / Cats.*

- Students decide which category each animal belongs to. You can lengthen the list by asking them to name more animals that they know.

Answers:

They are mammals, except the birds.
The lions and tigers are cats.

C Cassette/Whole class

- Tell students they are going to hear a boy and a girl doing a quiz. They have to guess which animal is being described.

- Play the tape, pausing after every description.

- At the end of the quiz, play the tape again.

Answers:

2 elephant, 3 parrot

 TAPESCRIPT:

Module 1, Lesson 3, Exercise C. Listen and guess the animals from exercise A. One.

GIRL: Where is it from?
BOY: Asia.
GIRL: Is it big?
BOY: Yes, it is.
GIRL: What colour is it?
BOY: Yellow and black.
GIRL: Is it a lion?
BOY: No, it isn't.
GIRL: Is it ...
NARRATOR: Two.
BOY: Where is it from?
GIRL: Mm, Africa.
BOY: Is it big?
GIRL: Er, yes, it's big.
BOY: What colour is it?

GIRL: It's grey.
BOY: Is it a .....
NARRATOR: Three
BOY: Where is it from?
GIRL: South America, I think.
BOY: Is it big?
GIRL: No, it's not very big.
BOY: Is it a cat?
GIRL: No, it's not.
BOY: Is it a bird?
GIRL: Yes, it is.
BOY: Is it a .....

Language Focus: Questions

D Cassette/Individual

- Before doing this exercise, you may wish to revise word order in questions with the class.

- Students look at the examples in the box. Then they listen to the first part of the quiz again and match the questions and answers. Check orally.

Answers:

1c; 2b; 3d; 4a

E Writing/Individual

- Students match the questions and answers in their notebooks.

- For extra writing practice, ask them to copy out the questions and the answers in full.

- Correct orally, one student reading out the question and another the answer.

Answers:

2d; 3f; 4c; 5a; 6e

F Writing/Individual

- Students write a question for each answer.

- Go over the example first and remind them to look at the language boxes if necessary.

- Correct the exercise by having students come up to the board and write the questions.

Answers:

2 Is he from Vigo? 3 Are kangaroos from Australia? 4 Who is your teacher? 5 How old is Elena? 6 Are you a good student? 7 What colour is an elephant?

Pronunciation: Questions

G Cassette/Whole class

- Students check their answers to exercise F with the tape and repeat them. Make sure their intonation goes up for *yes/no* questions and down for *wh-* questions.

 TAPESCRIPT:

Module 1, Lesson 3, Exercise G. Listen and check your answers to Exercise F. Then repeat the questions. One.

READER: Where are you from?
NARRATOR: **Two.**
READER: Is he from Vigo?
NARRATOR: **Three.**
READER: Are kangaroos from Australia?
NARRATOR: **Four.**
READER: Who is your teacher?
NARRATOR: **Five.**
READER: How old is Elena?
NARRATOR: **Six.**
READER: Are you a good student?
NARRATOR: **Seven.**
READER: What colour is an elephant?

H Speaking/Pairs

- Divide the class into pairs. Students think of an animal and their partners have to ask questions in order to guess what it is.
- Read the example with the whole class first and then individually to make sure that their intonation is correct.

Extra time!

- Students turn to *World Club Magazine* and do Activity 3 on page 88.

Answers:
1T; 2T; 3T; 4T

Reinforcement and extension activities

Animals: Writing/Individual

- For homework, ask students to try and write a list of animals beginning with each letter of the alphabet: *ant, bear, cat, dog,* etc.

- Draw the shapes of the continents on pieces of paper and fix them to the wall. Students cut out pictures of animals from magazines, label them and stick them on the appropriate continent.

Activity Book Key

A 2 the Arctic; 3 no; 4 seals; 5 a year

B 1 How old are you? 2 When is your birthday? 3 Where are you from? 4 Are you sporty? 5 Is your school big?

C 1 Twelve; 2 21st March; 3 Liverpool; 4 No, I'm not; 5 Yes, it is

D 1 How old are you? 2 What is your phone number? 3 What is your favourite animal? 4 Is your family big?

E 2 No, it isn't. 3 No, they aren't. 4 Yes, they are. 5 No, she isn't. 6 Yes, it is.

F Colours: blue, brown, green, pink, purple; **Animals:** elephant, kangaroo, panther, parrot, penguin; **Adjectives:** fantastic, modern, rich, sociable, strange

G 1 kangaroo (not a cat); 2 big (not a colour); 3 brother (not female); 4 class (not a subject); 5 person (not an adjective)

H 2 Danuta and Magdu are identical twins.
3 My favourite sport is tennis.
4 The house is very modern.
5 Paul is not very sociable.
6 She's a strange girl.
7 Parrots are very colourful birds.
8 Tigers are strong cats.

Time to Read:

A   Pedro ⊤ Maria

Laura (12)   Diego (8)

B 1 b; 2c; 3c; 4a; 5a

Extension Activity Key

1T; 2T; 3F; 4F; 5F; 6T; 7T; 8F

G

PRONUNCIATION: QUESTIONS
**Listen and check your questions from exercise F.
Then repeat the questions.**

H

GUESS THE ANIMAL

• Think of an animal. In pairs, ask questions about your partner's animal. Guess what it is.

Example:

A: Is it a bird?   B: Yes, it is.

A: What colour is it?   B: Black and white.

A: Where is it from?   B: Antarctica.

A: Is it a penguin?   B: Yes, it is.

E

Match these questions and answers.

Example: 1 b

1 What are your favourite animals?

2 Are you sporty?

3 How old are you?

4 Who is your favourite group?

5 Are penguins from the Arctic?

6 Where are they from?

a No, they aren't.

b Elephants and dolphins.

c Blur.

d No, I'm not.

e Antarctica.

f I'm twelve.

F

Write questions for these answers.

Example: 1 Where are you from?

1 I'm from Caceres. (Where ...)

2 No, he isn't from Vigo. (Is ...)

3 Yes, kangaroos are from Australia. (Are ...)

4 My teacher is Mrs Evans. (Who ...)

5 Elena is thirteen. (How old ...)

6 Yes, I'm a good student. (Are ...)

7 It's grey. (What colour ...)

Did you know?

There are more than 9,000 different types of birds.

EXTRA TIME

**Look at World Club magazine on page 88.
Do activity 3.**

Fluency

Writing: A Description

A

In groups, invent and describe a strange family.

Stage 1: Preparation

In groups, decide who is in the family. Write notes about the people in a table.

Example:

Name	Dr 'X-ray' Strange	Abnorma Strange	'Tiger' Strange	The twins: April + June
Age	43	31	12	2
Job	a doctor	basketball player	school pupil	
Favourite colours	black and white	purple and pink	black and orange	black and white
Hobby	collecting skeletons	playing chess	collecting spiders	swimming

Stage 2: Writing

Use your table to write a description. Each student in the group writes about one person in the family. Remember to use capital letters and full stops.

> The Strange family.
> Dr X-ray Strange is a doctor and he is forty-three. His hobby is collecting skeletons and his favourite colours are black and white.

Stage 3: Checking

Check your descriptions. Look at the Keyword Check and Grammar References 1 and 2 on page 16.

Stage 4: Display

Copy your descriptions neatly and draw pictures of the people. Show your friends or display them on the wall.

Speaking: Finding Out Information

B

In pairs with a student from a different group, ask questions about the families.

Where are they from?
Who is in the family?

What is his/her job?
How old is he/she?

What is his/her favourite colour?
What is his/her hobby?

Listening: A Quiz

C

Listen and answer the questions – choose a, b or c. Then check the answers with your teacher.

Writing: A description

A Writing/Groups

Stage 1: Preparation

- Explain to students that they are going to describe the strange family that is illustrated in their book and invent details about each person.
- Go through the different stages in the exercise with the whole class and make sure that they understand each one.
- Divide the class into small groups. Each group decides who is in the family and fills in a table with descriptive notes like the ones in the book.

Stage 2: Writing

- Students look at their notes and write their description. Each member of the group writes about one character. Remind them to use capital letters and full stops.

Stage 3: Checking

- Students check spelling and vocabulary with the help of their vocabulary books. They can also look at the Keyword Check and the Grammar Reference on page 16.

Stage 4: Display

- Students copy their descriptions and draw pictures of their characters.
- Display the finished compositions on the walls around the room. Make comments and ask questions.

Speaking: Finding out information

B Speaking/Pairs

- Pair students off with members from other groups so they can ask and answer questions about the strange families.
- Walk around the room to make sure that they are using the correct intonation. Remind them that it is not necessary to use complete answers.

Listening: Quiz

C Cassette/Individual

- Tell students they are going to hear a list of questions and will have to decide on the right answer. Play the tape, pausing after each question.
- Correct the exercise by asking for a show of hands first, and then giving students the answers.

Answers:

1b; 2a; 3 False; 4b; 5 True

 TAPESCRIPT:

Module 1, Fluency, Exercise C. Listen and answer the questions. Choose a, b or c. Question one.

READER: Name the daughter of Madonna. Is it a) Maria, b) Lourdes, or c) Magdalena?

NARRATOR: Question two.

READER: Name the actor who stars in Titanic. Is it a) Matt Damon, b) Brad Pitt, or c) Leonardo Di Caprio?

NARRATOR: Question three.

READER: True or false? All twins in Nigeria have the same names.

NARRATOR: Question four.

READER: How many different types of birds are in the bird family? a) More than 5,000, b) More than 9,000 or c) More than 20,000.

NARRATOR: Question five.

READER: True or false? The jaguar is in the cat family.

NARRATOR: Now check the answers with your teacher.

Reinforcement and extension activity

More questions: Speaking/Writing/Pairs

- Divide the class into pairs. Ask students to write two more questions like the ones they have just heard.
- When they have finished, have individual students ask questions to the rest of the class. Make sure everyone participates.

Consolidation

Grammar

A Writing/Individual

- Students find and correct the mistake in each sentence. Ask students to write the answers on the board so you can check the exercise with the whole class.

Answers:

2 Where is he from? 3 He is from Gdansk.
4 My mother is an engineer. 5 I'm not sporty.

B Writing/Individual

- Students complete the text. Check the answers with the whole class.

Answers:

2 is; 3 isn't; 4 is; 5 is; 6 are; 7 aren't; 8 is; 9 is; 10 isn't

C Writing/Individual

- Remind students to write the first word of each sentence with a capital letter. Check the answers with the whole class.

Answers:

2 What is your favourite music? 3 How old is he? 4 What is your name? 5 Are parrots from Africa?

Vocabulary

D Keywords/Individual

- Ask students to copy the table in their notebooks. They complete the *Job*, *Family* and *Adjective* columns with words from the box.
- Encourage them to add more words to the lists if they know them and to write the new words in their vocabulary books.

Answers:

Jobs: farmer, teacher, doctor, engineer
Families: husband, wife, nephew, uncle
Adjectives: rich, quiet, strange, sociable

Pronunciation: Contractions

E Cassette/Individual

- Students listen to the tape and write down the number of words there are in each sentence. Remind them that a contraction (such as *I'm*) counts as two words.
- Play the tape and check the answers. Play it again and ask students to repeat the sentences individually or chorally.

Answers:

2: 5; 3: 5; 4: 6; 5: 5

 TAPESCRIPT:

Module 1, Consolidation, Exercise E. Listen and count the words. One.

READER: I'm not very sporty.
NARRATOR: Two.
READER: We aren't from Britain.
NARRATOR: Three.
READER: She's twelve years old.
NARRATOR: Four.
READER: My house isn't very modern.
NARRATOR: Five.
READER: They're very good players.

F Cassette/Individual

- Explain that they are going to hear someone reading out the letters of the alphabet in random order. Play the tape. As they hear their letters, students cover them up or cross them off. The first person to cover the nine squares wins.
- If you wish to play the game again, the letters need to be called out in a different order. To do this, write letters on small pieces of paper and draw them out of a bag or box.

 TAPESCRIPT:

Module 1, Consolidation, Exercise F. Listen and cover the letters on your card when you hear them.

READER: B,H,S,M,F,A,W,T,L,X,G,N,P,E,R,Y,J,C,Q,U,Z,D,I,K,O,V.

Teacher's notes

# Consolidation

Grammar

A

Correct these sentences.

Example: 1 My father is thirty-five (or thirty-five years old).

1 My father is *thirty-five years.*
2 Where *he is* from?
3 *He from* Gdansk.
4 My mother *is engineer.*
5 I'm *no sporty.*

B

Complete the text with these words:

isn't (x2) / is (x5) / are (x2) / aren't

Example: 1 are

In our family, animals ¹... very important. Bouncer ²... a brown and white Cocker Spaniel. He ³... very active – his hobby is sleeping! Patch ⁴... a cat and he ⁵... twelve years old. Kate, Naomi and Claudia ⁶... goldfish. They ⁷... very sociable! Harry ⁸... my parrot. His favourite expression ⁹..., 'Can you repeat that, please? Can you repeat that, please? Can you repeat that, please?' – he ¹⁰... my favourite animal!

C

Order these words to make questions.

Example: 1 Are you from Turkey?

1 from / you / Turkey / are?
2 favourite / what / music / your / is?
3 how / old / he / is?
4 your / what / is / name?
5 Africa / parrots / are / from?

Vocabulary

D

Copy and complete the table with words from the box. Write new words in your vocabulary book.

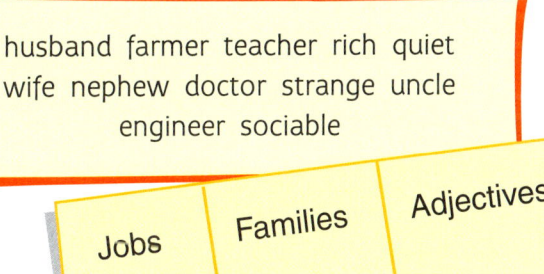

husband farmer teacher rich quiet wife nephew doctor strange uncle engineer sociable

Jobs
farmer

Families

Adjectives

Pronunciation: Contractions

E

Listen and count the words. Short forms count as two words.

Example: I'm not very sporty. 5 words

     1 2 3 4 5

Listen again and repeat the sentences.

F
ALPHABET BINGO

- Copy this square but write different letters.
- Listen to the letters on the cassette. Cover your letters when you hear them. If you cover nine squares, shout 'Bingo' ~ you are the winner!

F	G	A
I	E	B
C	L	O

Module check

Families

Grammar Reference

1 To be

I	Affirmative	Negative
I	am	am not ('m not)
you/we/they	are	are not (aren't)
he/she/it	is	is not (isn't)

To be is a **main verb** or an **auxiliary**.

As a **main verb** it is used to:

• Identify ourselves:

Hi! I'm Danuta and this is my sister Magda.

• Describe a state or a condition:

The parents are farmers. They aren't rich.

• Indicate a position:

Magda is with me in the photo. I'm on the right.

• Say where we come from:

My dad is from Rosario.

• Express age:

Jabu is thirteen years old.

2 Yes/no and *wh-* questions: *to be*

Questions		
Who	am	I?
What	are	you/we/they?
Where	is	he/she/it?
	Am	I
	Are	you/we/they
	Is	he/she/it

(British?)

• **Wh-** questions begin with **who** / **what** / **where** / **how**, etc.

• Yes/no questions begin with the verb *to be.*

• You can answer *yes/no* questions with *yes* or *no* or with a *short answer:*

Are penguins from Antarctica? Yes. / Yes, they are.
Is Jabu from Africa? No. / No, he isn't.

Keyword Check

Families: aunt, brother, daughter, father, granddaughter, grandfather, grandmother, grandson, mother, nephew, niece, parents, sister, son, uncle

Adjectives: bad, big, cold, different, fantastic, favourite, good, identical, moder quiet, rich, similar, small, sociable, sporty

Sports: basketball, badminton, cycling, football, swimming, tennis

School subjects: art, English, geography, history, maths, science

People: doctor, engineer, farmer, teacher

Animals: elephant, kangaroo, lion, parro penguin, tiger, polar bear, mammal

Colours: black, blue, brown, green, grey, orange, pink, purple, red, white, yellow

Classroom language:

Look at the photo.

Match the words and the names.

Draw your family tree.

Copy and complete the table.

Use the mini-dictionary.

Check your description.

Correct these mistakes.

---

1 Look at Grammar References 1-2 above and complete Grammar Files 1-2 in the Activity Book. Then do the *Test Yourself: Grammar* on page 11 of the Activity Book.

2 Look at the Keyword Check. Write important new words in your vocabulary book. Then do the *Test Yourself: Vocabulary* on page 11 of the Activity Book.

- This should help students to reflect on several aspects of their learning and to assess their progress themselves.

- First ask students to choose their favourite activity in this module and to give their reasons. (e.g. the quiz in Lesson 3)

- Ask them to assess a) their own participation in class, and b) their attitude to homework: good / okay / not very good

- Ask students to look at the *Grammar Reference*. Then, as this is their first *Module Check*, help them to find the *Grammar Files* and the *Test Yourself* section in the Activity Book. Ask them to complete the *Grammar File*, then do the *Test Yourself: Grammar* exercises.

- Ask them to look at the *Keyword Check* and write the important new words in their vocabulary books and then do the *Test Yourself: Vocabulary* exercises.

- Explain that these activities should be done **by** themselves and **for** themselves. However, also make it clear that you are always willing to revise problem areas in class.

- It is a good idea to spot check their work so you can get a better idea of each student's general attitude and progress.

2 Cartoons

Objectives

Talk and write about cartoon characters; describe what one can or cannot do and talk about possessions.

Contents

Language Aims

Functions:
- Using *can* to indicate ability
- Using *have/has got* to indicate possession
- Spelling words
- Expressing opinions
- Reviewing colours, physical descriptions and possessions
- Using classroom language
- Learning something about the production of cartoons

Target language:
- *Can you spell daughter?*
- *Yes, I can. D-A-U-G-H-T-E-R*
- *Grandma has got black hair.*
- *I think Spiderman is boring.*

- Check your writing.
- Draw your own cartoon character and write a description.

Vocabulary:

Opinions: *boring, excellent, funny, good, great, interesting, OK, terrible, useless*
Activities: *cook (hamburgers), count (to 100), do (mathematics), draw (pictures/cartoons), fly, jump (2 metres), play (sport), say (the alphabet), sing (songs), speak (French), swim (underwater)*
Parts of the body: *face, head, hair, ears, nose, mouth, eyebrows, moustache, eyes*
Colours: *black, blond, blue, brown, green, yellow*
Descriptions: *big, small, fair, dark, fat, thin, round, square, short, tall*
Possessions: *bicycle, car, cassette, computer, earrings, garden, glasses, hat, house, pet, poster, walkman*
Animals: *alligator, piranha fish, tarantula*

Pronunciation:
- Pronouncing the strong and weak forms of *can*
- Pronouncing the contraction *can't*

Activity types

- Talking about cartoons in small groups
- Reading a comic strip and saying whether the sentences are true or false
- Writing affirmative and negative sentences with *can*
- Asking and answering questions with *can* in pairs
- Playing a spelling game
- Doing the activities in the *World Club Magazine*
- Matching words with drawings
- Listening to a text and putting drawings in order
- Listening to oral instructions and drawing a cartoon
- Asking and answering questions about a cartoon character in pairs
- Reading an interview and finding the differences between the text and the picture
- Playing memory games in pairs and groups
- Playing an information-gap game in pairs
- Listening to questions about cartoon characters and answering a multiple choice quiz
- Completing the *Module Check*
- Organising the new vocabulary in a notebook
- Carrying out self-evaluation tasks

Attitudes to learning

- Showing interest in finding out about cartoons and their production
- Reflecting on the positive and negative subtexts of different cartoons
- Participating willingly in pair, group and whole-class activities
- Appreciating the importance of reflection and analysis in language learning

Moral and Social Values

- Non-sexism

Discussing with students the sexism, violence and racism found in many modern cartoons (Lead-In Lesson: *b*; Fluency: *My Cartoon Character*)

Lead-in

Module Objectives

Read and explain the module objectives to your students and make sure that they understand them.

Topic focus

- Ask students in their own language why they think cartoons are so popular. Which ones present heroes with positive attitudes? Which ones stereotype women, children and minority groups?

a Writing/Individual

- Ask students to list their five favourite cartoons. Help them with the spelling if necessary!

b Keywords/Speaking/Groups

- Divide the class into small groups. Go over the expressions in the box and read the example. Students then compare their lists, give their opinion on each cartoon and award points.

c Speaking/Whole class

- Groups agree on their favourite cartoons and report the results to their classmates.
- You can wrap up the activity by making a quick survey of the five most popular cartoons and writing them up on the board. Make sure students pronounce the names correctly (especially words like *Popeye* and *Spiderman*).

Cartoons

Lead-in

Module Objectives

In this module you will ...

- Read a comic story and an interview.
- Listen to descriptions and music.
- Talk about cartoon characters.
- Practise using *can* and *has got*.
- Draw a cartoon character and write a description.

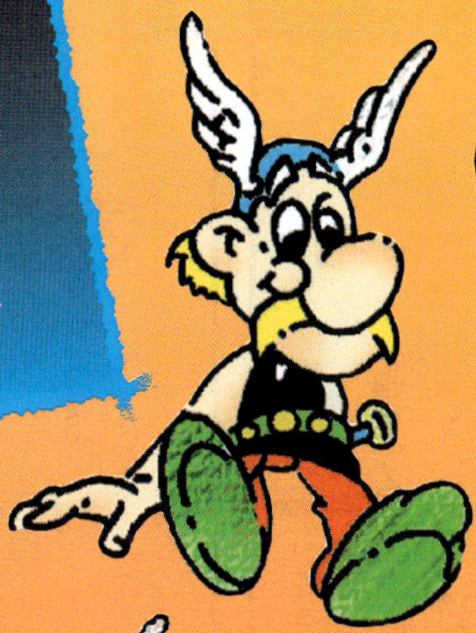

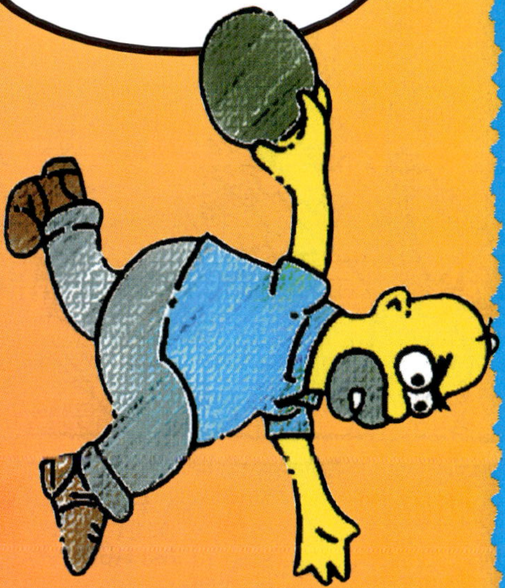

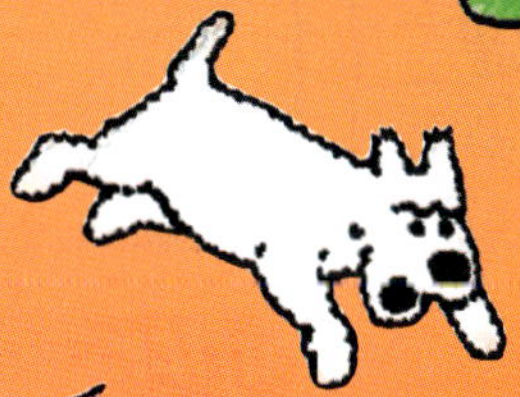

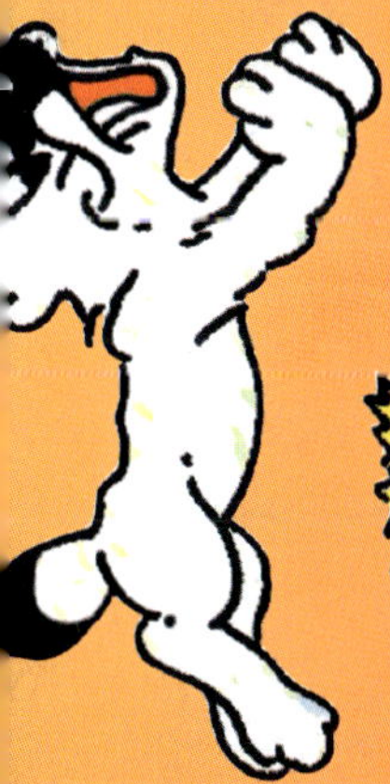

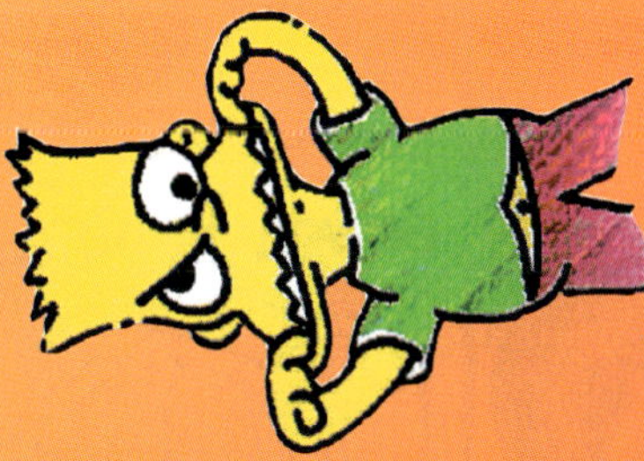

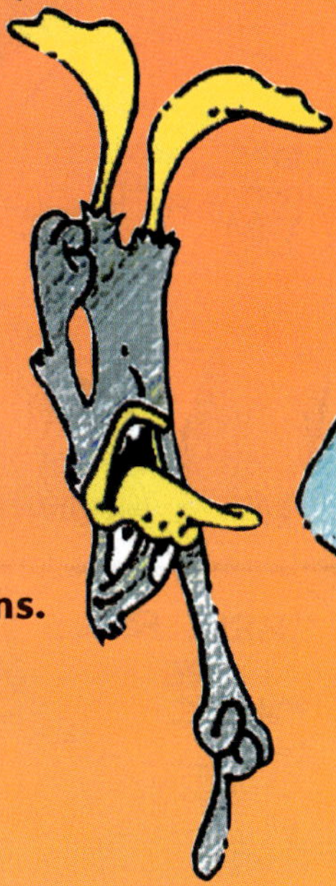

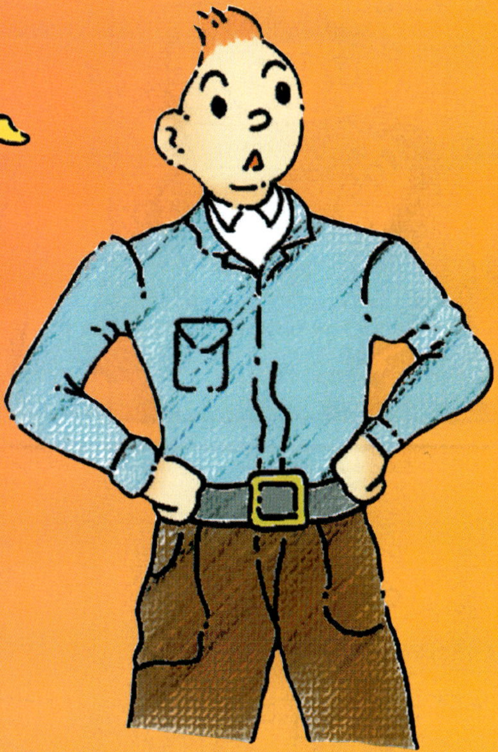

a

List your five favourite cartoons.

Example: The Pink Panther, The Simpsons

b KEYWORDS

In groups, read your list and give opinions. Use these words. Add up the points.

great / very funny - 5 points
OK / sometimes funny - 3 points
boring / terrible - 0 points

Example: A: Spiderman.
B: I think he's great. (5 points)
C: I think he's boring. (0 points)
D: I think he's OK. (3 points)

c

Tell the class about your group's favourite cartoons.

Example: Our favourite cartoons are Popeye and Scooby Doo.

4 Supertwins!

Topic focus

- Ask students to name as many cartoon "superheroes" as they can (*Superman, Batman, WonderWoman, Asterix*, etc.). What are their "superpowers" and where did they get them from?

A Reading/Individual

- Ask students to read the story and decide whether the sentences in the exercise are true or false. They can work in pairs if you wish.
- Remind them that at this stage it is more important to get the general idea than to understand every word.
- Check orally with the whole class.

Answers:
1F; 2F; 3F; 4T; 5T

Language Focus: *Can*

The verb *can* performs several functions in English (e.g. asking for permission, expressing possibility). Here it is used to express ability. Possible problems: *Can* is a modal verb, used with other verbs in the infinitive without *to: I can swim*, not *I can to swim*.

Can has the same form for all persons; it has no *s* ending in the third person singular. It is also unusual because negatives and questions are not formed with auxiliaries.

B Writing/ Individual

- Write two affirmative and two negative true sentences about yourself on the board and say them. Example: *I can speak English. I can't speak Japanese.*
- Ask students to read the comic again and find examples of *can* and *can't* in the text.
- Ask them to copy and complete the table. While they are doing this, draw the headings on the board yourself.
- Have one or two volunteers come to the board and complete the table with the help of the other students.

Answers:
can, can't, Can, can

- Focus students' attention on the completed boxes and ask the following questions:
  – does *can* change for *he/she/it?*
  – do we use *don't/doesn't* in negatives?
  – do we use *do/does* in questions?
- Finally, ask students to translate the example sentences into their own language.

C Writing/Keywords/Individual

- Students look at the activities listed in the box and write true sentences about what they can and cannot do. Remind them to use the mini-dictionary if they have problems with the vocabulary.
- Mark a few sentences and note any problems. If necessary, review the *Language Focus* section again and build up more examples on the board.

D Speaking/Pairs

- Divide the class into pairs and go over the example with a student. Partners then look at the drawings or at their own sentences and ask each other questions. Remind them to use short answers.
- Go round the class to monitor this activity.

E Speaking/Pairs

- Divide the class into pairs. Students look through modules 1 and 2 and write down five words each. Go over the example with a volunteer.
- Students test their partners and give them a mark out of five.
- Wrap up the activity by doing a quick spelling check with the whole class.

Extra Time!

- Students turn to *World Club Magazine* and do Activity 4 on page 89.

Answers:

1 a monkey; 2 an alligator; 3 a penguin; 4 a snake; 5 a lion

Extension activity

Superheroes: Writing/Groups

- Divide the class into small groups. Each group chooses a cartoon character and writes three true sentences about what he/she can or cannot do, and one false sentence.

- In turns, they read out their sentences to the rest of the class, who must decide which sentence is false and then rectify it.

Activity Book Key

A 1 Wanda can ride a bicycle.
  2 She can't swim.
  3 She can't play chess.
  4 She can't sing.
  5 She can speak French.

C 2 Can you play; 3 can't; 4 can you play; 5 can; 6 can; 7 Can she play; 8 can; 9 she can play; 10 can

D **Play:** tennis, badminton, rugby, volleyball, basketball; **Do:** mathematics, geography, science, French, history

E 2 count; 3 swim; 4 ride, ride; 5 jump; 6 play

F I/my; you/your; he/his; she/her; we/our; they/their

G 2 Her, She; 3 Our; 4 Their; 5 your/his/her; 6 I, my; 7 Her, She; 8 Their

Extension Activity Key

1T; 2T; 3T; 4F; 5T; 6T

A

Read the story. True or false?

1 On the first day, Mike can do the maths exercise.

2 Mandy can play volleyball well.

3 The alien gives them magic pens.

4 The next day Mike can do his maths exercises.

5 The next day Mandy can play basketball very well.

Language Focus: *Can*

B

Look at examples of *can* in the story. Copy and complete the tables.

AFFIRMATIVE		
I / you / he / she / it / we / they	¹...	fly.

NEGATIVE		
I / you / he / she / it / we / they	²...	fly.

QUESTION		
³...	I / you / he / she / it / we / they	fly?

SHORT ANSWER		
Yes,	I / you / he / she / it / we / they	⁴...
No,		can't.

C   KEYWORDS

Look at the activities in the box. Write sentences about what you *can* or *can't* do.

Example: I can ride a bicycle.

> ride a bicycle   play chess   draw cartoons
> cook a hamburger   sing a song in English
> swim underwater   swim 200 metres   jump two metres
> say the alphabet in English   count to 100 in English

D

In pairs, ask your partner questions from exercise C. Give short answers.

Example: A: Can you play chess?
B: No, I can't.

E

SPELLING GAME

- Write down five words from modules 1 and 2.
- In pairs, test your partner.

Example: A: Can you spell daughter?
B: Yes, I can. D-A-U-G-H-T-E-R.
A: Correct!

Did you know?
Batman can't fly.

EXTRA TIME

Look at World Club magazine on page 89. Do activity 4.

Cartoons

5 Drawing

A 🔑 KEYWORDS

Match the words in the box with the numbers on the drawings above.

long hair   short hair   pointed ears
hat small nose   big mouth   eyebrows
earrings   moustache   big eyes

A Keywords/Individual

- Go over the words in the box with the whole class. Then ask students to do the matching activity.
- Check the exercise orally.

Answers:

1 pointed ears; 2 big eyes; 3 long hair;
4 small nose; 5 big mouth; 6 earrings; 7 hat;
8 short hair; 9 eyebrows; 10 moustache

B Cassette/Individual

- Tell students that they are going to hear instructions on how to draw a cartoon character. Their task is to put the drawings in the correct order.
- Remind them that they do not need to understand every word in order to do the activity.
- Play the tape, more than once if necessary. Correct the exercise orally.

Answers:

2, 4, 1, 5, 3

 TAPESCRIPT:

Module 2, Lesson 5, Exercise B. Listen to the cartoonist and put the drawings in the correct order.

CARTOONIST: First, draw a head … and divide it into four with two lines. Now, on this line, draw the eyes … and the ears, big ears or small ears … like that. Right, now add the nose, a small nose … and the mouth … you can make the face happy or sad with the mouth. Okay, now hair … my character's got short hair … and some eyebrows. Oh, you can also add other things, like a hat or glasses. Maybe a moustache, if it's a man. Right, a cartoon face!

C Cassette/Individual

- Tell students that now they are going to follow instructions to draw a cartoon character. They can do this on a piece of paper or in their notebooks.
- Remind them that they do not need to understand every word in order to do the activity.
- Play the tape, more than once if necessary.

- Divide the class into pairs and play the tape again so students can check their partners' drawings. You could also ask a volunteer to come to the board and draw the character while the rest of the class check that the results are correct.

 TAPESCRIPT:

Module 2, Lesson 5, Exercise C. Listen to a description of a cartoon character. Draw the character as you listen.

READER: Are you ready? This character is a girl. Draw the head…
Her eyes are very big … big, enormous eyes.
Her ears are small … small ears … and her nose is small … small nose and ears.
Now her mouth - her mouth is very happy …
Now her hair. It's very long.
Her eyebrows are small and thin.
She's got big earrings.
If you want to colour the drawing, she's got green eyes, a yellow face and black hair.

Pronunciation: *Can/can't*

D Cassette/Whole class

- The main problem here will probably be the incorrect pronunciation of the affirmative form /kn/. Play the tape and ask students to repeat the sentences together.
- Play the tape and have individual students repeat the sentences.

 TAPESCRIPT:

Module 2, Lesson 5, Exercise D. Listen and repeat these sentences.

Cathy can play basketball. She can swim underwater. She can do mathematics. She can sing. She can speak French. Cathy can't play football. She can't fly. She can't do science. She can't sing in French. She can't speak Chinese.

E Writing/Individual

- Students imagine details about the girl in their drawing and complete sentences about her. If the drawings were done on sheets of paper, they could be displayed around the room along with the description after activity F.

MODULE 2 Cartoons

F Speaking/Pairs

- Divide the class into pairs. Go over the example with a student (make sure the rest of the class can see his or her drawing.) Students then ask and answer questions about their partners' characters.

- Go round the class to check that they are asking the questions with the correct intonation.

G Dictionary work

- Ask students first to look at spellings and think whether they are correct or not. If they are incorrect, students should write them correctly.

- Ask them to check each word in the mini-dictionary.

- Discuss their answers and write any difficult words on the board.

Answers:

1 favourite; 2 (correct); 3 bicycle;
4 geography; 5 different; 6 (correct)

Extra Time!

- Students turn to *World Club Magazine* and do Activity 5 on page 89.

Answer: b

Reinforcement activity

Can/can't tennis: Speaking/Whole class

- Divide the class into two teams. Give players a few minutes to think up sentences with *can* or *can't*. Tell them that the pace will have to be as brisk as in real tennis!

- The first player on team A says a sentence. The first player on team B must repeat it in the negative if it was in the affirmative and vice-versa.

- Set a time limit to the 'set' and keep score on the board.

Teacher's notes

Activity Book Key

A (example answers)

Mandy can do mathematics. She can't do science. She is good in geography. She is bad in history. She can play basketball. She can't play volleyball. She can swim.

B Across: nose, face, head, ears;
Down: mouth, eye, hair, eyebrows

C big, sad, small, pointed, long, white

D Bill is from Manchester. His hair is short and brown. He is twelve years old. His favourite hobby is swimming and he can swim 500 metres. He is not a very good student. He can't do mathematics and science but he's good at English.

Extension Activity Key

Sarah: She is tall. She's got long hair/Her hair is long. She's got small eyes/Her eyes are small. She's got big ears/Her ears are big. She is happy.

Sally: She is small/short. She's got short hair/Her hair is short. She's got big eyes/Her eyes are big. She's got small ears/Her ears are small. She is sad.

B

Match the sentences with the drawings. Listen to the cartoonist and put the drawings in order.

1 Add the nose and mouth.
2 Draw a head and divide it into four.
3 Add things ~ a hat, earrings or moustache.
4 Draw the eyes and ears.
5 Draw the hair and eyebrows.

C

Listen to a description of a cartoon character. Draw the character as you listen. Show the drawing to your partner.

D

PRONUNCIATION: CAN/CAN'T
Listen and repeat the sentences.

E

Imagine things about the girl in your drawing. Complete these sentences about her.

1 ... is from ...
2 *She* can play ...
3 *She* can't ... very well.
4 *Her* brother is called ...
5 *He* can ...
6 *He* can't ...

F

In pairs, ask and answer questions about the girl.

Example: A: What's her name?
B: Florence.
A: What can she do?

G  DICTIONARY SKILLS

Are these words correctly spelt? Use the mini-dictionary.

1 favourete
2 alphabet
3 bicicle
4 geograpy
5 diferent
6 similar

(EXTRA TIME)

Look at World Club magazine on page 89. Do activity 5.

Cartoons

6 The Silly Family

Gertrude
Grandpa
Horace
Grandma
Rudolf
Darlene
LIMO 1

Cartoons

A  KEYWORDS

Look at the picture. Choose the correct words.

1 Grandpa is *tall / short*.
2 Grandma is *fat / thin*.
3 Rudolf has got a *big / small* nose.
4 Horace has got *long / short* hair.
5 Gertrude has got *dark / fair* hair.
6 Rudolf and Gertrude have got *brown / green* eyes.

B

Read the interview with Rudolph. Find *five* differences between the text and the picture. Copy and complete the table.

In the picture ...	In the text ...
five piranha fish	ten piranha fish

Have you got any pets, Rudolf?

Yes, we have.

What animals have you got?

We've got a tarantula called Maggie, an alligator called Alistair and ten piranha fish.

Tell us about your house.

It's very silly, of course. It hasn't got a big garden. But our car is very big – it has got a TV in it!

Tell us about your family.

My mum is called Gertrude. She's 37. She is tall and she has got blonde hair. Her eyes are green and she's got a small nose. My dad is called Horace and he's 40. He is short and he

has got blue eyes. He's got very long, dark hair.

What about you?

My name is Rudolph Silly and I'm eleven. I've got black hair and green eyes.

And your sister?

Darlene is six. She is short and fat with fair hair and brown eyes. She's got a very big nose!

Tell us about your grandparents.

They are very old. They haven't got pets or a car, but they've got lots of interesting books. Grandpa is tall and he's got short, white hair. Grandma has got black hair.

Thank you, Rudolph

22

Topic focus

- Ask the class to tell you the name of any comic or cartoon families they know. Give them *The Simpsons* as an example.

A Keywords/Individual

- Ask students to look at the illustration. Check that they understand the vocabulary, then have them read the sentences and choose the correct word in each case.
- Correct orally with the whole class.

Answers:

1 tall; 2 thin; 3 small; 4 long; 5 fair; 6 green

B Reading/Individual

- In this exercise, students read the text and look at the picture in order to find the five discrepancies.
- Ask them to copy the table in their notebooks. Go through the example with them.
- They work individually to fill in the rest of the table. Remind them that they can consult their mini-dictionaries.
- Walk around the class, checking on progress and helping out where necessary.
- Ask two volunteers to complete the table on the board and check the results with the whole class.

Answers:

In the picture the house has a big garden, Gertrude's nose is big, Darlene has blue eyes, Grandma has got white hair.

Language Focus: *Has got/have got*

Students may confuse the short form in the third person singular with the similar short form of the verb *to be*. (For example: *She's got a car. She's big.*)

C Writing/Speaking/Individual

- Ask students to read the text again and find examples of *has got* and *have got* in the text.
- Ask them to copy and complete the table. Encourage them to use the contractions. While they are doing this, draw the headings on the board yourself.

- Have one or two volunteers come to the board and complete the table with the help of the other students.

Answers:

1 has; 2 's; 3 have; 4 've; 5 hasn't; 6 have not; 7 Have; 8 have; Short answer: have

- Focus students' attention on the completed boxes and ask the following questions:
  - does *have* change for *he/she/it?*
  - do we use *don't/doesn't* in negatives?
  - do we use *do/does* in questions?
- Finally, ask students to translate the example sentences into their own language.

D Writing/Individual

- Students complete each sentence with the appropriate form of the verb. Correct orally with the whole class.

Answers:

2 hasn't; 3 haven't; 4 've / haven't; 5 has; 6 have

E Writing/Individual

- Students complete the questions in their notebooks and add a few more to the list if they can.

Answers:

2 Has your house got a garden? 3 Have you got any pets? 4 Has your mother got long hair? 5 Have you got a lot of books? 6 Has your family got a car?

F Speaking/Pairs

- Divide the class into pairs. Go through an example with one student. Students then ask their partners the questions in exercise D.
- Go round the class to make sure that they are asking the questions with the correct intonation.

MODULE 2 Cartoons

G Speaking/Pairs

- Students remain in pairs. They write four questions about the Silly family and cover the picture and the text. They ask each other the questions about the Silly family.

- Encourage the early finishers to continue asking each other questions.

Extra Time!

- Students turn to *World Club Magazine* and do Activity 6 on page 90.

Answers:
1 b; 2 c; 3 a

Reinforcement activity

Word chains: Speaking/Groups

- Divide the class into groups of four. One student says a sentence, for example: *I can sing.* The next player adds another verb: *I can sing and dance.* The third adds a new element: *I can sing, dance and swim.* The aim is to keep adding to the previous student's sentence.

- When the chain breaks, they start with another verb: *I've got ...* or *I'm ...*

Activity Book Key

A 2 Yes, he has.
  3 No, she hasn't.
  4 Yes, they have.
  5 Yes, they have.
  6 No, she hasn't.

C Laura has got a bicycle.
  Claudia has got a dog.
  Brian has got a football.

D 2 Has she got a cat?
  3 Have they got a big garden?
  4 Has Freddy got a walkman?
  5 Has your mother got a radio in her car?

F 2 funny; 3 volleyball; 4 tennis; 5 football; 6 hobby

G 1 This; 2 That; 3 This; 4 That; 5 These; 6 Those; 7 Those; 8 These

Time to read:

A Gabriel

B 2F; 3F; 4T; 5T; 6F

C 2 Yes, it is. 3 No, I can't. 4 Yes, he has. 5 No, we haven't. 6 No, he can't.

Extension Activity Key
1T; 2F; 3F; 4F; 5T

Teacher's notes

Language Focus:
Has got/have got

C

Look at the text. Copy and complete the boxes.

AFFIRMATIVE

I	have ('ve)		black hair.
he			blue eyes.
she	[1]... ([2]...)		blond hair.
it		got	a TV in it.
we			a tarantula.
they	[3]... ([4]...)		lots of books.

NEGATIVE

It	has not ([5]...)	got	a garden.
They	[6]... (haven't)		pets.

QUESTIONS

	[7]...	you	got	any pets?
What	[8]...	you	got?	

SHORT ANSWERS

Yes, he has.	No, he hasn't.
Yes, we [9]...	No, we haven't.

D

Complete with *have/has* (+) or *haven't/hasn't* (-).

Example: We *have* got a small house.

1 We ... got a small house. (+)
2 It ... got a big garden. (–)
3 We ... got any pets. (–)
4 I ... got a Walkman (+), but I ... got a lot of cassettes. (–)
5 My big brother ... got a computer. (+)
6 My parents ... got two cars. (+)

E

Complete these questions.

Example: Have you got a computer?

1 you / got a computer?
2 your house / got a garden?
3 you / got any pets?
4 your mother / got long hair?
5 you / got a lot of books?
6 your family / got a car?

F

In pairs, ask your partner the questions.

G
MEMORY GAME

• Write four questions about the Silly family. Cover the picture and the text. In pairs, ask and answer the question.

Example: A: Have they got a dog?
B: No, they haven't.

Did you know?

Some people have got one brown eye and one blue eye!

EXTRA TIME

Look at World Club magazine on page 90. Do activity 6.

Cartoons

Fluency

Writing: My Cartoon Character

A

Draw your own cartoon character and write a description.

Stage 1: Preparation

Draw a simple cartoon character. Do not show it to your friends. Make notes about it.

Example:

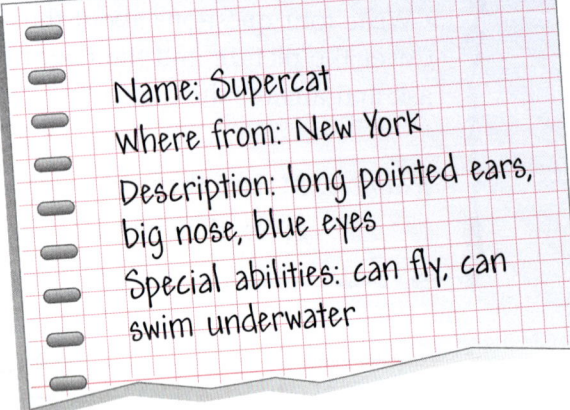

Name: Supercat
Where from: New York
Description: long pointed ears, big nose, blue eyes
Special abilities: can fly, can swim underwater

Stage 2: Writing

Write a description of your character.
Use adjectives, *has got* and *can*.

Stage 3: Checking

Check your descriptions for mistakes. Look at the Grammar Reference on page 26.

Speaking: Describe and Draw

B

Describe your cartoon character to your partner. He/she draws it.

Stage 1: Preparation

Practise saying your description. The words in the box will help you.

Example: My character is a cat. He has got long, pointed ears.

> head eyes ears nose earrings
> glasses mouth hair eyebrows h
> moustache face
> big/small green/blue/brown tall/sh
> pointed/round/square fat/thin

Stage 2: Speaking

Do *not* show your drawing to your partner.

Describe your character. Your partner draws it.

Compare the two drawings.

Listening: Cartoon Quiz

C

Listen and answer the questions a, b or c.

Example: 1 c

Writing: My Cartoon Character

A Writing/Individual

Stage 1: Preparation

- Explain to students that they are going to create their own cartoon character and write a description.

- Go through the different stages in the exercise with the whole class and make sure that they understand each one.

- Students draw a simple cartoon character and make notes about it.

Stage 2: Writing

- Students write a more complete description, using adjectives as well as the verbs *has got* and *can*.

Stage 3: Checking

- Students check their description for mistakes with the help of their vocabulary books. They can also look at the *Keyword Check* and the *Grammar Reference* on page 26.

Speaking: Describe and draw

B Speaking/Pairs

Stage 1: Preparation

- Tell students that they are going to describe their character to another student who will have to draw it.

- Read the example and remind them that while they are speaking, their partner will be drawing, so they have to pause once in a while. Ask them to practise saying their description.

Stage 2: Speaking

- Divide the class into pairs. Students look at their drawing again without showing it to their partners, and then describe it.

- When they have finished speaking and drawing, they compare both productions and circle the discrepancies if there are any.

- Monitor the activity, helping with vocabulary and structures.

Listening: Cartoon quiz

C Cassette/Individual/Pairs

- Tell students they are going to hear questions about popular TV cartoons. They have to answer a, b or c. Play the tape, pausing after each question.

- You may wish them to work in pairs or small groups to compare and discuss their answers.

- Correct the exercise by asking for a show of hands first, and then giving students the answers.

Answers:
1c; 2b; 3b; 4a; 5b

 TAPESCRIPT:

Module 2, Fluency, Exercise C. Listen and answer the questions. Choose a, b or c. Question One.

READER: Is Scooby Doo - a) a cat, b) a fish, or c) a dog?

NARRATOR: **Question Two.**

READER: What is the name of Batman's friend? Is it, a) Robert, b) Robin, or c) Roger.

NARRATOR: **Question Three.**

READER: In the cartoon Tom and Jerry, is Jerry a) a cat, b) a mouse, or c) a dog?

NARRATOR: **Question Four.**

READER: What colour is the famous cartoon panther? a) pink, b) brown, or c) black.

NARRATOR: **Question Five.**

READER: What is the name of Mickey Mouse's girlfriend? Is it a) Martha, b) Minnie, or c) Monica?

Consolidation

Grammar

A Writing/Individual

- In their notebooks, students complete the questions and then write the answer to each one. Remind them to write the first word in each sentence with a capital letter, and to add a question mark at the end. Check the answers with the whole class.

Answers:

2 Can you sing? Yes, I can. / No, I can't.
3 Can your mother speak English? Yes, she can. / No, she can't. 4 Can your father play chess? Yes, he can. / No, he can't. 5 Can you speak French? Yes, I can. / No, I can't.
6 Can Batman fly? No, he can't.

B Writing/Individual

- Students complete each sentence with the appropriate form of the verb. Check the answers orally with the whole class.

Answers:

1 have; 2 hasn't; 3 has; 4 haven't / hasn't; 5 has

C Writing/Individual

- Students complete the questions and then write the answer to each one. Remind them to write the first word in each sentence with a capital letter, and to add a question mark at the end. Check the answers with the whole class.

Answers:

2 Have the Flintstones got a pet? Yes, they have. 3 Has Bill Gates got a lot of money? Yes, he has. 4 Has Superman got fair hair? No, he hasn't. 5 Has Claudia Schiffer got long hair? Yes, she has. 6 Have the Sillies got a dog? No, they haven't.

D Speaking/Groups

- Divide the class into groups. Demonstrate the game first with two or three students. They must be careful when using the first and third persons singular!

- If a player makes a mistake, he or she is out.
- While the groups are playing, go round the class to make sure that both the word order and the intonation are correct.

Vocabulary

E Keywords/Individual

- Students look at the words in the two boxes and match the verbs and the nouns.
- Correct the exercise orally with the whole class. Then ask individual students questions with these expressions. For example: *Can you cook a hamburger?*

Answers:

2 play basketball; 3 do mathematics; 4 ride a bicycle; 5 draw cartoons; 6 sing songs; 7 read books; 8 cook a hamburger

Pronunciation: Contractions

F Cassette/Individual

- Students listen to the tape and write down the number of words there are in each sentence. Remind them that a contraction (such as She's) counts as two words.
- They listen to the tape again and write down the sentences. Then they repeat them individually or all together.

Answers

2: 6 words; 3: 6 words; 4: 5 words; 5: 6 words; 6: 6 words

 TAPESCRIPT:

Module 2, Consolidation. Exercise F. Listen and count the words in each sentence. Then write down the sentence and check your answers. One.

Boy: She's from London.
NARRATOR: **Two.**
Boy: Her brother's a good footballer.
NARRATOR: **Three.**
Boy: He hasn't got a car.
NARRATOR: **Four.**
GIRL: I'm twelve years old.
NARRATOR: **Five.**
GIRL: I haven't got a walkman.
NARRATOR: **Six.**
GIRL: My sister's got long hair.

Consolidation

Grammar

A

Write questions with *can* and then answer them using short answers.

Example: 1 Can penguins fly? No, they can't.

1 penguins / fly?
2 you / sing?
3 your mother / speak English?
4 your father / play chess?
5 you / speak French?
6 Batman / fly?

B

Complete the sentences with *have/has* (+), *haven't/hasn't* (-).

1 We ... got two dogs, a cat and three fish. (+)
2 My mother can't drive. She ... got a car. (–)
3 Sophie ... got a lot of cartoons on video. (+)
4 They ... got a big house. It ... got a small garden. (–)
5 Martin ... got a computer. (+)

C

Write questions with *has got* or *have got*. Then write short answers.

Example: 1 Has your school got a computer room?   Yes, it has.

1 your school / a computer room?
2 the Flintstones / a pet?
3 Bill Gates / a lot of money?
4 Superman / fair hair?
5 Claudia Schiffer / long hair?
6 the Sillies / a dog?

D

MEMORY GAME

• In groups, play this memory game. If you make a mistake, you are out.

Ana: I've got a dog called Jo.
Magda: Ana has got a dog called Jo and I've got a poster of Leonardo DiCaprio.
Juan: Ana has got a dog called Jo, Magda has got a poster of Leonardo DiCaprio, and I've got a computer.

Vocabulary

E

Match the verbs and nouns.

Example: speak English

speak play do ride draw sing read cook

a hamburger mathematics a bicycle
books cartoons songs basketball English

Pronunciation: Contractions

F

Listen and count the words in each sentence. Contractions count as two words. Then listen again and write down the sentences.

Example: She's from London. = 4 words
            1 2   3   4

Module check

Grammar Reference

3 Can

I/you/he/she/it/we/they	Affirmative	Negative
	can play	can't play (can not)

Questions				
What When Where	can	I/you/he/she/it/ we/they	read?
	Can		

- Can is used to express ability:

He can ride a bicycle. I can't play chess.

- Remember! You can answer can questions with *yes, no* or a *short answer*:

Can you spell 'daughter'? Yes. / Yes, I can.

Can you speak Japanese? No. / No, we can't.

4 Has / have got

	Affirmative	Negative	Questions			
I/you/ we/ they	have got	have not got (haven't got)	Have	I/you/ we/they	got	a car?
he/ she/it	has got	has not got (hasn't got)	Has	he/she/it	got	a car?

- Has/have got is used to indicate possession:

He's got ten piranha fish. They've got lots of books.
I've got black hair and green eyes.

- Remember! You can answer has/have got questions with *yes* or *no* or with a *short answer*:

Has he got an alligator? Yes. / Yes, he has.
Have you got a big nose? No! / No, I haven't.

Keyword Check

Opinions: I think it's boring / excellent / funny / good / great / interesting / OK / terrible / useless

Activities: cook (hamburgers), count (to 100), do (mathematics), draw (pictures / cartoons), fly, jump (two metres), play (sport), say (the alphabet), sing (songs), speak (French), swim (underwater)

Parts of the body: face, head, hair, ears, nose, mouth, eyebrows, moustache, eyes

Descriptions: big/small, fair/dark, fat/thin, round/square, short/tall, tall/sho

Possessions: bicycle, car, cassette, computer, earrings, garden, glasses, hat, house, pet, poster, Walkman

Animals: alligator, piranha fish, tarantula

Classroom language:
Tell the class.
Take turns to …
Put the pictures in order.
Choose the correct words.
Make notes about …
Complete the sentences with …
Check your writing.

1 **Look at Grammar References 3-4 above and complete Grammar Files 3-4 in the Activity Book. Then do the *Test Yourself: Grammar* on page 18 of the Activity Book.**

2 **Look at the Keyword Check. Write important new words in your vocabulary book. Then do *Test Yourself: Vocabulary* on page 18 of the Activity Book.**

- This should help students to reflect on several aspects of their learning and to assess their progress themselves.

- Ask them first to choose their favourite activity in this module (e.g: Lesson 5, exercise C - drawing the cartoon character).

- Ask them to assess their speaking in Fluency, exercise B: ✓✓✓= very well, ✓✓= quite well, ✓=OK, ✗=not very well.

- Ask students to look at the *Grammar Reference* and the *Grammar File* and then do the *Test Yourself: Grammar* exercises.

- Ask them to look at the *Keywords Check* and write the important new words in their vocabulary books and then do the *Test Yourself: Vocabulary* exercises.

- Remind them that these activities should be done **by** themselves and **for** themselves. However, also make it clear that you are always willing to revise problem areas in class.

- It is a good idea to spot check their work so you can get a better idea of each student's general attitude and progress.

3 Hobbies

MODULE 3 Hobbies

Objectives

Read and talk about different hobbies; listen to interviews and to a song; describe habitual actions and write a questionnaire.

Contents

Language Aims

Functions:

- Using the present simple
- Asking for specific information
- Expressing opinions
- Understanding collocation
- Talking about popular hobbies

Target language:

- *Miriam makes model aeroplanes.*
- *We don't watch TV in the evenings.*
- *Does he play computer games?*
- *Yes, he does. / No, he doesn't.*
- *Where do you play football?*
- *In the park.*
- *I love quiz games.*
- *In the summer, I play tennis and I go cycling.*

Vocabulary:

Verbs: *attack, buy, choose, collect, crash, find out, fly, give, help, keep, kill, make, paint, play, read, stop*

Hobbies: *collect (badges, coins, dolls, posters, stamps, stickers), play (board games, cards, chess, computer games, dominoes, football, tennis), go (canoeing, cycling, horse riding, swimming), make (model aeroplanes, model cars), read (books, comics, magazines), play (the guitar, the piano, the violin)*

Times: *on Sunday, at weekends, in the evenings, after school, in the summer, in the winter*

Places: *at home, at school, in the park, in the garden, at my friend's house, on the coast, in the mountains, in the street, in the city*

Adjectives: *creative, exciting, expensive, interesting, marvellous, original, private, realistic, sinister*

Pronunciation:

- Recognising and producing the /s/, /z/ and /ɪz/ endings of the 3rd person singular in the present simple

Activity types

- Brainstorming for topic-related vocabulary
- Making lists of hobbies
- Talking about hobbies in pairs and small groups
- Making predictions and checking them with the help of the text
- Completing sentences with the correct form of the verb in brackets
- Writing sentences about hobbies
- Doing the activities in the *World Club Magazine*
- Reading about computer games and choosing one
- Matching adjectives and their definitions
- Writing a letter to the *World Club Magazine* about games
- Drawing Venn diagrams
- Matching words and drawings
- Writing *yes/no* and *wh-* questions about favourite activities
- Doing a survey about hobbies in groups
- Listening to a song and singing it
- Completing the module check
- Organising the new vocabulary in a notebook
- Carrying out self-evaluation tasks

Attitudes to learning

- Reflecting on the enriching nature of hobbies and sport
- Participating willingly in pair, group and whole-class activities
- Showing respect for classmates' opinions
- Showing interest in overcoming learning problems
- Accepting and viewing errors as a natural part of the learning process

Moral and Social Values

- Health and Sex Education

Discussing with students the benefits of hobbies and physical activity to increase mental well-being (Lesson 7: *B*; Lesson 9: *G*; Fluency: *A Survey*).

Lead-in

Teacher's notes

Module Objectives

Read and explain the module objectives to your students and make sure that they understand them.

Topic focus

- Before opening the book, write the word *hobby* on the board and explain it. Tell the class what your hobbies are.
- Then write the verbs *play, make, collect, read* and *watch* on the board as column headings.
- Ask students to open their books and look at the hobbies in the pictures.
- Ask the class to tell you in which column to write the hobbies (e.g. *play chess, collect badges)* and complete the table on the board.
- Discuss with students if hobbies are similar or different in their area.
- Briefly ask two or three students to tell you their hobbies. For example: *I collect stamps.*

a Keywords/Individual

- Ask students to look at the items on the page and at the words in the box. Then have them make a list of their hobbies in their notebooks.
- Tell them the names of any other hobbies they wish to know in English and add them to the correct column on the board. (For example: *collect football cards, read music magazines.)*

b Speaking/Groups

- Divide the class into small groups. Students compare their lists and make a general list of the group's favourite hobbies.
- You can wrap up the activity by making a quick survey of the five most popular hobbies in the class and writing them up on the board. If an unusual hobby turns up on a list, ask the student to describe it briefly in his or her own language.

Hobbies

MODULE OBJECTIVES

IN THIS MODULE YOU WILL ...

Read	about collectors and computer games.
Listen	to interviews and a song.
Talk	about your hobbies and free time.
Practise	the present simple tense.
Write	a questionnaire.

Lead-in

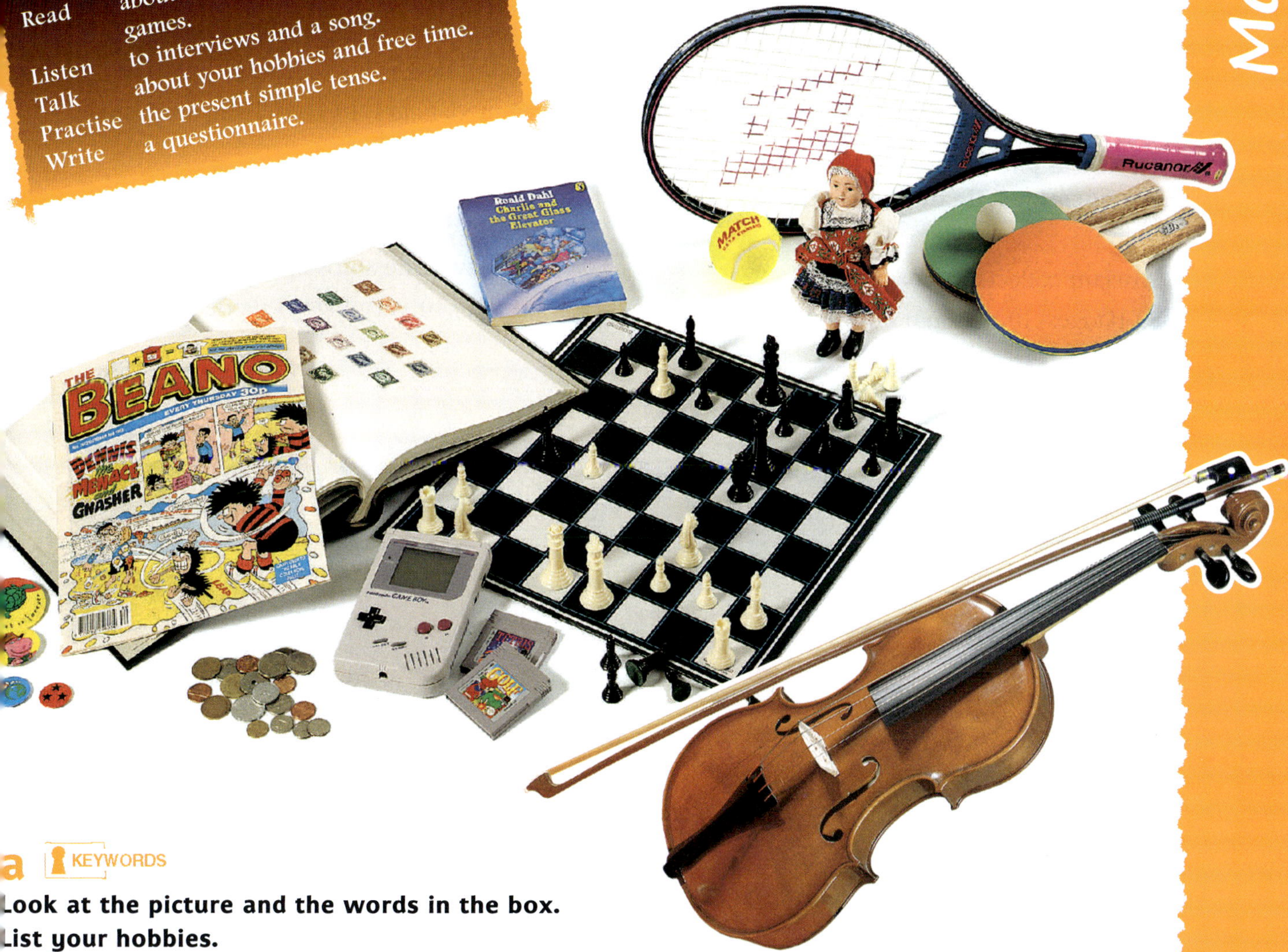

a KEYWORDS

Look at the picture and the words in the box. List your hobbies.

Example: football

play: basketball, football, computer games, tennis, table tennis, chess
collect: keyrings, stickers, stamps, coins, badges
make: model planes, model cars
read: comics, books, magazines
play: the violin, the piano, the guitar

b

In groups, read your list. What are the favourite hobbies in each group?

Example: football (3 people)
comics (2 people)

7 Collecting

A

What do you collect? Tell the class.

Example: I collect badges. I've got about 50.

B

Look at the photos. Guess the answers to these questions. Read and check.

1 Miriam collects
   a) badges b) national dolls c) coins

2 She has got
   a) fifteen b) twenty c) twenty-five

3 Her favourite doll is
   a) Japanese b) Spanish c) Russian

4 Simon makes and collects
   a) model cars b) model ships c) model aeroplanes

5 He has got
   a) fifteen b) twenty-five c) thirty

6 His favourite ships are
   a) old b) very big c) modern

LETTERS PAGE

This week - collecting things

I collect national dolls. I have got about twenty dolls from different countries like Greece, Holland and Japan. My favourite doll is from Japan. My parents give me dolls on my birthday. I also buy dolls when we go on holiday. I keep the dolls in my bedroom – I don't want my little brother to play with them!
Miriam Davies, Swansea

I make and collect model ships. I have got about thirty models of old boats (I don't collect modern ships). I make them from kits and paint them. I've also got three radio-controlled ships – my dad helps me make them. My favourite boat is a tall ship – it's fantastic! On Sundays we sail the ships in the park. My dad doesn't sail the tall ship because it's expensive and he doesn't want to crash it!

Simon Bartlett, Belfast

A Speaking/Whole class

- Ask students to tell their classmates briefly about the things they collect.
- If they seem to hesitate, help them by asking a few questions. For example: *Do you collect anything? Do you like football cards?* etc.

B Reading/Individual

- Students look at the photos, read the multiple choice questions and predict the answers.
- Ask them to read the text to check their answers. Correct orally with the whole class.

Answers:
1b; 2b; 3a; 4b; 5c; 6a

Language Focus: Present simple

This tense is presented here to express habitual actions or routines.

Students tend to forget the *s* ending of the third person singular, especially in oral work.

In the negative, the concept of using an auxiliary may be strange for some students. In English, there are two auxiliary forms for the present simple: *don't* and *doesn't*. The contracted form of the auxiliary is more common in both spoken and written English. The full form is used more formally.

C Writing/Individual

- Ask students to copy and complete the table. While they are doing this, draw the headings on the board yourself.
- Ask a volunteer to come to the board and complete the table.

Answers:
1 collect; 2 doesn't want

- Focus students' attention on the completed boxes and ask the following questions:
  - does *collect* change for *he/she/it?*
  - what do we use for *he/she/it* in negatives?
- Finally, ask students to translate the example sentences into their own language.

D Writing/Individual

- Students complete the sentences with the correct form of the verb in brackets. Remind them to use the mini-dictionary if they have problems with the vocabulary.
- Monitor the activity and note any problems. If necessary, review the *Language Focus* section again and give more examples on the board.

Answers:
2 goes; 3 don't play; 4 collect; 5 doesn't go; 6 make; 7 don't play; 8 buys; 9 helps; 10 doesn't fly

E Writing/Individual

- First explain how sentences are made by starting in the centre of the diagram and moving outwards. Demonstrate the activity by eliciting a sentence from the class or by writing one yourself on the board. For example: *She reads books.*
- Students write at least six sentences.
- Walk round the class and monitor the activity, marking as many sentences as you can. Note any problems and deal with them on the board when the students have finished.
- Ask students to read out their sentences – enough to give examples of different endings and auxiliaries.

F Speaking/Pairs

- Demonstrate the activity by saying a sentence about yourself and a sentence about a member of your family. The class guesses if the sentences are true or false.
- Divide the class into pairs to play the game.
- You can make the game competitive by awarding points for correct guesses. The first student to get five points is the winner.

G Dictionary work

- Look together at the mini-dictionary and elicit that the parts of speech are listed for all entries. Give a few examples orally.
- Ask students to think about the words listed and then look them up to check.
- Check the answers together.

Answers:

1 noun; 2 verb; 3 noun; 4 adjective;
5 verb; 6 adjective

Extra Time!

- Students turn to *World Club Magazine* and do Activity 7 on page 90.

Answers:

1 b; 2 a; 3 c; 4 c; 5 b

Extension activity

Venn diagrams: Speaking/ Writing/Pairs

- Divide the class into pairs. If your students are unfamiliar with the Venn diagram, draw two large intersecting circles on the board and call a student to the front of the room to demonstrate the activity. Write your name in one of the circles (outside the area of intersection) and your partner's name in the other.

- By asking and answering questions with *Are you ... ?/ Can you ... ?/ Have you got ... ?/ Do you collect ... ?*, the intersecting part of the circles is filled with things that are common to both partners. If only one person answers in the affirmative, the action or the object is written in his/her circle.

- Go round the class and help out where necessary. You may wish to keep or display these diagrams for additional oral work.

Activity Book Key

A 2 make, 3 goes, 4 gets, 5 make, 6 don't play, 7 collect, 8 doesn't understand, 9 wants, 10 don't give

B 2 His mum doesn't buy the models for him.

  3 Marcin and his brother don't play with the models.

  4 Marcin doesn't give his brother models to play with.

C 2 Eddie collects stamps.

  3 Mandy makes cars.

  4 Steve reads books.

  5 Elena has got a cat.

D 2 coins; 3 dolls; 4 badges; 5 stickers, 6 key rings

E 1 hobbies, dolls, countries, dresses;

  2 people, birthdays;

  3 children, matches, Saturdays

F 1 enjoys; 2 buys; 3 tries; 4 plays; 5 flies

Extension Activity Key

1F; 2T; 3T; 4F; 5F

Language Focus: Present Simple

C

Copy and complete the tables. Look at examples in the text.

AFFIRMATIVE		
I / you / we / they	[1]...	national dolls.
He / she / it	collects	

NEGATIVE		
I / You / We / They	don't want	to crash it.
He / She / It	[2]...	

D

Complete these sentences with the correct form of the verb.

Example: 1 gives

My mum [1] ... *(give)* me dolls on my birthday. She [2] ... *(go)* to lots of different places for her work. My friends [3] ... *(not play)* with dolls. They ... *(collect)* pop posters. My brother ... *(not go)* in my room.

[6] ... *(make)* model aeroplanes. I [7] ... *(not play)* with them ~ they are not toys. My dad [8] ... *(buy)* me kits. He [9] ... *(help)* me to make them, but he [0] ... *(not fly)* them.

E

Write sentences about hobbies.

Example: We don't watch TV.

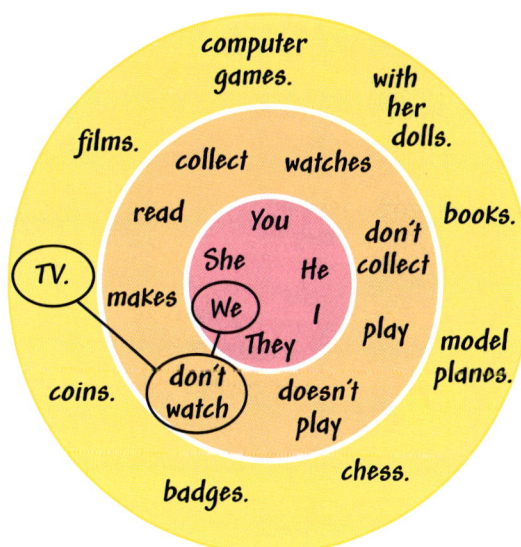

F

In pairs, say true and false sentences about your friends. Your partner guesses the false sentences.

Example: A: Alicia collects dolls.

　　　　　B: True.

　　　　　A: No, false!

G

LONGMAN DICTIONARY SKILLS

Are these words nouns, verbs or adjectives? Look them up in the mini-dictionary.

1 badge　　　　4 interesting
2 make　　　　5 speak
3 song　　　　6 thin

EXTRA TIME

Look at World Club magazine on page 90. Do activity 7.

8 Game Power

£32

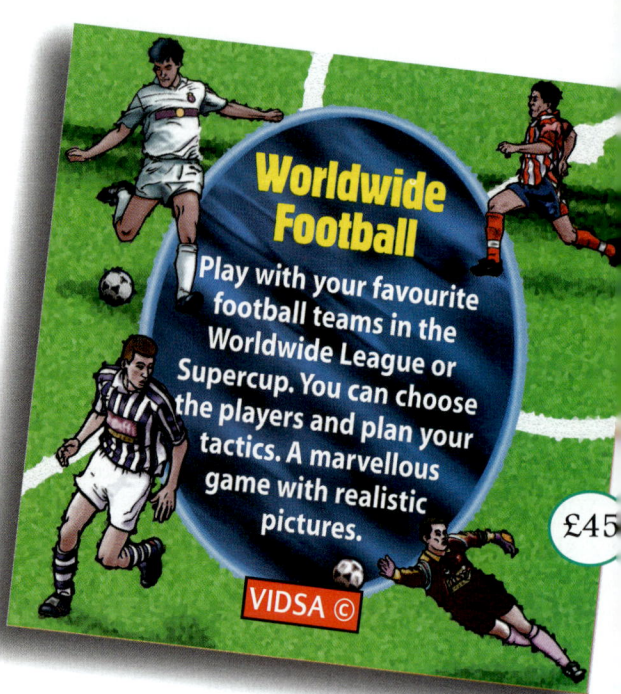

£45

Hobbies

A  KEYWORDS

Choose your three favourite games.

> card games chess dominoes ludo
> Game Boy Monopoly Scrabble
> interactive computer games
> Trivial Pursuit word puzzles

B

In pairs, talk about your favourite games.

Example:

A: My favourite game is a computer game called Haunted House. It's brilliant.

B: My favourite is Trivial Pursuit. I love quiz games.

A: I also like ...

C

Look at the computer game covers quickly. Match them with these topics:

- sport
- war
- clothes

D

Read about the games and choose your favourite. Copy the table and make notes.

	Planet Zenda	Worldwide Football	Fashion Show
Interesting	no	yes	yes
Original			
Creative			
Expensive			

30

Topic focus

- Ask the class what *indoor* games they play. They should try to tell you in English; if they can't, help them with vocabulary.

A Keywords/Individual

- Go over the words in the box with the whole class. Then ask students to choose and write down their three favourite games.

B Speaking/Pairs

- Divide the class into pairs and read the example with the students.
- Encourage them to tell each other about their favourite games. If an unusual game comes up, write it on the board and ask for an explanation, either in English or in the student's own language.

C Reading/Individual

- Students look at the computer game covers and match them with the three topics. Check their answers orally.

Answers:
1 war; 2 sport; 3 clothes

D Reading/Writing/Individual

- Ask students to copy the table in their notebooks.
- Next, they read about the games, make notes in their tables and decide which one they like best. Remind them to use the mini-dictionary if they need help with the vocabulary.
- This activity can also be done in pairs. When everyone has finished, write the names of the three games on the board and have the class vote which is their favourite.

E Keywords/Individual

- Students match the adjectives with the definitions. This can also be done orally with the whole class but make sure they add the new words to their vocabulary books.

Answers:
1b; 2a; 3d; 4c

F Writing/Individual

- Look at the Keyword box with students and explain any unfamiliar expression such as *on my own*.
- Explain the use of *also* (used to include an additional element in a sentence or paragraph).
- Read Montse's letter with the class and ask students to write something similar to *World Club Magazine* about the games they play.
- Divide the class into pairs so they can check each other's work before copying the text in their notebooks.
- Go round the class and help where necessary.

Extra Time!

- Students turn to *World Club Magazine* and do Activity 8 on page 91.

Answers:
1 computer game; 2 word puzzle; 3 cards; 4 dominoes; 5 Trivial Pursuit; 6 Game Boy

Reinforcement activity

The miming game: Speaking/ Whole class

- This is a miming game played in teams.
- Demonstrate the game by pointing to an invisible object and asking *What's this?* Then mime an action using the object. The class guess what the object is.
- Give players a few minutes to come up with words. They have thirty seconds to mime them in front of their own team, and lose a point if their side can't guess the word. They lose two points if the other team guesses it.
- Each team starts out with 20 points. The first team to reach 0 loses.

MODULE 3 Hobbies

Activity Book Key

A 1 crashes; 2 don't have; 3 try; 4 take;
5 swim; 6 follows; 7 tries; 8 doesn't speak;
9 play

B 1F; 2T; 3F; 4F; 5T

C Positive: exciting, educational, great,
realistic, marvellous, brilliant, creative;
Negative: expensive, boring, dangerous,
sinister, terrible

D 1 doesn't; 2 tennis; 3 beautiful; 4 different;
5 hobbies

Extension Activity Key

Sports: basketball, football, tennis

Hobbies: stickers, badges, books, stamps,
coins, dolls, guitar

Fashion Show

You are an international fashion designer. You make clothes for top models. Choose materials, colours and designs. This game gives you realistic images of supermodels like Claudia Schiffer and Cindy Crawford – with your clothes! Give your friends a private fashion show!

BFG©

£65

E  KEYWORDS

Match the adjectives with the definitions.

1 exciting
2 sinister
3 marvellous
4 private

a strange and nasty
b very interesting
c personal
d very good

F

Write a letter to *World Club Magazine* about the games you play. Use the words in the box to help you and include the word *also*.

Where? at home / at school / at my friend's house
When? at weekends / in the evenings / after school / on holiday
Who with? with my friends / with my family / on my own

Example:

I love Game Boy. I play at home after school. I play on my own and also with my friends. I also like computer games. I play with my sister in the evenings. Our favourite games are Bermuda Triangle and Art Mania.

Natalia Gómez, Río Gallegos

Did you know?

The game of dominoes is originally from China, and chess is from Iran.

EXTRA TIME

Look at World Club magazine on page 91. Do activity 8.

31

 **Outdoors**

Hobbies

A 🔑 KEYWORDS

Match the drawings below with the words in the box.

> swimming sailing canoeing
> cycling horse riding surfing skiing
> tennis football beach volleyball

B

Look at the photos and questions and guess the answers for Silvia and Paul.

Example: 1 Silvia = a, Paul = c

1 When do they go canoeing/play football?
   a) summer b) winter c) all the year
2 Where do they do the sports?
   a) on the coast b) in the mountains
   c) in the city
3 Who do they do them with?
   a) with their friends b) with their family
   c) with a club

Listen to the interviews and check your answers.

A Keywords/Individual

- Ask students to look at the small drawings and match them with the words in the box. Remind them to use the mini-dictionary if they are unsure of the meaning of a word.
- Correct orally with the whole class.

Answers:

1 horse riding; 2 football; 3 cycling; 4 skiing;
5 canoeing; 6 tennis; 7 swimming;
8 volleyball; 9 sailing; 10 surfing

B Cassette/Individual

- Students look at the two pictures and read the questions. Then they try to guess the answer for each one.
- Quickly review the expressions students saw in exercise F of lesson 8. Then play the tape so they can check their answers.

Answers:

2 Silvia: a, Paul: c; 3 Silvia: b, Paul: a

 TAPESCRIPT:

Module 3, Lesson 9, Exercise B. Listen to the interviews and check your answers. Interview one.

INTERVIEWER: Silvia, you like canoeing...
SILVIA: Yea, that's right.
INTERVIEWER: So when do you go canoeing?
SILVIA: Well, I go in the summer really, at weekends, and when I am on holiday.
INTERVIEWER: Mm, and where do you go?
SILVIA: On the coast. My grandparents live in Wales, and we go there. I canoe on the river and sometimes in the sea.
INTERVIEWER: And who do you go canoeing with?
SILVIA: With my family – my mum, dad and two brothers – they're good at canoeing.
INTERVIEWER: Thanks very much, Silvia.
SILVIA: Not at all.

NARRATOR: **Interview two.**
INTERVIEWER: Paul, you're a football fan, aren't you?
PAUL: Yea, I love the game.
INTERVIEWER: When do you play?
PAUL: All the year... in the summer, winter... I play when I can.
INTERVIEWER: Where do you play?
PAUL: At home in the garden, in the street or in the park.
INTERVIEWER: Who do you play with?
PAUL: I play with my friends from school.
INTERVIEWER: Thanks very much, Paul.

Language Focus: Present simple: *yes/no* questions

A serious error is to put an *s* on third person endings in questions (e.g. *Does he sings?* instead of *Does he sing?*) Point out that the auxiliary *does* already fulfils this function.

Other common errors are to confuse *do* and *does* or to omit it altogether.

C Learning to Learn/Individual

- Ask students to look at the *yes/no* questions box and tell you in their own language what differences they can see between it and the affirmative box in lesson 7. (*Do/does* have been added as well as a question mark.)
- Ask students to translate the sentences into their own language.

D Writing/Individual

- Ask students to look at the *yes/no* questions box again and remind them that *does* is used in the third person singular. All other persons use *do*.
- Also point out that there is no *s* on the verb (in this case *play*) for *he, she* or *it*.
- Students then write the example and the five other questions in their notebooks using the cues.
- Correct on the board with the whole class.

Answers:

2 Do they go canoeing?
3 Does he play beach volleyball?
4 Does her brother go sailing?
5 Do you play in the evenings?
6 Does she go to a club?

E Speaking/Pairs

- Divide the class into pairs. Partners ask each other questions with the words in the box.
- Make sure that they are using a rising intonation for each question. As a reminder, draw arrows going up on the board.

Language Focus: Present simple: *wh-* questions

F Writing/Individual

- Write the affirmative *you play* on the board. Then add *do, so* you have *do you play?* Now add a column at the beginning, so you have

  What

  Where do you play?

  When

- Do the same on the board with *he plays,* so you have

  What

  Where does he play?

  When

- Point out that with *he, she* or *it,* we drop the *s* on the main verb in questions.

- Also point out the word order for *wh-* questions.

- Ask students to look at the table and then complete the exercise in their notebooks using the cues.

Answers:

2 Where do you go skiing?
3 Who does he play football with?
4 When does she go canoeing?
5 Where do you play football?
6 Where does he go cycling?

G Speaking/Pairs

- Go through the example dialogue with a volunteer and then divide the class into pairs. Partners ask each other questions about their favourite activities.

- Encourage the early finishers to continue asking each other questions.

Extra Time!

- Students turn to *World Club Magazine* and do Activity 9 on page 91.

Reinforcement activity

Hobbies: Speaking/Groups

- In groups, students think of three sentences about their hobbies, (two true and one false). They take turns to say their sentences and the others have to guess the false one.

Activity Book Key

A Where do you play?
  What team do you like?
  Does your dad like them?
  Do you go to matches?
  Who do you go with?

B 2 Who do you play with?
  3 Do you play tennis?
  4 What does she play?
  5 Does her brother go sailing?

D **Play:** tennis, football, basketball
  Ride: a horse, a motorbike, a bicycle
  Go: swimming, cycling, fishing
  Read: comics, magazines, books
  Watch: television, videos, films

E 2 Do you play chess?
  3 Is Steve a good player?
  4 I don't know what to do.
  5 What's your favourite sport?

F 1 on; 2 at; 3 in; 4 at; 5 on; 6 in; 7 in, in; 8 at

Time to read:

A 1 He does sports every day.
  2 Stamp collecting.

B 2 matches; 3 story books; 4 footballer;
  5 atlas; 6 stamp album

C 2 Does; 3 Who does; 4 What is;
  5 Where do; 6 What does

Extension Activity Key

1b; 2a; 3c; 4c; 5b; 6c; 7b; 8b

Language Focus: Present Simple: *Yes/No* Questions

C

Look at the tables. What are the questions and answers in your language?

YES/ NO QUESTIONS			
Do	I / you / we / they	**play**	football?
Does	he / she / it		

SHORT ANSWERS		
Yes,	I / you / we / they	**do.**
No,		**don't.**
Yes,	he / she / it	**does.**
No,		**doesn't.**

D

Use the words to write *yes/no* questions.

Example: 1 Do you play tennis?

1 you play tennis?
2 they go canoeing?
3 he play beach volleyball?
4 her brother go sailing?
5 you play in the evenings?
6 she go to a club?

E

In pairs, ask and answer questions.

> play football   go swimming   play tennis
> go skiing   go cycling   play basketball

Example: A: Do you play football?
  B: No, I don't.

Language Focus: Present Simple: *Wh-* Questions

F

Look at the table. Then write questions.

WH- QUESTIONS			
When Where	**do**	I / you / we / they	**play?**
What	**does**	he / she / it	

Example: 1 What sport do you play?

1 What sport / you play?
2 Where / you go skiing?
3 Who / he play football with?
4 When / she go canoeing?
5 Where / you play football?
6 Where / he go cycling?

Write five more *Wh-* questions about sports.

G

In pairs, ask and answer questions about your favourite activities.

Example: A: What do you do?
  B: I play tennis.
  A: Who do you play with?
  B: My friend, Sam.

 EXTRA TIME

Look at World Club magazine on page 91. Do activity 9.

Hobbies

 # Fluency

Writing: A Questionnaire

A

Write a free-time questionnaire.

Stage 1: Preparation

Copy the diagram and add to it.

stamps

tennis

collect things

play sports

play instruments

FREE TIME

piano

do indoor activities

do outdoor activities

watch videos

read books

Stage 2: Writing

Choose four activities. Write two questions for each one.

Example: 1 Do you collect things?   Yes / No
2 If yes, what do you collect?
....

Stage 3: Checking

Check your questions. Look at the Grammar Reference on page 36

Speaking: A Survey

B

Do your hobbies survey.

Stage 1: Preparation

In pairs, practise your questions.

Example: A: Do you collect things?
B: Yes, I do.
A: What do you collect?

Stage 2: The Survey

Ask other students in your group or class.
Write down the answers in your notebook.

Example: collect things: total 6 (coins 3, stickers 2, stamps 1)

Stage 3: The Results

Put the information on a graph and list the favourites.

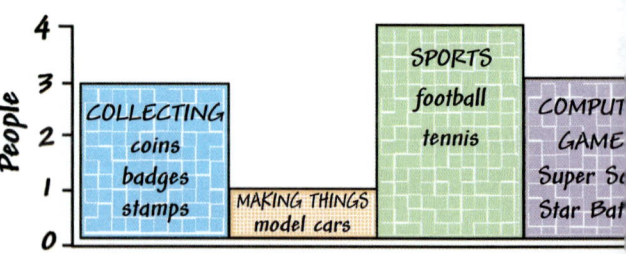

Listening: A Song

C

Listen to the song. Write down five freetime activities you hear.

34

Writing: A questionnaire

A Writing/Individual

Stage 1: Preparation

- Explain to students that they are going to do a survey on free time activities. Go through the different stages in the exercise with the whole class and make sure that they understand.

- Ask them to copy the diagram and add as many possible answers to the ones already there.

Stage 2: Writing

- Students write two questions like the ones in the example for four activities.

- Allow slower students to use the two questions already on the page.

Stage 3: Checking

- Students check their questions for mistakes with the help of their vocabulary books. They can also look at the *Keyword Check* and the *Grammar References* on page 36.

Speaking: A survey

B Speaking/Pairs

Stage 1: Preparation

- Go through the example with a volunteer. Remind students that they can also answer with just the information. In this case, *stickers* would be a perfectly acceptable reply.

- Divide the class into pairs. Students practise asking each other their questions.

Stage 2: The survey

- Students now ask other students their questions. Since the results are going to be reflected in individual graphs, decide at the outset how many people each student is going to interview.

- Students write the answers in their notebooks. The easiest way is to prepare a grid beforehand.

Stage 3: The results

- When students have got all the necessary information, they transfer it onto a graph. If you are short of time, they could do the activity at home.

Listening: A song

C Cassette/Individual/Pairs

- Tell students they are going to hear a rap song about free time activities.

- The task is to write down the activities they hear. This may be easier if they are allowed to work in pairs or groups, as one student can act as note taker.

- Play the tape, more than once if necessary. Pause between verses.

- You may wish students to compare their answers with another pair or group.

- Correct the exercise orally with the whole class.

Answers:

drawing; writing poems and letters; making models; swimming; playing football; surfing; surfing the Internet; collecting stamps, coins, dolls, badges, stickers, keyrings; playing dominoes and chess; playing the keyboard, the violin, the guitar

TAPESCRIPT:

Module 3, Fluency, Exercise C. Listen to the song. Write down five free time activities you hear.

Hey, boy, you need a hobby.
Hey, girl, you need a hobby.
School time, lunch time, home time, free time,
Draw a picture, write a poem, try to make the words rhyme.
Write a letter to a friend: make a connection.
Make a model, buy a stamp: start a collection.

If you're feeling energetic and you wanna stay cool,
Get yourself into the water, swim around in the pool.
Or try kicking a football, see how good you can get,
Take a free kick or penalty, put the ball in the net.
Football net, Internet, just surf where you can,
Free time is your time, be your best fan.
Hey, boy ... (etc.)

Stamp collectin', coin collectin', dominoes or chess,
It really doesn't matter, just relieve your stress.
Collect some dolls or badges or stickers or keyrings,
Autographs or photographs, a thousand other things.
Learn to play the keyboard, the drums or guitar,
Write a song, join a group, be a big star.
Hey, boy ... (etc.)

Module 3 Hobbies

Consolidation

Grammar

A Writing/Pairs/Groups

- Read the instructions with the whole class and check students understand how to play.

- Divide the class into groups and let them play the game.

- After each student has collected ten words (or more if you wish), stop the game. Students then write as many sentences as they can using the words they have collected.

- They can hand in their final list of sentences for you to correct. At a later date you can announce the winner.

B Writing/Individual

- Students correct the mistake in each sentence. When they have finished, ask one or two students to write the answers on the board so you can check the exercise with the whole class.

Answers:

2 does she like; 3 collect; 4 does he; 5 play

Vocabulary

C Keywords/Individual

- Students match the verbs with the nouns in the box.

- Students then look at the words in the box and classify them as *indoor* or *outdoor* activities. Remind them to use the mini-dictionary if they need help with the vocabulary.

- Correct the exercise orally.

Answers:

1 collect dolls, coins, stamps, (comics, magazines, books)
2 play tennis, the piano, basketball, the guitar, dominoes
3 go cycling, swimming, skiing, horse riding
4 read comics, magazines, books

Pronunciation: Final *s*

D Cassette/Individual/Whole class

- Copy the group headings and the example words onto the board.

- Say the words and emphasise the different endings: walks /s/ runs /z/ dances /iz/

- Play the examples on the tape, pausing between the words for students to repeat together.

- Explain that now they will hear a list of words. They listen and put them in the correct column.

- Check the answers and write the words in the correct column on the board.

- Play the list of words again pausing while students repeat the words.

Answers:

Group 1: collects / makes / looks
Group 2: plays / gives / reads
Group 3: watches / chooses

 TAPESCRIPT:

Module 3, Consolidation, Exercise D, Pronunciation. Listen to these words. Group 1.
READER: walks
NARRATOR: Group 2.
READER: runs
NARRATOR: Group 3.
READER: dances
NARRATOR: Listen and put these words in group 1, 2 or 3.
READER: plays, collects, makes, watches, gives, looks, chooses, reads
NARRATOR: Listen again and repeat the words.

Teacher's notes

Consolidation

Grammar

A
BOARD GAME

- You need dice and counters.
- When you land on a square, write the word on a piece of paper.
- Stop when you have ten words.
- Make sentences with your words. You can use the words again for different sentences. You get one point for every sentence.

B

Correct the underlined mistakes.

Example: 1 collects

1 My sister <u>collect</u> dolls.
2 What hobbies <u>she like</u>?
3 Does he <u>collects</u> coins?
4 Where <u>he does</u> play football?
5 Ana and Sandra <u>plays</u> computer games.

Vocabulary

C KEYWORDS

Match these verbs with the words in the box: *collect, play, go, read*.

Example: collect dolls

cycling dolls comics coins tennis the piano
magazines swimming basketball stamps skiing
books the guitar dominoes horse riding

Now classify the activities: indoor (I) or outdoor (O).

Pronunciation: Final '*s*'

D

Listen to these words.

Group 1: (/s/) walk*s*   **Group 2:** (/z/) run*s*
Group 3: (/ɪz) danc*es*
Listen and put these words in group 1, 2 or 3.

plays / collects / makes / watches / gives / looks / chooses / reads

Listen again and repeat the words.

Module check

Hobbies

Grammar Reference

5 Present simple: affirmative and negative

	Affirmative	Negative
I/you/we/they	make	do not make (don't)
he/she/it	makes	does not make (doesn't)

- The **present simple** is used to **express habitual actions**:

George **makes** model cars. They **give** her presents.

- We use **don't** and **doesn't** to form the **negative** and we don't add s to the main verb:

He **doesn't** go sailing in the winter.

We **don't** watch TV in the evenings.

- **Remember!** Verbs in the **third person singular** end with **s**. The ending of the verb can change a little:

he watche**s** / she goe**s** / it flie**s**.

6 Present simple: questions

Questions				
	Do	I/you/we/they	collect	dolls?
	Does	he/she/it		
What	do	I/you/we/they	read?	
When				
Where	does	he/she/it		
How				

- For questions, we use the auxiliary do and does.
- You can answer *do/does* questions with *yes* or *no*, or with a *short answer*:

Does he play tennis? **Yes.** / Yes, he does.

Do you play with dolls? **No.** / No, I don't.

- You can answer *wh-* questions with *just the information* or a *sentence*:

Where do you play football? **In the park.** / I play **football in the park.**

Keyword Check

Verbs: attack, buy, choose, collect, crash, find out, fly, give, help, keep, kill, make, paint, play, read, stop

Hobbies: *collect* badges, coins, dolls, poste keyrings, stamps, stickers

play board games, cards, chess, computer games, dominoes, football, tennis

go canoeing, cycling, horse riding, swimming

make model aeroplanes, model cars

read books, comics, magazines

play the guitar, the piano, the violin

Times: *on* Sundays, *at* weekends, *in* the evenings, *after* school, *in* the summ *in* the winter

Places: *at* home, *at* school, *at* my friend' house, *in* the park, *in* the garden, *in* the mountains, *in* the street, *in* the city, *on* the coast

Adjectives: creative, exciting, expensive, interesting, marvellous, original, private, realistic, sinister

1 Look at Grammar References 5-6 above and complete Grammar Files 5-6 in the Activity Book. Then do the *Test Yourself: Grammar* on page 25 of the Activity Book.

2 Look at the Keyword Check. Write important new words in your vocabulary book. Then do the *Test Yourself: Vocabulary* on page 25 of the Activity Book.

- This check should help students to reflect on several aspects of their learning and to assess their progress themselves.
- First, ask them to choose their favourite activity in this module (eg: the board game on page 35).
- Ask students to look at the *Grammar Reference* and the *Grammar File* and then do the *Test Yourself: Grammar* exercises.
- Ask them to tell you if a grammar structure is still a problem for them so that you can review it in class.

- Ask them to look at the *Keyword Check* and write the important new words in their vocabulary books and then do the *Test Yourself: Vocabulary* exercises.
- Remind them that these activities should be done **by** themselves and **for** themselves. However, also make it clear that you are always willing to revise problem areas in class.
- It is a good idea to spot check their work so you can get a better idea of each student's general attitude and progress.

4 Parties

Objectives

Talk about parties and festivals; read a questionnaire and some letters; listen to a song; design a party poster and describe habitual actions and possessions.

Contents

Language Aims

Functions:

- Talking about likes and dislikes
- Using subject and object pronouns
- Using possessive adjectives
- Using the Saxon genitive
- Contrasting elements in a sentence with the conjunction *but*
- Reviewing the days of the week, the months of the year and clock times
- Reviewing clothes and professions
- Discussing reading strategies

Target language:

- *He loves dancing.*
- *Jazz is OK.*
- *She can't stand rap music.*
- *I sometimes play tennis with them.*
- *Your books are on the shelf.*
- *My friend's parents are going to Austria.*
- *I work inside but I don't work in an office.*

Vocabulary:

Clothes: *boots, dress, fancy dress, hat, jacket, jeans, mask, t-shirt, shirt, shoes, skirt, trainers, uniform*
Food and drink: *burger, coke, crisps, hot dog, sandwich, sausage, soft drink, sweets*
Music: *heavy metal, rap, reggae, techno*
People: *air hostess, astronaut, bus driver, cowboy, dentist, gangster, jockey, nurse, pirate, police officer, punk, schoolmate, soldier, vampire, waiter, witch*
Places: *café, home, indoors, outdoors, office, restaurant, street*
Activities: *dancing, drinking, eating, meeting (people), playing (games), talking*
Festivals: *carnival, celebration, costume, figure, present, procession, season*
Months: *January, February, March, April, May, June, July, August, September, October, November, December*
Days: *Monday, Tuesday, Wednesday, Thursday, Friday, Saturday, Sunday*
Times: *7 o'clock, 8 o'clock*
Verbs / nouns: *carry (a bag), have (a party), know (a person), meet (a person), wear (clothes)*

Pronunciation:

- Using rising intonation in *yes/no* questions
- Recognising and producing two sounds associated with the letter *e*

Activity types

- Describing one's ideal party
- Reading a questionnaire and listening to young peoples' answers
- Completing sentences with the appropriate expressions
- Matching sentences with drawings
- Doing the questionnaire with a partner
- Completing a dialogue
- Asking and answering questions in pairs
- Doing the activities in the *World Club Magazine*
- Listening to a description and matching people with their costume
- Playing guessing games in pairs
- Playing vocabulary games
- Reading about different festivals worldwide
- Telling a partner about a familiar festival
- Designing a party poster
- Acting out a dialogue in groups
- Listening to a song and singing it
- Completing the *Module Check*
- Organising the new vocabulary in a notebook
- Carrying out self-evaluation tasks

Attitudes to learning

- Showing interest in finding out about different festivals and celebrations
- Being willing to share one's knowledge and experiences with the rest of the group
- Understanding the importance of developing adequate reading skills in order to make the most of a text
- Showing interest in overcoming learning problems
- Developing confidence in one's own ability to understand and communicate in English

Moral and Social Values

- Consumer Education

Being aware of the importance of using free time in worthwhile leisure pursuits (Fluency: *A Party Poster*; Listening: *Dancing in the Street*).

- Health and Sex Education

Encouraging students to develop healthy relationships with young people of the opposite sex (Lead-in: *b*; Lesson 10: *A*).

Lead-in

Module Objectives

- Read and explain the module objectives to your students and make sure that they understand them.

Topic focus

- Students look at the picture of the party. Ask them when we have parties. For example: *birthdays, end of the school year, weddings, christenings,* etc.

- Also ask what they usually do at parties. For example: *dance, eat, play games,* etc.

a Keywords/Speaking/Pairs

- Divide the class into pairs. Explain to students that the list of elements in the box can help them plan their ideal party. Remind them to use the mini-dictionary if they have problems with the vocabulary.

- Ask them to write down their preferences.

b Speaking/Pairs

- Each pair tells the class about their ideal party. After everyone has spoken, you can write a class list of favourite party elements on the board, including the best day, the best place, etc.

Parties

Lead-in

MODULE OBJECTIVES

IN THIS MODULE YOU WILL ...

Read   a questionnaire and some letters.
Listen   to a survey, descriptions and a song.
Talk   about parties and festivals.
Practise the present simple, personal
             pronouns and possessive adjectives.
Design   a party poster.

a 🔑 KEYWORDS

In pairs, plan your ideal party. Use the mini-dictionary to help you.

Our ideal party is *(at home/in a restaurant/ in a café/in a garden)* on *(Monday/Tuesday/ Wednesday/Thursday/Friday/Saturday/Sunday)* night from *(6/7/8/9 o'clock)* to *(8/9/10/ 11/12 o'clock)* with our *(friends/family/ schoolmates)*. We have *(crisps/sandwiches/ sweets/soft drinks)*. We wear *(smart/informal)* clothes. We *(play games/dance/sing/talk)*.

b

In pairs, tell the class.

Example: A: Our ideal party is at home on a
            Saturday night.
          B: It starts at eight o'clock and it
             finishes at ...

Are you a Party Person?

1 Do you like parties?

a) Yes, I love parties.

b) They're OK.

c) No, they're boring. I hate parties.

2 Do you like dancing at parties?

a) Yes, dancing is great fun. I love it.

b) It depends on the music. I don't mind.

c) No, I don't. I sit down all the time.

3 Do you like playing games at parties?

a) Yes, they're good fun.

b) I don't mind playing games.

c) No, I hate party games.

4 Do you like fancy dress parties?

a) Yes, I love them.

b) I don't mind them.

c) No, I don't like them at all.

5 Do you talk a lot at parties?

c) No, I don't talk much.

a) Yes, I talk to a lot of people.

b) I talk to one or two friends.

YOUR SCORE	TOTAL	
a) 3 points	0-4: You don't like parties.	
b) 2 points	5-9: You like parties.	
c) 0 points	10-15: You're a party person!	

A

Read the questionnaire. Then listen and write down Mark's answers. Is he a party person?

Example: 1 a

Parties

A Reading/Cassette/Individual

- Ask students to read the questionnaire to themselves and check that they understand the vocabulary.

- Explain that they will hear two teenagers doing the questionnaire. They have to make a note of Mark's choices and then calculate his score.

- Ask them to write the numbers 1 to 5 in their notebooks. Play the tape, more than once if necessary. Students write *a, b* or *c* next to each number.

- Finally they look at the key and add up Mark's points.

Answers:
2a; 3b; 4c; 5b; Total score: 10 points

 TAPESCRIPT:

Module 4, Lesson 10, Exercise A. Listen and write down Mark's answers. Is he a party person?

SUSAN: Mark, can I interview you for the school magazine?
MARK: Yeah, sure.
SUSAN: Right, first question. Do you like parties?
MARK: Oh yes. I love parties.
SUSAN: What about dancing? Do you like dancing at parties?
MARK: Yeah, I like dancing too, especially if the music's loud.
SUSAN: Er, do you like playing games at parties?
MARK: Well, I don't mind, I suppose. It depends.
SUSAN: Do you like fancy dress parties?
MARK: No, I hate them! I hate wearing silly clothes.
SUSAN: Now the final question. Do you talk a lot at parties?
MARK: Well, I don't like talking to *a lot* of people. I talk to one or two friends.
SUSAN: Thanks a lot, Mark.

Language Focus: Present simple: likes and dislikes

Explain or translate the expressions of like and dislike to the class, especially *I don't mind* and *I can't stand.*

B Cassette/Individual

- Students listen to the tape again and complete each sentence with the appropriate words.

- Correct the exercise orally with the whole class.

Answers:
1 parties; 2 dancing; 3 playing games;
4 wearing silly clothes; 5 talking to a lot of people

Pronunciation: Questions

C Cassette/Whole class/Individual

- Play the tape. Students listen to the questions and repeat them, first all together and then individually. Remind them that the voice rises in *yes/no* questions.

 TAPESCRIPT:

Module 4, Lesson 10. Exercise C. Listen to the questions and repeat them. One.

SUSAN: Mark, can I interview you for the school magazine?
NARRATOR: **Two.**
SUSAN: Right, first question. Do you like parties?
NARRATOR: **Three.**
SUSAN: What about dancing? Do you like dancing at parties?
NARRATOR: **Four.**
SUSAN: Er, do you like playing games at parties?
NARRATOR: **Five.**
SUSAN: Do you like fancy dress parties?
NARRATOR: **Six**
SUSAN: Now the final question. Do you talk a lot at parties?

D Speaking/Pairs

- Divide the class into pairs. Ask students to look at the questionnaire in exercise A again and to interview their partners, writing the score on a piece of paper.

- Wrap up the activity by making a quick survey to find out how many students like parties and how many don't.

E Writing/Individual

- Students complete the dialogue with the appropriate expression. You may need to explain or translate the question *What about... ?*

- Correct orally with the whole class.

Answers:
1 Do; 2 love; 3 don't mind; 4 hate; 5 don't;
6 love; 7 don't like

F Writing/Individual

- Students read the dialogue again and copy the questions in their notebooks. They also add three of their own to the list.
- Remind them to check their tables if they are not sure about word order.

G Speaking/Pairs

- Divide the class into pairs. Read the example with one student. Students then ask their partners the questions they have prepared.
- Go round the class to make sure that they are asking the questions with the correct intonation.

H Dictionary work

- Explain that the aim of this activity is to help students use the mini-dictionary to find the meaning of words. Ask them to look up the three words in number 1. Then discuss which word makes sense in the context of the sentence.
- Ask them to continue on their own or in pairs.
- Check orally.

Answers:

1 fishing; 2 keep; 3 attractive

Extra Time!

- Students turn to *World Club Magazine* and do Activity 10 on page 91.

Answers:

She likes playing games.
She hates dancing.
She doesn't mind singing.

Reinforcement activity

Fizz-Buzz: Speaking/Groups/ Whole class

- *Fizz-Buzz* is a party game and can be played in groups or with the whole class.
- Students take turns to say numbers, in counting order. However, if a number can be divided by three (e.g. 3, 6, 9), they don't say the number but say *fizz*. Also, if the number can be divided

by five (e.g. 5, 10, 15), they say *buzz*. If the number can be divided by both five and three, they say *fizz-buzz*.

- Players are out if they say the number when they should say *fizz* or *buzz*, and the game continues until only one person is left.
- Example of the beginning of the game: 1, 2, *fizz*, 4, *buzz*, *fizz*, 7, 8, *fizz*, *buzz*, 11, *fizz*, 13, 14, *fizz-buzz*, 16, 17, *fizz*, 19, *buzz*, *fizz*, 22 ... etc.

Activity Book Key

B 2 She loves skiing.
   3 She doesn't mind maths.
   4 She hates horse riding.
   5 She loves (playing) tennis.

C 2 hate; 3 does she like; 4 loves; 5 Does she like; 6 does; 7 does she like; 8 likes; 9 does Karen go

D 1 Monday; 2 Tuesday; 3 Wednesday; 4 Thursday; 5 Friday; 6 Saturday; 7 Sunday

E 2 It starts at four o'clock. It finishes at seven o'clock.

   3 It starts at seven o'clock. It finishes at ten o'clock.

F 2 Where do you live?
   3 Does your brother like parties?
   4 What music does he like?
   5 Who do you dance with at parties?

G (example answers)
   Who does she dance with?
   Where does he come from?
   What games do you play?
   Who do you like?
   Where does she live?

Extension Activity Key

Sally doesn't like TV or school. Sally collects coins and makes model aeroplanes. Sally can play tennis, she can swim and she can ride a bicycle. Sally can speak French and English. Sally doesn't like English, but she likes French.

Language Focus: Present Simple - Likes and Dislikes

B

Listen again and complete the sentences with these words.

talking to a lot of people / playing games / wearing silly clothes / dancing / parties

Example: 1 b

> 1 I love ...
> 2 I like ... too.
> 3 I don't mind ...
> 4 I hate ...
> 5 I don't like ...

How do you say these sentences in your language?

C

PRONUNCIATION: QUESTIONS
Listen to the questions and repeat them.

D

Use the questionnaire in exercise A to interview your partner. What is his/her score?

E

Complete the dialogue with these words:

don't mind / don't like / love (x2) / do / don't / hate

A: First question. ^{1} ... you like parties?

B: Yes, of course! I ^{2} ... them!

A: And what about school lunches?

B: They're okay, I suppose. I ^{3} ... them.

A: Really? Most people think they're horrible – they ^{4} ... them. Next question. What do you think of Leonardo DiCaprio?

B: I ^{5} ... like him much.

A: Oh, most girls ^{6} ... him. Finally, what about rap music?

B: No, I ^{7} ... it.

F

Copy the questions from exercise E and add three more.

Examples: Do you like basketball?
Do you like going to the cinema?

G

In pairs, ask and answer your questions.

Example: A: Do you like basketball?
B: I don't mind it.

H

Choose the correct word to complete the sentences. Use the mini-dictionary.

1 His favourite activity is evening / boring / fishing.
2 Where does he ... his models? give / keep / help
3 She loves collecting dolls because they are incredible / horrible / attractive.

Look at World Club magazine on page 91. Do activity 10.

11 Fancy Dress

A 🔑 KEYWORDS

Match these words with the numbers on the drawings.

> T-shirt long dress skirt jeans trainers shoes boots spiky hair shirt mask hat jacket

Example: 1 spiky hair

B 📼

Listen and match these people with the different kinds of fancy dress.

1	punk	a	Paul
2	witch	b	Miriam
3	cowboy	c	Tracy
4	policewoman	d	Patricia
5	vampire	e	Richard

C ✏️ 🔑 KEYWORDS

Join the sentences with *but*. Which jobs are the sentences about?

> bus driver air hostess dentist pirate waiter soldier gangster jockey nurse clown

Example: I wear a uniform, but I don't wear a hat

1 I wear a uniform. I don't wear a hat.
2 I work with machines. I don't drive.
3 I work inside. I don't work in an office.
4 I work with people. I don't work with animals.
5 I examine people's mouths. I don't examine their eyes or ears.

Parties

A Keywords/Individual

- Go over the words in the Keyword box with the whole class. Then ask students to match the words with the numbers on the drawing. Correct orally with the whole class.

Answers:

2 T-shirt; 3 boots; 4 long dress; 5 hat;
6 jacket; 7 skirt; 8 shoes; 9 mask; 10 trainers;
11 shirt; 12 jeans

B Cassette/Individual

- Ask students to write the numbers 1 to 5 in their notebooks. Tell them that they are going to listen to the tape and match the people in the picture with their fancy dress costumes.

- Play the tape, more than once if necessary, and pause after every description. Correct the exercise orally with the whole class.

Answers:

1c; 2d; 3e; 4b; 5a

 TAPESCRIPT:

Module 4, Lesson 11, Exercise B. Listen and match the people with the different kinds of fancy dress. One.

BOY 1: My name's Paul. I've got a white shirt and black jeans. I've also got a mask. My character is not a very nice person. It likes the night, but it doesn't like the day. It comes from Transylvania.

NARRATOR: **Two.**

GIRL 1: My name's Miriam. I've got a special uniform. I've got a black jacket and skirt and a hat. I've also got a badge. I think I'm very smart.

NARRATOR: **Three.**

GIRL 2: I'm Tracy. I like fancy dress parties because you can wear what you want. I've got a t-shirt, an old pair of jeans and my favourite boots. I think spiky hair is great, especially this colour.

NARRATOR: **Four.**

GIRL 2: My name is Patricia. I've got an old black dress from my sister. I made the big, pointed hat from black paper and put make-up on my face.

NARRATOR: **Five.**

BOY 3: My name's Richard. This costume is easy. I've got some old jeans, a pair of old boots, and a cowboy hat and toy gun from my little brother.

C Writing/Individual

- Students join the sentences with the conjunction *but,* which is used to indicate an opposition or a contrast between two elements.

- Next to each sentence, they indicate which character the sentence is about.

- Correct orally with the whole class.

Answers:

2 I work with machines but I don't drive.
3 I work inside but I don't work in an office.
4 I work with people but I don't work with animals.
5 I examine people's mouths but I don't examine their eyes or ears.

D Speaking/Pairs

- Ask students to look at exercise C again and choose one of the jobs.

- Students try to find out which job their partner chose by asking a maximum of five questions. The answers can only be *yes, no* or *sometimes.*

- Demonstrate the game first with a student. While the pairs are playing, go round the class to make sure that both the word order and the intonation are correct.

E Keywords/Groups

- Divide the class into small groups. Each player needs five small pieces of paper. In their own language, players write down five things that they usually wear.

- All the papers are placed face down on the table. Players take turns picking up a paper and trying to give the equivalent in English.

- The student with the most points wins.

- You will need to monitor the activity and act as referee when players disagree. It would also be a good idea to have a bilingual dictionary on hand to settle arguments!

MODULE 4 Parties

Extra Time!

- Students turn to *World Club Magazine* and do Activity 11 on page 92

Answers:

1 waiter; 2 air hostess; 3 farmer; 4 journalist; 5 lawyer; 6 nurse.

Extension activity

Jobs: Speaking/groups

- In groups of 5 or 6, one student thinks of a job. The others have to ask a maximum of 10 questions to guess the job. You can limit the jobs to those mentioned in the module or open it, as you feel appropriate.

Activity Book Key

B 2 She doesn't like boots but she doesn't mind trainers.
3 She likes black skirts but she hates red skirts.
4 She doesn't mind long hair but she loves short hair.

C 2 trousers; 3 jacket; 4 air hostess; 5 waiter; 6 shoes

D 2 friends; 3 Wednesday; 4 people; 5 questions; 6 mountains

Extension Activity Key

hat, office, animals, street, gun, catch, prison. A policeman.

E  KEYWORDS

Test Your Vocabulary.

- Write five things you wear on five small pieces of paper in your own language.
- In groups, put all the words face down on the table.
- In turns, take a word and say it in English (1 point).
- The student with the most points wins.

Did you know?

On special occasions, Scottish men wear a skirt called a kilt.

D

WHO AM I?

- Choose one of the jobs from exercise C. In pairs, ask your partner five questions.

Examples: Do you wear a uniform? / Do you wear a hat? / Do you work inside? / Do you work with machines? / Do you help people? / Do you work with animals? / Do you like ...?

- You can only answer *yes*, *no* or *sometimes*. Guess who your partner is.

EXTRA TIME

Look at World Club magazine on page 92. Do activity 11.

Parties

YOUR LETTERS

1

We have a special celebration every year on 8th December. It is called Beach Day. We have a big party to celebrate the start of the beach season.
Hugo, Montevideo, Uruguay

2

My grandmother is from Trinidad. Every year in August we go to the Notting Hill Carnival. It is a big street party. We watch the processions – my grandmother's favourite procession is the Masquerade Players. We also dance to reggae music.
Sammy, London, UK

3

Our big celebration is Diwali. For us it is the start of a new year, but it is in October or November. We eat special food. It is also a time to meet your friends and give them presents!
Madhur, New Delhi, India

4

Carnival is usually in February. We elect a Carnival Queen. We dance and carry her through the streets.
Maria, Santa Cruz de Tenerife, Spain

A  KEYWORDS

When are the main festivals you know?

Example: in July - San Fermín in Spain

in October - Halloween in the USA

January	February	March	April	May
June	July	August	September	October
November	December			

Topic focus

- Look at the lesson title: *Festivals*. Elicit or explain the meaning of the word. Ask students to give any examples of famous festivals in their area or other countries. For example: *San Fermines in Pamplona, the carnival in Brazil*, etc.

A Keywords/Whole class

- Ask students when the main festivals in their area are celebrated. Then go through the months of the year to see if they can name other important festivals in their country or in the rest of the world.

B Reading/Individual

- Students read the letters and say in what month each festival is held. Remind them to use the mini-dictionary if they need help with the vocabulary.
- Correct orally with the whole class.

Answers:

2 in August; 3 in October or November; 4 in February

C Reading/Individual

- Ask students to read the letters again and answer the five questions. This can be done in writing, or orally with the whole class. In both cases, students can use short answers.

Answers:

1 in Uruguay; 2 the Masquerade Players; 3 reggae; 4 eat special food, meet friends and give presents; 5 the Carnival Queen

Language Focus 1: Personal pronouns and possessive adjectives

This is a revision of the subject and object pronouns and the matching possessive adjectives.

Possessive adjectives always precede a noun and always come first in a list of adjectives before a noun. Like all adjectives, they have no plural form.

D Writing/Individual

- Students copy and complete the table in their notebooks.

Answers:

Object pronouns: you / her / us / them; Possessive adjectives: my / his / our

- Point to individual students and have them say one pronoun (or adjective) at a time and in order. Increase the pace until the word comes automatically.

E Writing/Individual

- Students complete the sentences with one of the words in brackets. To give them additional writing practice, you can ask them to copy out the whole sentence.
- Correct by having students write the answers on the board.

Answers:

1 we; 2 me; 3 you / your; 4 She / her; 5 Our / us

Language Focus 2: Possessive 's

F Speaking/Whole class

- Ask students to look at the expressions in the box and translate them. Once you are satisfied that they understand the difference between possessor and possession, they complete the sentences with the correct form of the possessive.
- Correct the exercise by having volunteers write out the sentences on the board.

Answers:

2 Fred's sister; 3 Mrs Smith's class; 4 Alice's hair; 5 friends'

Reinforcement activity

The Saxon genitive: Speaking/ Whole class

- This is a team game to practise the Saxon genitive. Hand out small pieces of paper to the students and write the following examples on the board: *the father of Diego* and *the pencil of the teacher.*

- Ask them to write similar possessive expressions with *of.*

- Collect the pieces of paper and divide the class into teams.

- Read out the first expression. The first player on team A must quickly give out the equivalent Saxon genitive expression for two points: *Diego's father; the teacher's pencil.* If he or she hesitates or is wrong, the first player on team B gets a chance for one point.

- Set a time limit to the game. The team with the most points wins.

Extra Time!

- Students turn to *World ClubMagazine* and do Activity 12 on page 92.

Answers:

1 Carnival; 2 Valentine's Day; 3 Diwali; 4 Guy Fawkes (Bonfire) Night

Activity Book Key

A 2 us; 3 her; 4 him; 5 you; 6 them

B 2 He doesn't like them.
3 They love it.
4 We listen to it with her.
5 She helps us with our homework.
6 They like him.

C My, I, they, me, I, them, we, I, we, I, them, my

D 2 I like Lucy's hair.
3 I've got Patrick's telephone number.
4 I love Mrs Green's lessons.
5 Tom's dog is called Nero.

E 2 The children's bicycles are new.
3 Lucy's dolls are expensive.
4 The stamps are yours.
5 Lucy's cat is called Tammie.

G It's fantastic - I love it; I like them; I don't mind it; I don't like him; I hate it

H 2 an; 3 an; 4 a; 5 a; 6 an; 7 a; 8 an

Time to Read:

A b

B 1 Hallowe'en; 2 broomstick; 3 pumpkin; 4 ghost; 5 apple; 6 trick or treat

C 1 On October 31st.
2 At school.
3 A witch's costume.
4 No, he doesn't.
5 At 7 o'clock.
6 In America.

B

Read the letters. When are the festivals?

Example: 1 in December

C

Read the letters again. Answer the questions.

1 Where do they have a big party on 8th December?
2 What procession does Sammy's grandmother like?
3 What music do they have at the Notting Hill Carnival?
4 What do people do in Diwali in India?
5 Who do they carry through the streets in Tenerife?

Language Focus 1: Personal Pronouns and Possessive Adjectives

D

Copy and complete this table:

my / her / them / us / our / his / you

Subject pronoun	Object pronoun	Possessive adjective
I	me	...
you	...	your
he	him	...
she	...	her
it	it	its
we	...	...
they	...	their

E

Complete each sentence.

Example: 1 my

1 In (me/my) town in July (we/us) have a festival.
2 My parents take (I/me/my) to the procession.
3 Do (you/your) have a good festival in (you/your) town?
4 (She/her) always wears (she/her) red dress.
5 (We/Us/Our) parents take (we/us/our) to the dance.

Language Focus 2: Possessive 's

F

How do *you* say these expressions?

> my grandmother's favourite procession
> Sammy's grandmother   my parents' friend

Complete the sentences.

Example: 1 dad's

1 My dad has got a new car. My ... car is new.
2 Fred has got a sister called Jane ... sister is called Jane.
3 My teacher is Mrs Smith. I am in ... class.
4 Alice has got lovely hair. I like it. I like ... hair.
5 My friends have got nice clothes. My ... clothes are nice.

EXTRA TIME

**Look at World Club magazine on page 92.
Do activity 12.**

Fluency

Writing: A Party Poster

A

In pairs, design a poster for a party at your school.

Stage 1: Preparation

Look at the poster above and write notes for your party.

Stage 2: Writing

Use your notes to make a poster on a big sheet of paper.

Stage 3: Checking

Check the spelling of words. Use a dictionary. Display your posters. Choose the best.

Speaking: A Role-play

B

In groups, act out a party situation.

Stage 1: Preparation

Write a name, a place, an age and a job on separate pieces of paper. Use your imagination.

In groups, put the pieces of paper in four sets (names, places, ages, jobs).

Take turns to choose one piece of paper from each set. This is your new identity!

Stage 2: Speaking

Now imagine you are at a party. Ask the other 'party people' questions.

Tell the class about someone.

Example: Nancy is a bus driver from India and she's 87.

Listening: A Song

C

Listen to the song 'Dancing in the Street'. Which of these places do you hear?

London / Chicago / New Orleans / Rome / New York / Barcelona / Brazil / the USSR / L.A. / China

Parties

Writing: A party poster

A Writing/Pairs

Stage 1: Preparation

- Explain to students that they are going to design a poster for a school party. Go through the different stages of exercise with the whole class and make sure that they understand each one.

- Divide the class into pairs. Partners write notes about the time, place, food and drink, activities and any other details they want to include.

- Next they discuss the design of the poster: the lettering, layout, pictures and colour, etc.

Stage 2: Writing

- Students use their notes and designs to make the posters on large sheets of paper.

Stage 3: Checking

- Students check their spelling carefully with the help of their vocabulary books and of the class dictionary.

- Display the finished compositions on the walls or pass them around the class.

- Finally, students decide which are the three best posters.

Speaking: A role-play

B Speaking/Groups

Stage 1: Preparation

- Make sure that each student has four small pieces of paper. Tell them to write a name, a place, an age and a job on the pieces.

- Divide the class into small groups. Students put their pieces of paper in four sets: names, places, ages and jobs.

- They take turns to pick one piece of paper from each set and read them. This is their new identity.

Stage 2: Speaking

- Students now pretend that they are at a party and ask other members of their groups questions.

- Go through the example with a volunteer first and encourage students to use a 'party-going' intonation when speaking.

- Finally, as many students as possible describe another person in their group to the rest of the class.

Listening: A song

C Cassette/Individual/Pairs

- Tell students they are going to hear a song about dancing and celebrating in the streets.

- The task is to write down the names of the places they hear. This may be easier if they are allowed to work in pairs or groups.

Answers:

Chicago, New Orleans, New York, the USSR, L.A., China

 TAPESCRIPT:

Module 4, Fluency, Exercise C. Listen to the song 'Dancing in the Street'. Which places do you hear?

Calling out around the world
Are you ready for a brand new beat?
Summer's here and the time is right
For dancing in the streets,
They're dancing in Chicago,
Down in New Orleans, in New York City,
All we need is music, sweet music,
There'll be music everywhere,
They'll be swinging, swaying, records playing,
Dancing in the street, oh
It doesn't matter what you wear, just as long as you are there,
So come on every guy, grab a girl, everywhere around the world,
They'll be dancing, dancing in the street.
It's an invitation across the nation,
A chance for folks to meet,
They'll be laughing and singing, music swinging,
Dancing in the street,
Philadelphia P.A., Baltimore DC now,
Can't forget the motor city,
All we need is music...
Way down in L.A., every day
Dancing in the streets,
'Cross in China too,
Me and you,
Dancing in the street.
Back in the USSR, no matter where you are.

MODULE 4 Parties

Consolidation

Grammar

A Writing/Individual

- Students put the verbs in brackets in the correct form. To give them extra writing practice, you can ask them to copy out the sentences in full.
- Correct orally with the whole class.

Answers:

2 doesn't mind; 3 watching; 4 hate;
5 drawing; 6 likes / doesn't like; 7 wearing;
8 dancing

B Writing/Individual

- Students write the numbers 1 to 12 in their notebooks and complete the letter with the words given.
- Correct the exercise orally.

Answers:

2 my; 3 us; 4 our; 5 his; 6 she; 7 her; 8 me;
9 Their; 10 John's; 11 Mark's; 12 your

Vocabulary

C Keywords/Individual

- Students match the verbs and the nouns in the box.
- Correct the exercise orally with the whole class. Then ask individual students to give nouns to complement the verbs on the list. For example: *carry / a box.*

Answers:

2a; 3e; 4b; 5d; 6c

D Keywords/Individual

- Students add the missing vowel or vowels to each item of clothing.
- Correct the exercise by having them spell out each word, either individually or all together.

Answers:

2 jeans; 3 shirt; 4 trousers; 5 dress; 6 boots;
7 trainers; 8 jacket

Pronunciation: Vowel sounds

E Cassette/Writing/Individual/ Whole class

- First contrast the vowel sounds in *Tess / dentist* and *Steve / teacher.* Ask students to repeat the words several times.
- Tell them to copy the table in their notebooks and match the vowel sounds in the words to the sounds in the names *Tess* and *Steve.*
- Play the tape so that students can correct the exercise.
- Finally have them repeat each word, first all together and then individually.

Answers:

1 Steve: teacher; 2 Tess: tennis / Steve: reading; 3 Tess: red; 4: Tess: eggs / Steve: sweets

 TAPESCRIPT:

Module 4, Consolidation. Exercise E. Listen to the descriptions and check your answers.

READER: Tess is a dentist. She loves playing tennis. Her favourite colour is red. Her favourite food is eggs. Steve is a teacher. He likes reading. His favourite colour is green. His favourite food is sweets.

Consolidation

Grammar

A

Put the verb in the correct form.

Example: 1 hates

1 My sister ... (hate) fancy dress parties.
2 She ... (not mind) playing party games.
3 He likes ... (watch) cartoons.
4 We ... (hate) rap music.
5 They love ... (draw).
6 She ... (like) dancing but she ... (not like) playing sport.
7 I can't stand ... (wear) formal clothes.
8 We really love ... (dance) to that music.

B

Complete the letter with these words:

my / I / us / his / her / John's / our / she / Mark's / me / your / their

Example: 1 I

Dear Laura,
My name is Stella. 1 ... am your new penfriend.
Here is a photo of 2 ... family. You can see all of 3 ... in it. We are in 4 ... garden. Dad is on the left – 5 ... name is Arthur. And Mum is on the right – 6 ... has got short hair in the photo, but now 7 ... hair is long. You can see 8 ... with my dog, Ben. You can also see my two brothers. 9 ... names are John and Mark. 10 ... hair is dark and 11 ... hair is blond.
Please send a photo of 12 ... family.
Best wishes,
Stella

Vocabulary

C KEYWORDS

Match the verbs and the nouns.

Example: 1 f

1	meet	a	a present
2	give	b	a party
3	wear	c	a bag
4	have	d	a person well
5	know	e	a uniform
6	carry	f	a person at a party

D  KEYWORDS

Here are some clothes with no vowels. What are they?

Example: 1 shoes

1 shs	**2** jns	**3** shrt	**4** trsrs
5 drss	**6** bts	**7** trnrs	**8** jckt

Pronunciation

E

Copy and complete. Match the vowel sounds to the sounds in the names.

teacher / dentist / tennis / reading / red / green / sweets / eggs

	Tess	Steve
Job	dentist	...
Hobby	...	...
Favourite colour	...	green
Favourite food	...	...

Listen to the descriptions and check your answers.

Module check

Grammar Reference

7 Likes and dislikes

- To talk about things that **you like**:
He loves dancing. I like playing games.
- To talk about things that **don't interest you very much**:
We don't mind football. Parties are OK.
- To talk about things that **you don't like**:
I don't like dancing. They hate parties.

8 Pronouns and possessive adjectives

Subject pronouns	Object pronoun	Possessive adjective
I	me	my
you	you	your
he	him	his
she	her	her
it	it	its
we	us	our
you	you	your
they	them	their

- **Pronouns** replace **nouns**.
John and Louise love tennis. They play after work.
I play with them.

- **Possessive adjectives** indicate **possession**.
On Fridays, Fred goes to the disco with his friends.
Your books are on the shelf.

- **'s** also indicates **possession**. For singular nouns we use **'s**.
For plural nouns we **only** add the apostrophe.
Mary's dress = The dress belongs to Mary.
('Mary' is singular)
My friends' dog = The dog belongs to my friends.
('My friends' is plural)

Keyword Check

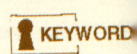

Clothes: boots, dress, fancy dress, hat, jack
jeans, mask, T-shirt, shirt, shoes, skirt,
trainers, uniform

Food and drink: burgers, coke, crisps, ho
dogs, sandwiches, sausages, soft drinks, swo

People: air hostess, astronaut, bus driver,
cowboy, dentist, gangster, jockey, nurse,
pirate, police officer, punk, schoolmates,
soldier, vampire, waiter, witch

Places: café, home, indoors/outdoors, offi
restaurant, street

Activities: dancing, drinking, eating, mee
people, playing games, talking

Festivals: carnival, celebration, present,
procession

Months: January, February, March, April,
May, June, July, August, September, Octob
November, December

Days: Monday, Tuesday, Wednesday,
Thursday, Friday, Saturday, Sunday

Times: 7 o'clock, 8 o'clock

Verbs/nouns: carry a bag, have a party,
know a person, meet a person, wear cloth

---

1 Look at Grammar References 7-8 above
and complete Grammar Files 7-8 in the
Activity Book. Then do the *Test Yourself:
Grammar* on page 32 of the Activity Book.

2 Look at the Keyword Check. Write
important new words in your vocabulary
book. Then do the *Test Yourself: Vocabulary*
on page 32 of the Activity Book.

Parties

- This check should help students to reflect on several aspects of their learning and to assess their progress themselves.

- First, ask them to choose their favourite activity in this module (eg. writing a party poster).

- Ask them to think about how they read. Do they look at the pictures and think about the text? Ignore difficult words? Use the mini-dictionary?

- Ask students to look at the *Grammar Reference* and the *Grammar File* and then do the *Test Yourself: Grammar* exercises.

- Ask them to look at the *Keyword Check* and write the important new words in their vocabulary books and then do the *Test Yourself: Vocabulary* exercises.

- Remind them that these activities should be done **by** themselves and **for** themselves. However, also make it clear that you are always willing to revise problem areas in class.

- It is a good idea to spot check their work so you can get a better idea of each student's general attitude and progress.

5 Planet Earth

Objectives

Talk about our planet and about aliens; read a tourist brochure; listen to a tourist guide and a song, and describe what is taking place now.

Contents

Language Aims

Functions:

- Using the present continuous
- Describing habitual actions in the present simple
- Giving advice
- Reviewing animals, parts of the body and the names of countries
- Learning or reviewing the names of key geographical features
- Discussing listening strategies

Target language:

- *The baby is smiling.*
- *It is not raining.*

- *Why is the alien laughing?*
- *Because humans look funny.*
- *We sleep eight hours a day.*
- *When you are crossing the road, look left and right.*
- *Don't ask to watch TV.*

Vocabulary:

Countries: *Argentina, Brazil, China, France, Germany, Greece, Italy, Mexico, Portugal, Russia, Spain, the United States, the UK*
Geography: *Africa, the Alps, the Amazon, America, the Andes, the Arctic, Asia, the Atlantic, Europe, the Gobi, the Himalayas, the Nile, the Pacific, the Sahara*
Geographical features: *forest, mountain, river, desert*
Animals: *camel, gorilla, leopard, monkey, parrot, penguin, polar bear, scorpion, seal, snake*
Parts of the body: *arm, ear, eye, finger, leg, mouth*
Actions: *give (someone a kiss), have (tea), run, say (hello), shake (hands), sit down, smile, stand, walk*

Pronunciation:

- Recognising and producing two sounds associated with the letter *a*

Activity types

- Doing a geography quiz in pairs
- Listening for specific information in a text
- Completing sentences with the appropriate verbs
- Drawing street scenes and describing them in pairs
- Matching activities with pictures
- Reading and answering a questionnaire in pairs
- Describing acceptable and unacceptable behaviour in one's country
- Writing advice for aliens visiting planet Earth
- Listening to a text and ordering the information
- Looking at an illustration and saying what is wrong
- Playing a memory game in pairs
- Doing the activities in the *World Club Magazine*
- Drawing a diagram of a spaceship
- Describing the aliens in the spaceship to a partner
- Listening to a song and singing it
- Completing the *Module Check*
- Organising the new vocabulary in a notebook
- Carrying out self-evaluation tasks

Attitudes to learning

- Showing interest in learning more about our planet
- Understanding the difference between acceptable and unacceptable behaviour
- Understanding the importance of developing adequate listening skills in order to make the most of an oral text
- Accepting and viewing errors as a natural part of the learning process

Moral and Social Values

- Moral and Social Development

Discussing what constitutes appropriate behaviour with students and encouraging them to use it in class (Lesson 14: C, D, E, F and G).

Lead-in

Module Objectives

Read and explain the module objectives to your students and make sure that they understand them.

Topic focus

- The idea of this module is to encourage students to think about themselves as inhabitants of the *Planet Earth*, rather than merely of particular countries.
- This module also presents information about the planet and touches on the topic of the environment.

a Keywords/Individual

- Look at the title of the module: *Planet Earth* and elicit the meaning of this in the students' own language.
- Tell them to match the words in the two boxes. They may do this in pairs if you wish.
- Ask them to add as many names to the list as they can.

Answers:

Continents: Asia / Europe;
Countries: Spain / the United States;
Oceans: the Atlantic / the Pacific;
Mountains: the Andes / the Himalayas;
Rivers: the Mississippi / the Nile;
Deserts: the Gobi / the Sahara

b Speaking/Pairs

- If students did not do the first part in pairs, divide the class now. On a separate piece of paper, partners write five questions about the places they have listed. Go through the examples with them first.
- Divide the class into different pairs so that students can quiz their new partners. After the exercise, collect the questions and save them for the reinforcement activity at the end of lesson 15.

54

Planet Earth

Lead-in

MODULE OBJECTIVES
IN THIS MODULE YOU WILL ...
Read   a tourist brochure.
Listen   to a tourist guide, a quiz and a song.
Talk   about our planet.
Practise the present continuous tense.
Write   a description.

a KEYWORDS

Match the words in the two boxes.

> the Andes   Asia   the Atlantic   Europe
> the Gobi   the Himalayas   the Mississippi
> the Nile   the Pacific   the Sahara   Spain
> the United States

> continents   countries   oceans
> mountains   rivers   deserts

Can you add more words to the lists?

b

GEOGRAPHY QUIZ

> • In pairs, write five questions.
>
> *Example:*
>   Where is the Mississippi?
>   What is the capital of the USA?
>
> • Now test another pair.

13 Galactic Tours

A  KEYWORDS

Look at the aliens. What is funny about them?

> ear eye head mouth
> leg arm finger

Example: They've got one eye.

B

Read and listen to the alien tourist guide's presentation. Complete the text with *is*, *isn't*, *are* or *aren't*.

Example: 1 are

Good morning.
This is the first planet on our tour.
This planet is called Earth. It is not very important, but it is good fun to visit. The people are very strange. They've got two eyes, two legs and two arms!

Please look at the screen. We ¹ ... looking at a city. At the moment it ² ... raining. Many people ³ ... driving cars. And over there is a school bus. The children ⁴ ... going to work, they ⁵ ... going to school.

And there you can see a man in a park. He ⁶ ... going to work. He ⁷ ... walking with a strange animal called a dog. Dogs live in houses with people! Here is a house. The mother and father ⁸ ... eating meat and vegetables. The children ⁹ ... eating. They ¹⁰ ... watching television. And that is a baby. It ¹¹ ... sleeping.

Now, before we begin our visit ...

Planet Earth

Topic focus

- This lesson introduces a group of visitors travelling from the planet Zorg to Earth. On the tape, students will hear how our planet is being described to the Zorgons and what they think of our living conditions.

A Keywords/Whole class

- Ask students to look at the aliens and say what is funny about them. For example: *She's got one eye. She's got four arms.*

B Cassette/Writing/Individual

- Go through any vocabulary students may be unfamiliar with before playing the tape.
- When students have listened to the tape, ask them to complete the text. Check their answers with the whole class.

Answers:

2 is; 3 are; 4 aren't; 5 are; 6 isn't; 7 is; 8 are; 9 aren't; 10 are; 11 is

 TAPESCRIPT:

Module 5, Lesson 13, Exercise B. Listen to the alien tourist guide. Complete the text in your books with *is, isn't, are* or *aren't*.

Good morning. this is the first planet on our tour. This planet is called Earth. It is not very important, but it is good fun to visit. The people are very strange. They've got two eyes, two legs and two arms!

Please look at the screen. We are looking at a city. At the moment it is raining. Many people are driving cars. And over there is a school bus. The children aren't going to work, they are going to school.

And there you can see a man in a park. He isn't going to work. He is walking with a strange animal called a dog. Dogs live in houses with people! Here is a house. The mother and father are eating meat and vegetables. The children aren't eating. They are watching television. And that is a baby. It is sleeping.

Language Focus: Present continuous

The present continuous is used to talk about something that is happening now. Usually the main problem with this tense is leaving out the auxiliary.

C Writing/Individual

- Write a couple of sentences in the present continuous on the board. For example: *I am teaching a new lesson today. Pablo and María are listening to me.* Explain that the present continuous is used to describe what is happening now.
- Ask students to copy and complete the tables with the auxiliaries.

Answers:

Affirmative: are going / is sleeping; Negative: aren't going / isn't sleeping

- Once they have finished, ask the following questions:
  - how many parts are there in the verb? What are they?
  - what ending do we use for the main verb?
  - how do we form the negative?
- Ask students to translate the example sentences into their own language. Then play the second part of the tape again, more than once if necessary. Students listen to the dialogue and raise their hands every time they hear a verb in the present continuous.

D Writing/Individual

- Students complete the sentences with the correct form of the verb. For extra writing practice, have them copy them out in full.
- Correct the exercise by having students write the verbs on the board.

Answers:

2 isn't raining; 3 are working; 4 are looking; 5 is wearing; 6 aren't making / are working; 7 is doing; 8 isn't sleeping / is reading

E Keywords/Individual

- Students look at the verbs in the box and draw a street scene with stick figures performing the actions. (They may need a bit of help in drawing stick figures: demonstrate first on the board.)

Module 5 Planet Earth

F Speaking/Pairs

- Divide the class into pairs. Students take turns describing their scenes so that their partners can draw it. When they finish, they compare pictures.

- Monitor the activity to make sure that they are using the present continuous (rather than the present simple) and including the auxiliary.

G Dictionary work

- Make sure students understand the activity. Ask them to write the three headings in their notebooks.

- Let them work on their own, thinking about each word and then checking in the mini-dictionary.

- Check together on the board.

Answers:

nouns: river people street celebration
verbs: pull wear carry eat
adjectives: expensive pretty little marvellous

Extra Time!

- Students turn to *World Club Magazine* and do Activity 13 on page 92.

Answers:

Zig is listening to music. Zeeta is eating. Zed is reading the newspaper

Reinforcement activity

What am I doing?: Speaking/ Groups/Whole class

- This is a miming game played in teams.

- Demonstrate the game by miming an action and asking *What am I doing?* The class guess what the action is.

- Give players a few minutes to come up with suitable actions. They have thirty seconds to mime them in front of their own team, and lose a point if their side can't guess the verb. They lose two points if the other team guesses it.

- Each team starts out with 20 points. First team to reach 0 loses.

Activity Book Key

A Age: 36; Home: Glasgow; Job: computer programmer; Family: married with 2 daughters; Car: BMW; Free time: playing guitar, reading, Italian food, rock music

B 2 am watching; 3 isn't working; 4 is sitting; 5 aren't talking; 6 is listening; 7 is reading; 8 are drinking; 9 are swimming; 10 aren't wearing

C 2 is playing; 3 isn't wearing; 4 is making; 5 aren't talking; are studying; 6 is sitting

D 1 continents; 2 mountains; 3 rivers; 4 countries; 5 oceans

E 2 Mount Everest is in the Himalayas.
3 The Sahara is in Africa.
4 We go to London every August.
5 They are climbing the Andes in Peru.
6 I live near the Mississippi in the USA.

F 1 getting; 2 swimming; 3 sitting; 4 winning; 5 putting; 6 running

Language Focus: Present Continuous

C

Copy and complete the tables.

AFFIRMATIVE

	¹am eating (eat)	my dinner.
you / we / they	²... (go)	to school.
I / she / it	³... (sleep)	now.

NEGATIVE

	⁴... not eating (eat)	my dinner.
you / we / they	⁵... (go)	to school.
he / she / it	⁶... (sleep)	now.

D

Complete these sentences with the verbs in the present continuous.

Example: I am studying

1 Please be quiet. I ... (study) for the exam.

2 It ... (not rain) now. It's sunny!

3 My parents ... (work) at the moment.

4 Those tourists ... (look) at a monument.

5 She ... (wear) a coat because it's very cold today.

6 The pupils ... (not make) a lot of noise. They ... (work) very hard.

7 Carla ... (do) her English project at the moment.

8 Pete ... (not sleep) – he ... (read) in his bedroom.

E

Quickly draw a street scene. Use these ideas.

walking   standing   sitting   eating

going to school   driving   looking at

F

Describe your scene to your partner. He/she draws it.

Example: Four children are going to school.

When you finish, compare your pictures.

G

Look up these words in the mini-dictionary and put them into three groups: nouns, verbs and adjectives.

river   expensive   pull   people
wear   pretty   street   carry   little
eat   marvellous   celebration

**Look at World Club magazine on page 92.
Do activity 13.**

Planet Earth

14 Meeting Humans

A  KEYWORDS

Match the activities with the pictures.

smiling   having tea   kissing
watching TV   offering food   reading
shaking hands

Example: smiling 4

B

In pairs, test your partner about the pictures.

Example: A: She is having tea.
B: Picture 6.
A: Yes, correct.

C

In pairs, read and answer the questionnaire.

Example: A: Number 1 – I kiss them.
B: I don't – I say hello.

Meeting People

1 **You are meeting some people for the first time. Do you:**
a) kiss them?
b) shake hands?
c) say 'hello'?

2 **A person is talking to you. Do you:**
a) look at him/her?
b) close your eyes?
c) look at the floor?

3 **You are visiting a person's house. Do you:**
a) say nice things about his/her house?
b) ask to watch the TV?
c) read a magazine?

4 **A person is offering you food, but you don't like it. Do you:**
a) say you are not hungry?
b) take some food, but not eat it?
c) say you hate it?

Topic focus

- This lesson looks at what people do when they meet each other and enables students to think about what is polite and what is impolite social behaviour.
- Focus on the lesson title and elicit or explain the meaning of the title. Ask who in the lesson is meeting humans (the aliens that are travelling to Earth in their spaceship).

A Keywords/Individual

- Go over the words in the Keyword box with the whole class. Then ask students to match the activities with the pictures. Correct orally with the whole class.

Answers:

having tea 6; kissing 1; watching TV 5; offering food 3; reading 7; shaking hands 2

B Speaking/Pairs

- Divide the class into pairs. Go through the example with a student first and then have partners test each other about the pictures.

C Reading/Pairs

- Divide the class into pairs. Students read the questionnaire and note their answers in their notebooks.
- Remind them to use the mini-dictionary if they need help with the vocabulary.
- Encourage them to discuss and compare their answers.

D Speaking/Whole class

- When they have finished, go through the answers with the whole class. In their own language, ask students what they think constitutes polite behaviour and what constitutes rudeness in their country.
- You may also indicate that for British and other English-speaking persons, the expressions *please, excuse me* and *thank you* are very important (and encourage their use in class!)

E Reading/Individual

- This exercise can also be done in pairs. Students read the advice for the Zorgons and find the three examples of bad advice. They can explain in their own language why they think it is bad.
- Remind them to use the mini-dictionary if they need help with the vocabulary.

Answers:

Bad advice: c, d, f

F Writing/Individual

- Read the three examples with the whole class and then ask students to write similar advice for aliens visiting their area. Tell them to include some bad suggestions too.
- They should come up with at least four sentences. Go round the class and help with structures and vocabulary if necessary.

G Speaking/Groups

- Divide the class into pairs. Students read their sentences to their partners who must decide which advice is good and which is bad.
- Wrap up the activity by asking volunteers to read their sentences to the whole class.

Extra Time!

- Students turn to *World Club Magazine* and do Activity 14 on page 92.

Answers:

The Zorgon family are visiting a human, Mrs Smith, at her house. Mrs Smith is talking to Zed but he is watching television. His wife, Zeeta, is sitting on the television. Zig is listening to music and eating rocks. His sister, Zizi, is drinking petrol and sleeping. Mrs Smith is not very happy.

Did you know?

- Encourage students to draw their own version of what they believe a spaceship to look like.

MODULE 5 Planet Earth

Reinforcement activity

Building sentences: Speaking/ Groups

- On separate pieces of paper students write three verbs, a person and three objects. In groups of four they combine the verbs, the people and the objects in three piles.

- They take turns taking a paper from each pile and saying a sentence in the present continuous, negative or positive as makes best sense.

Activity Book Key

A 2 Zip is eating rocks.
  3 Zop is drinking petrol.
  4 Zed and Zud are sitting on the ceiling.
  5 They are smiling.
  6 Zak is reading.
  7 Zim and Zam are kissing.

B 1 eyes, hair; 2 hands; 3 neck; 4 fingers; 5 ears; 6 mouth

C 1 match; 2 listen, don't write; 3 look at, talk about; 4 write, don't put

Extension Activity Key

2 Australia isn't a city.
3 London isn't a country.
4 Japan isn't a desert.
5 Brazil isn't a river.

D

Which things in the questionnaire are rude in your country? Tell the class.

Example: I think it is rude to watch TV when you are visiting a friend.

E

Read the advice for Zorgon visitors. Find three examples of bad advice. Use the mini-dictionary.

G

In pairs, read your advice to your partner. He/she says which is good and bad.

Example:

A: Don't dance the Zorgon Tango when you go to the toilet.

B: Good advice?

A: Yes, it is very dangerous!

Advice for Zorgon visitors to Planet Earth

a HELLO!

• Smile and say hello when you meet a human.

b

• Don't give a human a Zorgon kiss – this is very dangerous.

c BLA BLA BLA

• Close your eyes when a human is talking to you.

d I HATE YOUR FOOD! I EAT ROCKS!

• Say, 'I hate your food – I eat rocks' when a human is offering you food.

e

• Don't drink petrol in the kitchen – this is also dangerous!

f

• Sit on the ceiling when you are in a human's house.

Planet Earth

F

Write good and bad advice for aliens visiting your area.

Examples:

Don't eat the ducks when you are in the park. (good advice)

Don't wear clothes when you go out. (bad advice)

Look left and right when you are crossing the road. (good advice)

Did you know?

Every year hundreds of people say they see alien spaceships.

EXTRA TIME

Look at World Club magazine on page 92. Do activity 14.

15 The Living Planet

Rainforest

Polar re

Desert

Planet Earth

Language Focus: Present Continuous Questions

C

Listen. Copy and complete the questions.

Example: 1 doing

> 1 What is it ... ?
> 2 Is it ... on the ground?
> 3 Where are you ... ?
> 4 Why is that bird ... ?
> 5 What are they ... ?

D

Put the words in order to make questions.

Example: 1 What are you doing?

1 what / you / are / doing?
2 talking to? / she / who / is
3 they / going? / are / where
4 running? / why / he / is
5 they / swimming / in the river? / are
6 that monkey / eating? / what / is
7 thinking about? / I / am / what
8 those people / why / are / looking at us?

A  KEYWORDS

Match the animals with the habitats in the photos. Use the mini-dictionary.

Example: Camels live in deserts.

> camel gorilla leopard monkey parrot
> penguin polar bear scorpion seal snake

B

Listen to the Zorgon tourists. In what order do they visit the regions in the photos?

Topic focus

- As part of a travel brochure for Zorgon visitors, basic information is given in this lesson about climate, flora and fauna.
- Look at the title of the lesson. Elicit or explain the meaning: Earth is the living planet because it is full of plants and animals, whereas Mars and Venus have no life on them.

A Keywords/Individual

- Students look at the animals in the box and match them with the habitats in the photos. Remind them to use the mini-dictionary if they need help with the vocabulary.
- Correct orally with the whole class.

Answers:

2 gorillas / rain forests; 3 leopards / rain forests; 4 monkeys / rain forests; 5 parrots / rain forests; 6 penguins / polar regions; 7 polar bears / polar regions; 8 scorpions / deserts; 9 seals / polar regions; 10 snakes / rain forests, deserts

B Cassette/Individual

- Ask students to look at the three photos on the page. They are going to hear dialogues about Zorgon tourists visiting the different places and the task is to say in what order they visit them.
- Play the tape, pausing after each dialogue so that students have time to look at the photos.
- Correct orally with the whole class.

Answers:

1 desert; 2 polar region; 3 rain forest

 TAPESCRIPT:

Module 5, Lesson 15, Exercise B. Listen to the Zorgon tourists. In what order do they visit the places in the photos? One.

ZED: Look at those rocks! I feel really hungry.
ZEETA: Look at that animal!
ZIGGY: Mum, what is it doing?
ZEETA: It's drinking some water. It's a ...
ZEETA: ... an elephant.
ZED: No, it isn't! It's a camel.
ZEETA: Ah, yes.
ZIGGY: Look at that strange animal. It hasn't got legs.

ZEETA: Is it moving on the ground?
ZIGGY: Yes, it is.
ZEETA: I think it's a snake.
NARRATOR: Two.
ZED: Wow, it's all white here!
ZEETA: Oh fantastic! Look.
ZED: Where are you looking?
ZEETA: Over there.
ZIGGY: Why is that bird walking? Birds fly.
ZED: It's a parrot. They can talk.
ZEETA: No it isn't. It's a penguin. They can't fly and they live in the Antarctic.
NARRATOR: Three.
ZED: Look at those trees. Millions of trees!
ZEETA: I can see animals in that tree. What are they doing?
ZED: They're monkeys. They're eating fruit.
ZIGGY: What's that noise?
ZED: It's a gorilla, I think. It's not dangerous.
ZEETA: It isn't a gorilla, it's a leopard! It's coming here, run ... aaghh.

Language Focus: Present continuous questions

C Cassette/Individual

- Students listen to the tape again and complete the questions with the appropriate verb.
- Correct the exercise by having volunteers write the answers on the board.

Answers:

2 moving; 3 looking; 4 walking; 5 doing

D Writing/Individual

- In their notebooks, students reorder the words to make questions. Remind them to write the first word of each sentence with a capital letter, and to add a question mark at the end. Check the answers with the whole class.

Answers:

2 Who is she talking to?
3 Where are they going?
4 Why is he running?
5 Are they swimming in the river?
6 What is that monkey eating?
7 What am I thinking about?
8 Why are those people looking at us?

E Keywords/Writing/Individual

- Students read the words in the box and look up the ones they don't know in the mini-dictionary. Revise the names of all the animals.

- Ask them to look at the picture of the Zorgon tourists in the Antarctic and say what is wrong with the details.

- Ask them to write sentences in the present continuous to describe what the animals are doing. They can work in pairs if you wish.

Answers:

A leopard is hunting a penguin. A penguin is flying. A parrot is eating a fish. A snake is eating eggs. A camel is drinking with a polar bear. A gorilla is sitting on the ice.

F Speaking/Pairs

- Divide the class into pairs and go through the example. Tell students to look at the picture for one minute and then close their books.

- Partners ask each other questions about the picture. They get one point per correct answer.

- Encourage the early finishers to continue asking each other questions.

Extra Time!

- Students turn to *World Club Magazine* and do Activity 15 on page 93.

Answers:

1 To explore space in their parents' spaceship. 2 Enormous trees, snakes and giant insects. 3 They don't have any water and the Dargans attack them. 4 To their village. 5 Because a big spaceship appears.

Reinforcement activity

Quiz: Speaking/Whole class

- Take out the questions you collected at the end of exercise *b* of the Lead-in. Divide the class into teams.

- Read out the first question. The first player on team A can answer for two points. If he or she is wrong, the first player on team B gets a chance for one point.

Activity Book Key

A 2a Is she sitting down? No, she isn't.
2b Is she dancing? Yes, she is.
3a Are they eating dinner? No, they aren't.
3b Are they watching TV? Yes, they are.
4a Are they kissing? Yes, they are.
4b Are they smiling? No, they aren't.

B 2 What is she doing? 3 Are you listening to me? 4 Who are they talking to? 5 Is she smiling?

C Polar region (B); Desert (C); Rain forest (A)

D **Left to Right:** penguin, camel, rabbit; **Right to Left:** snake; **Down:** polar bear, elephant, gorilla, panther, parrot; **Up:** rat, scorpion, monkey, seal, lion, fox

E 1 panther; 2 parrot; 3 penguin; 4 pig; 5 polar bear; 6 puma

F 1 They fish in the Atlantic ocean.
2 She lives in Italy.
3 We're sailing on the Mississippi.
4 She goes on holiday to the UK.
5 They are climbing the Andes in Peru.
6 We fly across the Pacific to Japan.
7 They cross the Sahara desert to Morocco.
8 The USA is part of North America.

G 1 He's learning English.
2 They aren't talking.
3 She isn't working very hard.
4 We're living in Barcelona now.
5 What's Alice doing?

Time to Read:

A India, Iran, Turkey, Greece, England

B 1 In India.
2 In Iran.
3 At Istanbul.
4 Mountains.
5 Because it's cloudy.

C 2 What are her parents doing?
3 What is she drinking?
4 Where does she want to have a holiday?
5 What can she see over the north of Europe?

Extension Activity Key

1T; 2F; 3F; 4F; 5T

E 🔑 KEYWORDS ✏️

**Look at the picture of the Zorgons in the Antarctic.
What is wrong? Write sentences with these words.**

biting hunting flying eating drinking sitting

Examples: A scorpion is biting Ziggy.
Zorgons have four arms, not two.

Planet Earth

F
MEMORY GAME

- Look at the picture for one minute, then close your book.
- In pairs, ask questions about the picture.
- You get a point if your answer is correct.

Example: A: What is Zed doing?
   B: He is taking photos.
   A: Correct – one point for you.
      What is the scorpion doing?

Did you know?

There are about ten million kinds of animals and plants on our planet, but hundreds are disappearing every week!

EXTRA TIME

Look at World Club magazine on page 93. Do activity 15.

Fluency

Writing: A Description

A

Write about some aliens on a spaceship.

Stage 1: Preparation

Copy this diagram of a spaceship.

Draw your own aliens in each room. Give them names. What are they doing?

eat drink sleep look at read study
play make do write

Stage 2: Writing
Write your description.

Example:

These aliens are from the planet Bop. They are travelling to the planet Earth. Biff is in room 1. She is looking at a map of the world. Baff and Beff are in room 2. They are playing a strange game called ...

Stage 3: Checking

Check your description. Look at Grammar References 9 and 10 on page 56.

Speaking: Finding Out

B

Stage 1: Preparation

Draw another copy of the spaceship diagram.

Stage 2: Speaking

In pairs, ask and answer questions about your spaceships.

Draw your partner's aliens in the spaceship.

Example: A: Where are your aliens from?
B: The planet Bop.
A: Who is in room 1?
B: Biff. She is the mother.
A: What is she doing?

Listening: A Song

C

Read the questions and use the mini-dictionary to check vocabulary. Listen to the song and choose the correct answers.

Example: 1 b

1 Ground Control to a) Major John
b) Major Tom.
2 Ten, nine, eight, seven, six, five, four, three, a) two, one, lift-off
b) one, two, lift-off.
3 This is Major Tom to Ground Control, a) I'm walking through the door b) I'm stepping through the door.
4 Planet Earth is
a) green b) blue.
5 I'm feeling very
a) still b)ill.

Planet Earth

Writing: A description

A Writing/Individual

Stage 1: Preparation

- Go through the different stages in the exercise with the whole class and make sure that they understand each one.
- Ask students to copy the drawing of the spaceship. Next, they draw aliens in each of the four rooms, give them names and explain what they are doing. The verbs in the box can give them some ideas.

Stage 2: Writing

- Students use their drawings to write a description of the aliens' activities aboard the spaceship. Read the example first.

Stage 3: Checking

- Students check their spelling with the help of their vocabulary books and mini-dictionary. If they have doubts about structures, they can also look at the *Grammar Reference* on page 56.

Speaking: Finding out

B Writing/Speaking/Pairs

Stage 1: Preparation

- Ask students to draw another copy of the spaceship diagram.

Stage 2: Speaking

- Divide the class into pairs. Partners ask each other questions about their spaceships and draw the aliens in the appropriate rooms.
- Read the example and monitor the activity.

Listening: A song

C Cassette/Individual

- Tell students they are going to hear a song about an astronaut. The task is to read the questions and choose the correct answer.
- Ask students to check the vocabulary in the mini-dictionary before playing the tape.

- Play the tape, more than once if necessary. Pause between verses.
- Correct the exercise orally with the whole class.

Answers:

2a; 3b; 4b; 5a

 TAPESCRIPT:

Module 5, Fluency, Exercise C. Listen to the song and answer the questions in your book.

Ground Control to Major Tom,
Ground Control to Major Tom,
Take your protein pills and put your helmet on.
Ground Control to Major Tom,
Commencing countdown, engines on.
Check ignition and may God's love be with you.
Ten, nine, eight, seven, six, five, four, three, two, one, lift-off.
This is Ground Control to Major Tom,
You've really made the grade,
And the papers want to know whose shirts you wear.
Now it's time to leave the capsule if you dare.
"This is Major Tom to Ground Control,
I'm stepping through the door,
And I'm floating in a most peculiar way,
And the stars look very different today.
For here
Am I sitting in a tin can,
Far above the world.
Planet Earth is blue
And there's nothing I can do.
Though I'm past one hundred thousand miles,
I'm feeling very still,
And I think my spaceship knows which way to go,
Tell my wife I love her very much, she knows."
Ground Control to Major Tom,
Your circuit's dead, there's something wrong.
Can you hear me, Major Tom?
Can you hear me, Major Tom?
Can you hear me, Major Tom?
Can you....
 "Here I am floating round my tin can,
 Far above the Moon.
 Planet Earth is blue
 And there's nothing I can do."

Consolidation

Grammar

A Cassette/Individual

- Tell students they are going to hear five sounds that are typical in a Zorgon family. Play the tape so that they can identify them silently first.
- Play the tape again and ask the question: *What are they doing?* Students answer using the present continuous.

Answers:

2 reading the paper; 3 dancing; 4 playing a computer game; 5 driving a car

---

 TAPESCRIPT:

Module 5, Consolidation, Exercise A. Listen to a Zorgon family. What are they doing? One. The family.

Sounds of the family eating rocks.
NARRATOR: Two. The father.
Rustling of newspaper. Occasional chortle.
NARRATOR: Three. The daughter.
Sound of samba. Sounds of someone dancing.
NARRATOR: Four. The son.
Sound of computer game being played.
NARRATOR: Five. The mother.
Sound of car driving.

B Writing/Individual

- In their notebooks, students write five sentences about what their family and friends are probably doing now.

C Writing/Individual

- Students look at the answers and write suitable questions in the present continuous. They can work in pairs if you wish.
- Correct the exercise by having volunteers write the questions on the board. The rest of the class decides whether the answer is right or wrong.

Answers:

2 Where are you going? 3 Who are you talking / writing to? 4 What are you reading? 5 What are you watching?

D Writing/Individual

- Students choose an illustration from their book and describe it in writing. Remind them to use

the present continuous and to check their mini-dictionary if they need help with the vocabulary.

E Speaking/Groups

- Divide the class into small groups. Students take turns reading their descriptions while the others try to find the page number of the illustration. If they aren't sure, they can ask more *yes/no* questions. For example: *Is the mother wearing a red dress?*
- Wrap up the activity by asking a few students to read their descriptions to the whole class.

Vocabulary

F Keywords/Individual

- Students do the matching exercise. Correct it orally with the whole class.

Answers:

2a; 3f; 4b; 5c; 6d

Pronunciation: Letter *a* sounds

G Cassette/Individual

- Focus on the two words and play the tape. Students listen and repeat the two sounds all together.
- Students look at the words given and try to say them aloud. Then they put them in group 1 or 2. They can do this in pairs if you wish.
- Play the tape so that students can check their answers.
- Play the tape again. Students listen and repeat the words all together.

Answers:

Group 1: parrot, camel, Africa, kangaroo, planet, Atlantic;
Group 2: Arctic, Argentina, banana, arm, fast, Sahara

 TAPESCRIPT:

Module 5, Consolidation, Exercise G. Listen to these words.
Group 1: animal. **Group 2:** dance.
Listen and put the words in the correct group.
Argentina / Arctic / parrot / camel / Africa / banana / kangaroo / arm / planet / fast / Atlantic / Sahara.

Consolidation

Grammar

A

Listen to a Zorgon family at home. What are they doing?

Example: 1 They are having lunch.

1 family   **2** father   **3** daughter
4 son   **5** mother

B

What are people you know doing now? Write five sentences.

Example: My grandfather is taking the dog for a walk.

C

Write questions for these answers.

Example: 1 What are you eating?

1 A banana. (What ...)
2 Home. (Where ...)
3 To Anna. (Who ...)
4 A computer magazine. (What ...)
5 A sports programme. (What ...)

D

Choose a picture from *World Club Magazine*. Write a description.

Example: Picture a, page 90

The family are on the beach. You can see a forest and the sea. One boy is reading a book...

E

In groups, read your description. The others find the picture.

Vocabulary

F  KEYWORDS

Match the words below.

Example: 1 e

1	have	**a**	hello
2	say	**b**	a jacket
3	turn on	**c**	a person
4	wear	**d**	a bag
5	meet	**e**	tea
6	carry	**f**	the TV

Pronunciation

G

Listen to these words:

Group 1 (/æ/): *a*nimal   **Group 2** (/ɑː/): d*a*nce

Listen and put these words in the correct group.

Argentina / Arctic / parrot / camel / Africa / banana / kangaroo / arm / planet /fast / Atlantic / Sahara

Module check

Grammar Reference

9 Present continuous: affirmative and negative

	Affirmative	Negative	
I	am	am not ('m not)	
you/we/they	are	are not (aren't)	looking
he/she/it	is	is not (isn't)	

- We use the **present continuous** to talk about actions **happening** now.

The baby **is smiling**. The aliens **are travelling** to Earth. It **is not raining**. They **are not learning** English.

10 Present continuous: questions

Questions			
	Am	I	
	Are	you/we/they	going?
	Is	he/she/it	
Where	am	I	
When	are	you/we/they	going?
How	is	he/she/it	

- We use the **present continuous** to ask questions about things **happening** now. You can answer with *yes* or *no*, or with a *short answer*.

Are the children **going** to school? Yes. / Yes, they are. Is the Zorgon **kissing** a human? No. / No, he isn't.

- You can answer *wh-* questions with *just the information* or a *sentence*.

What **are** the Zorgons **drinking?** Petrol. / They're drinking petrol.

Keyword Check

Countries: Argentina, Brazil, China, Franc Germany, Greece, Italy, Mexico, Portugal, Russia, Spain, the United States, the UK

Geography: The Andes, the Arctic, Asia, th Atlantic, Europe, the Gobi, the Himalayas, t Nile, the Pacific, the Sahara, Spain, the Uni States

Geographical features: continent, country desert, mountain, ocean, polar region, rainforest, river

Animals: camel, gorilla, leopard, monkey, parrot, penguin, polar bear, scorpion, seal, snake

Body: arm, ear, eye, finger, leg, mouth

Actions: carry something drive a car, give someone a kiss, have tea, meet a person, ru say hello, shake hands, sit (down), smile, stand, walk

Advice: visit the park, say 'thank you', sm look left and right, don't ask to watch TV

1 **Look at Grammar References 9-10 above and complete Grammar Files 9-10 in the Activity Book. Then do the *Test Yourself: Grammar* on page 39 of the Activity Book.**

2 **Look at the Keyword Check. Write important new words in your vocabulary book. Then do the *Test Yourself: Vocabulary* on page 39 of the Activity Book.**

- This check should help students to reflect on several aspects of their learning and to assess their progress themselves.
- First, ask them to choose their favourite activity in this module (eg: listening to the aliens in Lesson 13).
- Ask them to think about what they do when they listen. Do they think about the topic before they listen? Use the pictures to help them? Keep calm when they don't understand?
- Ask students to look at the *Grammar Reference* and the *Grammar File* and then do the *Test Yourself: Grammar* exercises.

- Ask them to look at the *Keyword Check* and write the important new words in their vocabulary books and then do the *Test Yourself: Vocabulary* exercises.
- Remind them that these activities should be done **by** themselves and **for** themselves. However, also make it clear that you are always willing to revise problem areas in class.
- It is a good idea to spot check their work so you can get a better idea of each student's general attitude and progress.

6 Villages

Objectives

Read about villages in Britain and write about an imaginary village; talk about one's own area; practise shopping and play a shopping game.

Contents

Language Aims

Functions:

- Indicating the presence of something with the expressions *there is / there are*
- Indicating that something is not present or missing with the expressions *there isn't / there aren't*
- Using the determiners *some / any*
- Giving reasons with *because*
- Asking for things in shops
- Discussing writing strategies

Target language:

- There are many restaurants here.
- There isn't a swimming pool.
- I'd like some lemonade, please.
- There aren't any crisps in the cupboard.

- My sister goes to ballet classes because she loves dancing.
- Good morning. Can I help you?
- Yes, I'd like some sweets, please.
- How much is that, please?

Vocabulary:

Buildings: *art gallery, bank, bar, beach, castle, church, cinema, disco, golf course, harbour, health centre, hotel, market, park, restaurant, school, shop, supermarket*
Location: *east, north, south, west*
Adjectives: *beautiful, busy, excellent, famous, historic, interesting, marvellous, pretty, unusual*
Activities: *fishing, sailing, surfing*
Jobs: *businessperson, dentist, doctor, journalist, lawyer, mechanic, police officer, teacher, waiter*
Shopping: *cake, can (of cola / lemonade), cassette, clothes, comics, computer games, crisps, fizzy drink, ice cream, packet (of sweets / crisps), sweets*

Pronunciation:

- Recognising and pronouncing the contractions *isn't* and *aren't*
- Contrasting and pronouncing the /i/ and /iː/ sounds

Activity types

- Talking about places near one's home with a partner
- Matching places and symbols
- Reading the description of villages and answering questions
- Writing descriptive sentences
- Asking and answering questions about different places in pairs
- Writing about one's ideal holiday village
- Doing the activities in the *World Club Magazine*
- Reading letters and completing a table with the appropriate information
- Listening to a text and reading it in order to find the differences
- Completing dialogues in a shop
- Practising dialogues in pairs
- Inventing a village and describing it in pairs
- Playing a shopping game with the whole class
- Listening to a quiz
- Completing the *Module Check*
- Organising the new vocabulary in a notebook
- Carrying out self-evaluation tasks

Attitudes to learning

- Showing interest in finding out about village life around the world
- Showing critical judgement when shopping for leisure products
- Understanding the importance of developing adequate writing skills in order to improve communication
- Developing confidence in one's own ability to understand and communicate in English

Moral and Social Values

- Consumer Education

Discussing the need to budget one's money and spend it rationally (Lesson 18: *B*; Fluency: *Shopping*).

- Health and Sex Education

Encouraging students to avoid excessive consumption of fast / junk food (Lesson 18: *F* and *G*).

Lead-in

Module Objectives

- Read and explain the module objectives to your students and make sure that they understand them.

Topic focus

- Ask students to explain in their own language what they perceive to be the main differences between cities and villages. However, keep the discussion short.

a Keywords/Writing/Individual

- Ask students to look at the words in the box and then write a list of places near their home. Help them with additional vocabulary if they need it.

b Speaking/Pairs

- Divide the class into pairs. Partners tell each other about the places they visit, and when. Go through the examples with them first.
- Then ask a few volunteers to tell the rest of the class where they usually go, when and with whom.

Teacher's notes

Villages
Lead-in

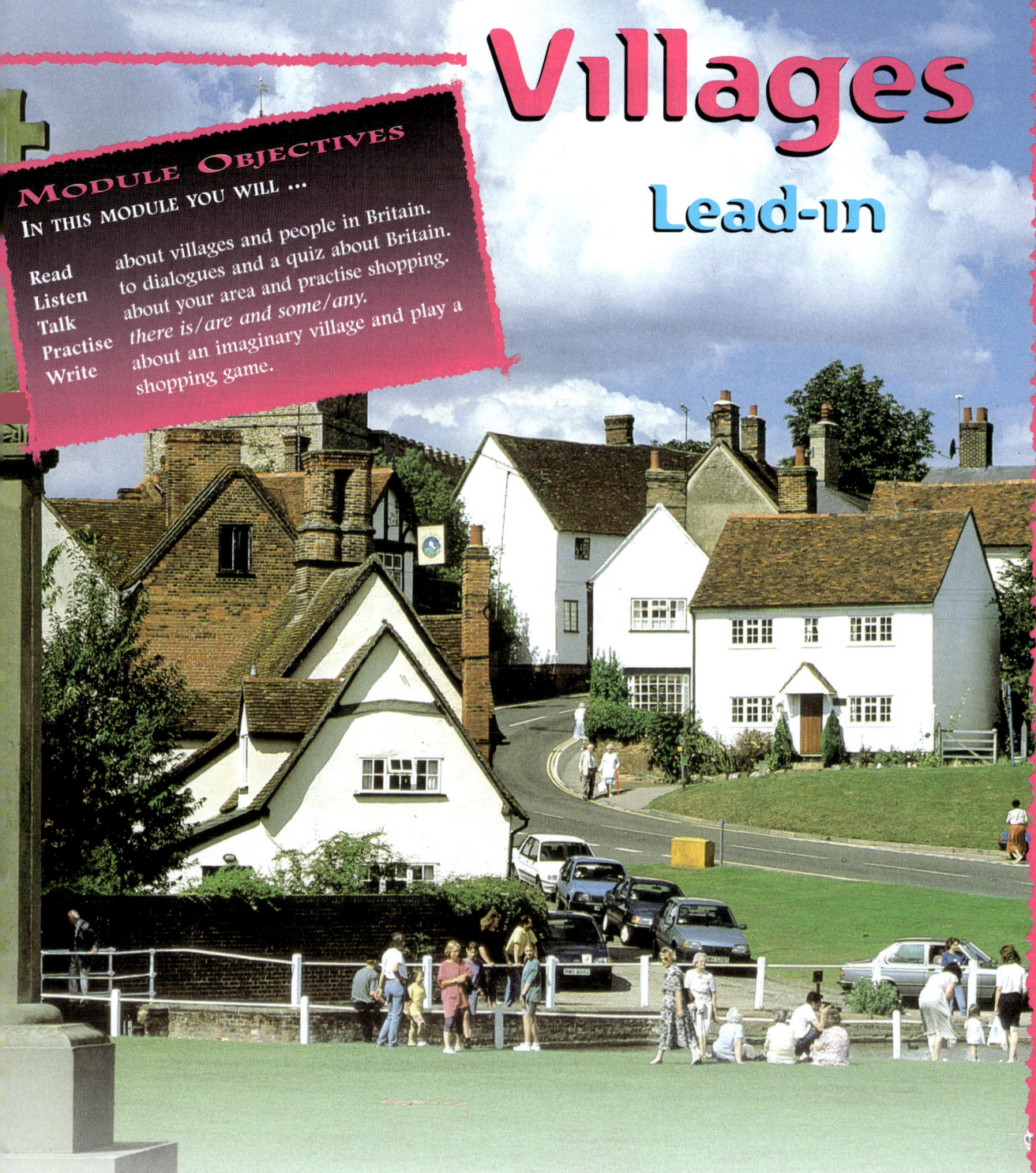

a KEYWORDS

Write a list of places near your home.

Example: a Chinese restaurant, two banks, an old church

bank bar bus station church cinema disco
ealth centre hotel park restaurant art gallery
school sports centre supermarket

b

In pairs, tell your partner about places you visit.

Example: A: I go to the supermarket with my dad. After school, I go to the park with my friends. And you?

B: I go to the church on Sundays. I go to the sports centre with my mum every Friday.

16 Around Britain

Clovelly is a beautiful fishing village in Devon, in the southwest of England. There is a historic harbour with white houses. Near Clovelly there are excellent beaches for swimming and surfing and marvellous countryside. One unusual thing – there is a car park, but there aren't any cars in the village - transport is by foot or by donkey!

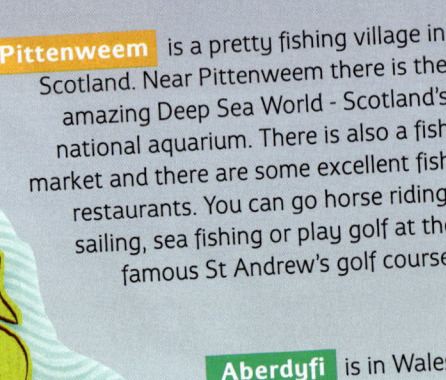

SCOTLAND

ENGLAND

WALES

Pittenweem is a pretty fishing village in Scotland. Near Pittenweem there is the amazing Deep Sea World - Scotland's national aquarium. There is also a fish market and there are some excellent fish restaurants. You can go horse riding, sailing, sea fishing or play golf at the famous St Andrew's golf course.

Aberdyfi is in Wales. There are good shops in the main street and there is an art gallery. There is a great beach and a yacht club. There are fantastic places to visit near Aberdyfi - for example, there are some activity centres, there is pony trekking, there is a beautiful lake and a historic castle.

A KEYWORDS

Match the places with the symbols.

art gallery car park beach fish market
castle golf course yacht club harbour

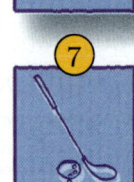

A Keywords/Individual

- Ask students to read the words in the box and give them a few minutes to look up the ones they don't know in the mini-dictionary.
- They match the places with the symbols shown. Correct orally with the whole class.

Answers:

1 carpark; 2 beach; 3 art gallery; 4 yacht club; 5 castle; 6 fish market; 7 golf course; 8 harbour

B Reading/Individual

- Students skim the three texts (remind them that it is not necessary to understand every single word) and answer the five questions.
- Check the answers orally with the whole class.

Answers:

1 Pittenweem; 2 Aberdyfi; 3 Clovelly; 4 Pittenweem; 5 Clovelly and Pittenweem

C Reading/Keywords/Individual

- Students match the words from the text with the definitions. Correct orally with the whole class.

Answers:

1 beautiful; 2 historic; 3 marvellous; 4 unusual; 5 famous

Language Focus: *There is/are*

There is and *there are* are used to say that something exists, with the real subject of the sentence coming after the verb. For example: *There is a school.* Students may have problems of word order and with the use of singular and plural forms, as in several languages there is only one form. Possible mistakes: *A school is in my village. There is two churches.*

To indicate what is not present or missing, we use *there isn't/aren't.*

D Writing/Individual

- First explain the difference between *there is/isn't* and *there are/aren't: there is/isn't* is used with singular subjects and *there are/aren't* with plural ones.

- Students complete the sentences with the given words and indicate which verbs are singular and which are plural.
- They translate the sentences in their language.

Answers:

1 is; 2 isn't; 3 are; aren't

E Writing/Individual

- Students write six sentences about places near their house with *there is/there are*. Read the example with them first and remind them that they can also write negative sentences.

F Speaking/Pairs

- Divide the class into pairs. Students take turns asking and answering questions about places near their partners' houses.
- Monitor the activity to make sure that they are using the new expressions correctly.

G Writing/Speaking/Individual/Group

- Tell students that they are going to describe their ideal holiday village.
- Read the example with them and focus their attention on the use of *there is/are*. While they are writing, go round the class and help with structures and vocabulary if necessary.
- Divide the class into small groups. Students read their descriptions to the rest of the group. Encourage listeners to ask questions and make comments (preferably in English!).

Extra Time!

- Students turn to *World Club Magazine* and do Activity 16 on page 93.

Answers:

England: London; Scotland: Edinburgh; Wales: Cardiff; Ireland: Dublin

Reinforcement activity

There is/there are: Speaking/ Groups

- Divide the class into small groups. Each student has to say a sentence about things they can see in the classroom, for example: *There are thirty desks.*

- When one of the students cannot think of a sentence, he or she gets 'time out' to think some more and write one down!

Activity Book Key

A 2 Are there any shops? Yes, there are.
3 Are there any banks? Yes there are.
4 Is there a school? No, there isn't.
5 Is there a restaurant? Yes, there is.
6 Is there a cinema? Yes, there is.
7 Are there any hotels? No, there aren't.
8 Is there a toy shop? Yes, there is.

C 2 There is a good restaurant.
3 There are nice pubs.
4 There isn't a golf course.
5 There aren't any shoe shops.

D 2 supermarket; 3 school; 4 doctor;
5 restaurant; 6 bank

E on; by; on; in; in; in; in

F 2 at; 3 on; 4 at; 5 on/under/next to; 6 in;
7 in; 8 on

G 1 church; 2 cinema; 3 hotel; 4 restaurant;
5 school; 6 supermarket; 7 station;
8 sports centre

Extension Activity Key

1 Yes, it is. 2 No, he isn't. 3 Yes, he does.
4 Yes, there is. 5 No, he doesn't.

B

Read about the villages. Which village:

1 is in Scotland?
2 has got an art gallery?
3 has got good beaches for surfing?
4 is near a famous golf course?
5 has got white houses?

C KEYWORDS

Match these words from the text with the definitions.

| historic unusual beautiful famous marvellous |

1 nice to look at
2 important in history
3 very good
4 strange
5 well-known

Language Focus: *There is/are*

D

Copy and complete these sentences about Clovelly with these words:

is / are / isn't / aren't

There	¹...	a historic harbour.
There	²...	a hotel.
There	³...	excellent beaches.
There	⁴...	any cars.

Which verbs are singular and which are plural?

E

Write six sentences about places near your house.

Example: There is a bank. There are four shops.
There isn't a cinema.

F

In pairs, find out about places near your partner's house. Answer like this:

Yes, there is. / No, there isn't. / Yes, there are. /
No, there aren't.

Example: A: Is there a cinema?
B: No, there isn't.

G

Write about an ideal village for a holiday. Then tell your partner.

Example:

My ideal village is near the sea. There is a fantastic beach for swimming and surfing. There are places to go at night like cinemas and discos. There is also...

Look at World Club magazine on page 93.
Do activity 16.

Villages

17 Village People

Dear Oscar,

Hi! I'm called David. I live in Llanfair PG on the island of Anglesey in Wales. The name in Welsh is Llanfairpwllgwyngyllgogery-chrwyrndrobwllllantysiliogogogoch! You can see why we call it Llanfair PG! There are lots of shops and one hotel in the village. My dad is a mechanic and my mum is a businesswoman. I love music and I play the cello. I am in the school choir too. Every year I sing in the Eisteddfod festival with the school. I'm also learning to surf, because in Anglesey there are great beaches for surfing. Sometimes I go fishing to the river at

Dear Alicia,

I'm your new penfriend. My name is Elaine. I'm from Catterline in Scotland. It's a very small village – there is only one shop and a pub! I go to school in Stonehaven by bus – there isn't a secondary school in my village. There's a harbour, but there aren't any fishing boats now. My mum is a doctor and my dad is a police officer. What do your parents do? I love Highland dancing and I go to classes. In the summer I dance at different Highland games. It's great fun. Tell me about

A

Read the letters. Copy and complete the table.

	Places in village	Parents' jobs	Hobbies	Festivals
Elaine	shop			Highland games
David				

Topic focus

- A positive attitude to encourage in this lesson is tolerance towards people living in different environments. In some countries, city dwellers may look down on 'villagers' so it is important to point out the positive aspects of village life.
- Look at the lesson title: *Village people.* Find out if any students live in villages or have families who do. Write the names of the villages on the board.

A Reading/Writing/Individual

- Ask students to copy the table in their notebooks. Next, they read the letters and complete the table with the required information. Remind them to use the mini-dictionary if they need help with the vocabulary.
- This activity can also be done in pairs. When everyone has finished, write the names of the two children on the board and have a couple of students write down the missing information. Check it with the whole class.
- Finally, ask students which of these villages they would like to live in and why.

Answers:

Elaine: shop, pub; mother: doctor, father: police officer; Highland dancing; Highland games; **David:** shops, one hotel; mother: businesswoman, father: mechanic; music; surfing; Eisteddfod Festival

B Reading/Individual

- Explain that the question word *why* is used to ask for an explanation. Read the example with the whole class and point out the use of *because* to introduce this explanation.
- Students read the texts again and answer the questions in their notebooks. Correct the exercise orally.

Answers:

2 Because it's great fun. 3 Because the complete name is very long. 4 Because there are great beaches for surfing in Anglesey.

C Cassette/Individual

- Ask students to look at the words in the box and tell them that they are going to hear the children reading their letters. There are five mistakes which they must discover: they are all about the parents' jobs and the keywords will help them do the task.
- Read the example. Play the tape, more than once if necessary, stopping after the first letter so they have time to write. Do the same with the second. Remind students that it is not necessary to understand every single word.
- Correct orally with the whole class.

Answers:

2 Elaine's dad isn't a police officer – he's a teacher.

3 David's dad isn't a mechanic – he's a journalist.

4 His mum isn't a businesswoman – she's a lawyer.

 TAPESCRIPT:

Module 6, Lesson 17, Exercise C. Listen to the children reading their letters. Find four mistakes in the texts. One.

ELAINE: Dear Alicia; I'm your new penfriend. My name is Elaine. I'm from Catterline in Scotland. It's a very small village – there is only one shop and a pub! I go to school in Stonehaven by bus – there isn't a secondary school in my village. There's a harbour but there aren't any fishing boats now. My mum is a dentist and my dad is teacher. I love highland dancing and I go to classes. In the summer I dance at different 'highland games'. It's great fun. Tell me about…

NARRATOR: **Two.**

DAVID: Dear Oscar; Hi! I'm called David. I live in Llanfair PG on the island of Anglesey in Wales. The name in Welsh is *Llanfairpwllgwyngyllgogerychwyrndrobwllllantysiliogog o- goch!* You can see why we call it Llanfair PG! There are lots of shops and one hotel in the village. My dad is a journalist and my mum is a lawyer. I love music and I play the cello. I am in the school choir too. Every year I sing in the 'Eisteddfod' festival with the school. I'm also learning to surf, because in Anglesey there are great beaches for surfing. Sometimes I go …

Pronunciation: Contractions

D Cassette/Individual

- Tell students to listen to the sentences and count the number of words. Play the example and stop the tape. Focus on the contraction *isn't*.

- Play the rest of the tape, more than once if necessary, stopping after every sentence so they have time to write.

- Play the tape again. This time students repeat the sentences, first chorally and then individually.

Answers:
2: 7 words; 3: 7 words; 4: 8 words;
5: 7 words; 6: 13 words

 TAPESCRIPT:

Module 6, Lesson 17, Exercise D. Listen and write the sentences. Then count the words. One.

READER: There isn't a disco in the village.
NARRATOR: **Two.**
READER: There're two shops in my village.
NARRATOR: **Three.**
READER: There's a cinema near my house.
NARRATOR: **Four.**
READER: There's a beautiful church in the village.
NARRATOR: **Five.**
READER: There're three banks and ten shops.
NARRATOR: **Six.**
READER: There's a yacht club and there're two good beaches for surfing.

E Writing/Individual

- Read the examples with the whole class and then ask students to write similar sentences about their families, using the word *because* in each one. Go round the class and help with structures and vocabulary if necessary.

F Speaking/Pairs

- Divide the class into pairs. Students read the first part of their sentences to their partners who must then ask for the reason by saying *Why?* Go through the example dialogue with a volunteer first.

- Wrap up the activity by asking volunteers to read their sentences to the whole class.

G Dictionary work

- Look at the entry *country* in the mini-dictionary. Elicit that it has two meanings. Discuss sentence number 1.

- Students continue on their own.

- Check orally.

Answers:
1 1; 2 2; 3 1; 4 1; 5 2;

Extension activity

Project about a real village: Speaking/Writing/Groups

- If students live in a village themselves, ask them to do a small project about the village. Alternatively, if students live in a city, they could do a project about their street or neighbourhood.

- They draw a map and draw the important places in it (or use photos).

- Then they write about some of the people they know: the postman, the doctor, teachers, etc.

- Finally, they produce a poster about the village.

Extra Time!

- Students turn to *World Club Magazine* and do Activity 17 on page 94.

Answers:

The Stott Family
house: Daphne and Eric - number 11
Lavinia - number 7
Daphne - job: teacher; car: number 10
Eric - job: dentist

The Darnley-Smith Family
house: Captain and wife - number 3
Rupert and Celia - number 2
Captain - job: businessman; car: number 4
Wife - job: policewoman; car: number 12
Rupert - car: number 6
Celia - car: number 9

Activity Book Key

A 1 is; 2 are; 3 is; 4 isn't; 5 aren't

B 2 doctor; 3 waiter; 4 dentist; 5 mechanic;
6 journalist; 7 farmer; 8 police officer

C 1 c; 2 a; 3 e; 4 b; 5 d

B

Read the letters again and answer these questions.

Example: 1 Because there isn't a secondary school in her village.

1 Why does Elaine go to school by bus?
2 Why does she go to the Highland games?
3 Why do people call David's village Llanfair PG?
4 Why is David learning to surf?

C KEYWORDS

Listen to Elaine and David to find four differences in the letters. Use the words below to help you.

Example: Elaine's mum isn't a doctor – she's a dentist.

> lawyer teacher waiter
> journalist businessman/woman
> police officer dentist mechanic

D

PRONUNCIATION: CONTRACTIONS

Listen and write the sentences. Then count the words. Contractions are two words.
Example: 1 There isn't a disco in the village. = 8 words

Listen again and repeat.

E

Write five sentences about you and your family or friends. Use the word *because*.

Example: I come to school by bus because I don't live in this town. My sister goes to ballet classes because she loves dancing.

F

In pairs, tell your partner about you, your family and friends.

Example: A: I come to school by bus.

 B: Why?

 A: Because I don't live in this town.

G  DICTIONARY SKILLS

The words underlined have more than one meaning. Look them up in the mini-dictionary and write the number of the appropriate meaning.

1 Poland is a large <u>country</u>.
2 That <u>poor</u> little bird is trying to fly, but it can't.
3 There is an <u>old</u> castle near the harbour.
4 I don't like <u>tea</u>. I prefer coffee.
5 It's a very <u>thin</u> book. You can read it quickly.

Did you know?

It is very bad to call people from Scotland or Wales 'English'. They are British (or Welsh or Scottish)!

 EXTRA TIME

Look at World Club magazine on page 94. Do activity 17.

Villages

18 Village Shops

A 🔑 KEYWORDS

Match the pictures with these words.

> clothes   comics   sweets   cassettes
> computer games   ice cream   crisps
> fizzy drinks   cakes

1 
2 
3

4 
5 
6

7 
8 
9

B 🗨️

In pairs, find out what things your partner buys.

Example: A: Do you buy computer games?
B: Yes, I do.

C 📼

Listen to a girl in a village shop. Answer these questions.

1 Which of the things from exercise A does she buy?
2 How much does she spend?
   a) £5.40   b) £8.40   c) £9.40

Topic focus

- This lesson looks at village shops, which are small shops that sell lots of different things. In Britain, village shops are often combined with the local post-office. Unfortunately, the growth of large shopping centres has meant the decline in number of these small shops.

A Keywords/Individual

- Students look at the words in the box and match them with the items in the photo. Remind them to use the mini-dictionary if they need help with the vocabulary.

- Correct orally with the whole class.

Answers:

clothes: 9; comics: 3; sweets: 5; cassettes: 2; computer games: 1; ice-cream: 4; crisps: 7; fizzy drinks: 6; cakes: 8

B Speaking/Pairs

- Divide the class into pairs and do the example dialogue with a student. Partners ask each other similar questions.

C Cassette/Individual

- Tell students to look at the photo of the girl in the village shop. Read the three quantities clearly and explain the question *How much does she spend?*

- Play the tape, more than once if necessary, and stop once in a while so that students can take notes.

- Correct the exercise by having a student write the total amount spent and the list on the board.

Answers:

1 a cassette, two packets of crisps and a can of cola; 2c

 TAPESCRIPT:

Module 6, Lesson 18, Exercise C. Listen to a girl in the village shop and answer the questions in your book.

SHOPKEEPER: Good morning. Can I help you?
GIRL: Yes, er, have you got any computer games?
SHOPKEEPER: No, I'm sorry, I haven't got any computer games at the moment.

GIRL: Well, have you got any cassettes?
SHOPKEEPER: Yes, I've got some music cassettes, over there.
GIRL: Mm, er, great, I'd like this cassette, please.
SHOPKEEPER: Right.
GIRL: And two packets of crisps, please. And have you got any fizzy drinks?
SHOPKEEPER: Yes, I've got cola, lemon and orange.
GIRL: A can of cola, please.
SHOPKEEPER: Anything else?
GIRL: No, that's all.
SHOPKEEPER: That's nine pounds forty pence, please. Thank you very much. Bye.
GIRL: Goodbye.

Language Focus: *Some/any*

Some languages do not have two different forms of *some/any* and students may use the 'zero' article on many occasions instead. For example: *Have you got crisps?* or confuse *some/any*.

D Writing/Individual

- Read out the example sentences from the dialogue stressing the use of *some* and *any*.

- Ask students to complete the rules. Check the exercise orally with the whole class.

Answers:

1 some; 2 any; 3 any

E Writing/Individual

- Students complete each sentences with the appropriate word.

- Correct the exercise orally. Ask students to give the reason for their choice. For example: *She hasn't got any computer games – because the sentence is negative.*

Answers:

1 any; 2 some; 3 any; 4 some; 5 any; 6 any; 7 some

F Cassette/Individual

- Students complete the shop dialogue with *some* and *any*.

- Play the tape, more than once if necessary, so they can check their answers.

Answers:

1 any; 2 any; 3 some; 4 any; 5 some; 6 some

TAPESCRIPT:

Module 6, Lesson 18, Exercise F. Listen and check your answers.

A: Good morning. Can I help you?
B: Yes. Have you got any comics?
A: No, I'm sorry, we haven't got any.
B: Well, I'd like some sweets. Two of those packets, please. And have you got any fizzy drinks?
A: Yes, we've got some cola and some lemonade.
B: A can of cola, please. How much is that?
A: The sweets are two pounds, the drink is 60p – that's two pounds sixty, please.
B: Thank you. Bye.
A: Bye.

G Speaking/Pairs

- Divide the class into pairs. Tell students that they are going to practise a dialogue like the one in exercise F.

- First ask them to repeat the expressions *Can I help you?; No, I'm sorry; Anything else?*, etc. with the correct intonation.

- Focus their attention on the list of items and repeat the prices with them.

- Go around the room and monitor the use of shopping language. Make notes of the mistakes you hear and discuss them with the class once the activity is over.

Extension activity

Shopping and prices: Speaking/ Groups

- Divide the class into small groups. Students copy the shopping list from exercise G.

- Groups choose one of two activities: they can either go to the local shops, check the price of the items and compare them with the English prices, or (especially if they live in a village) try to find the shop that sells a maximum of items on the list. Can they buy a baseball cap and a computer game in the same place?

- Give them a few days to do this. Then ask them to report their findings back to the rest of the class.

Extra Time!

- Students turn to *World Club Magazine* and do Activity 18 on page 95.

Answer:

50p

Activity Book Key

A 2 Is there any ice cream? No, there isn't.
  3 Are there any crisps? Yes, there are.
  4 Is there any chocolate? Yes, there is.
  5 Are there any fizzy drinks? Yes, there are.
  6 Are there any computer games? No, there aren't.

B 1 is; 2 any; 3 some; 4 isn't; 5 are; 6 aren't; 7 any; 8 are; 9 is

D **Fruit:** apple, banana, orange, melon; **Vegetables:** carrot, potato, cauliflower, cabbage; **Others:** ice-cream, sweets, rice, cakes

E 2 two pounds forty-five; 3 six pounds thirty; 4 three pounds fifty-five; 5 eighty-five pence; 6 two pounds twenty; 7 one pound eighty. Total change: two pounds ten pence.

Time to Read:

A 1 Australia
  2 Jim

B 1 He usually goes swimming in the sea.
  2 Because they are very cold.
  3 A Radio 523 T-shirt.
  4 In Grasmere
  5 A famous English poet.

C 1 snow; 2 are; 3 can't; 4 cold; 5 aren't; 6 are; 7 is; 8 Radio 523

Extension Activity Key

cinema, bank, castle, school, church, hotel, shops, disco, park, bar

Language Focus: *Some/Any*

D

Look at these sentences.

AFFIRMATIVE
I've got *some* music cassettes.

NEGATIVE
I haven't got *any* computer games

QUESTIONS
Have you got *any* cassettes?

Complete these rules with *some* or *any*.

1 For affirmative sentences we use ...

2 For questions we usually use ...

3 For negative sentences we use ...

E

Complete the sentences with *some* or *any*.

1 She hasn't got ... computer games.

2 He is eating ... sweets.

3 Have they got ... comics?

4 She is making ... cakes.

5 They haven't got ... ice cream.

6 Are there ... fizzy drinks in the fridge?

7 I'd like ... cakes, please.

F

Complete the shop dialogue with *some* or *any*. Then listen and check your answers.

A: Good morning. Can I help you?

B: Yes. Have you got [1] ... comics?

A: No, I'm sorry, we haven't got [2] ... .

B: Well, I'd like [3] ... sweets. Two of those packets, please. And have you got [4] ... fizzy drinks?

A: Yes, we've got [5] ... cola and [6] ... lemonade.

B: A can of cola, please. How much is that?

A: The sweets are two pounds, the drink is 60p that's two pounds sixty, please.

B: Thank you. Bye.

A: Bye.

G

In pairs, practise a shop dialogue like the one in exercise F. Use these prices to help you.

computer game	£35.00
cassette	£8.00
comic	£1.25
ice-cream	85p
sweets	£1.00
can of cola	80p
packet of crisps	40p
T-shirt	£10.00
baseball cap	£3.50

EXTRA TIME

Look at World Club magazine on page 95. Do activity 18.

Villages

# Fluency

Writing: Description of a Village

A

In pairs or groups, invent and write about a village.

Stage 1: Preparation

Look at the table. Then copy and complete it with information for your village.

Name:	Bigwig
Location:	Scotland, near the sea
Places:	supermarket, bank, park...
Tourist Attractions:	castle, church
Festivals:	ice-cream festival (August) – ice-cream statues
People:	Mrs Brice (teacher), Mr McDonald (fisherman)

Stage 2: Writing

Write about your village and some of the people. Divide the work between you.

Examples:

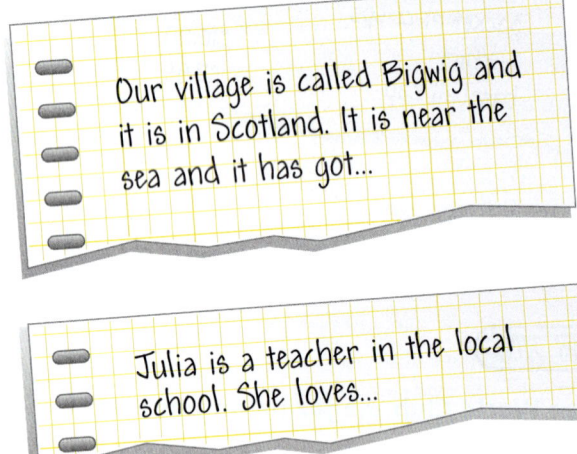
Our village is called Bigwig and it is in Scotland. It is near the sea and it has got...

Julia is a teacher in the local school. She loves...

Stage 3: Checking and presentation

Check your work for punctuation, spelling and grammar.

Make a poster. Draw the village neatly and include your descriptions.

Speaking: Shopping

B

Stage 1: Preparation

Half of the class (village shopkeepers) make a list of six things with a price to sell.

Example: a computer game, £45

The other half of the class (customers) make a list of six objects they want to buy.

Stage 2: Speaking

Form pairs (shopkeeper and customer).
Buy and sell objects.

Example: A: Good morning. Can I help you?
        B: Hello. Have you got a packet of crisps, please?
        A: No, I'm sorry.

You get one point for every object that you buy or sell.

Listening: A Quiz

C

Listen to the quiz and write down the answers to the questions - a, b or c. Then check the answers with your teacher.

Example: 1 c

Villages

Writing: Description of a village

A Writing/Pairs/Groups

Stage 1: Preparation

- Divide the class into pairs or small groups. Explain to students that they are going to write about an imaginary village. Go through the different stages in the exercise with the whole class and make sure that they understand each one.

- Ask students to copy the table and complete it with information for their village.

- Next, they draw a simple map of the village.

Stage 2: Writing

- Students use their notes to write a description of the village. Read the example with the whole class first.

- If they are working in groups, get each student to write about one particular area.

Stage 3: Checking and Presentation

- Students check their spelling with the help of their vocabulary books and mini-dictionary. If they have doubts about structures, they can also look at the Grammar Reference on page 66.

- Students make a poster. They include their description, as well as any additional details.

- Display the finished posters on the walls around the room. Make comments, ask questions, and encourage students to do the same about the productions of all the groups.

Speaking: Shopping

B Speaking/Groups

Stage 1: Preparation

- Divide the class into two groups: the shopkeepers and the customers.

- The shopkeepers make a list of six items with a price to sell.

- The customers make a list of six objects they want to buy.

Stage 2: Speaking

- Divide the class into pairs. The shopkeepers start the exchange with the question *Can I help you?* and customers go through their shopping lists.

- Both shopkeepers and customers get one point for every item they can buy or sell. Go round the class and monitor the activity, helping with vocabulary and structures whenever necessary.

Listening: A quiz

C Cassette/Individual

- Tell students they are going to hear a quiz about Great Britain. The task is to listen to the questions and choose the correct answer.

- Play the tape, more than once if necessary. Pause between questions. Students write a, b or c in their notebooks.

- You may want them to compare their answers with another pair or group.

- Read each question again and give students the correct answer.

Answers:

1c; 2a; 3b; 4b; 5a

 TAPESCRIPT:

Module 6, Fluency, Exercise C. Listen to the quiz and write down the answers to the questions - a, b or c.

READER: Hello. Welcome to the Britain Quiz. And here are the questions.
Number one. What is the capital of Scotland? a) Cardiff, b) Belfast, or c) Edinburgh.
Okay, now for question **number two.** What languages do they speak in Wales? a) Welsh and English, b) Gaelic and English, or c) Welsh and Scottish.
Right. Now, **question three.** Where do people wear kilts? Is it, a) Wales, b) Scotland, or c) England.
Question four. What is the population of Britain? Is it, a) 98 million, b) 58 million, or c) 38 million.
Question five. Where is the famous golf course, St Andrew's? Is it a) in Scotland, b) in England, or c) in Wales. Right, those are the first five questions tonight, and now ...

Consolidation

Grammar

A Writing/Individual

- Students complete the description with the words given. To give them additional writing practice, you can ask them to copy out the whole paragraph.
- Correct the exercise orally.

> **Answers:**
> 1 There are; 2 there is; 3 there isn't; 4 There are; 5 any; 6 some

B Speaking/Groups

- Divide the class into groups of four or five.
- Look at the examples and demonstrate the game with the whole class.
- If students make a mistake or hesitate too long, they are out of the game. (Set a maximum of five seconds.)

Vocabulary

C Keywords/Individual

- Students identify the buildings and places. Remind them to check the words in the mini-dictionary if they need help with the vocabulary.
- Correct the exercise orally with the whole class.

> **Answers:**
> 2 bank; 3 restaurant; 4 supermarket; 5 disco; 6 hospital; 7 school

D Keywords/Individual

- This is a spelling test. Ask students to look through the module and write down ten words that they find difficult to spell.
- They learn the spelling at home. In the next class, they exchange lists with a partner. Then they test each other.
- Wrap up the activity by asking which words were generally found most difficult.

Pronunciation: Difficult sounds

E Cassette/Individual

- First contrast the two vowel sounds in *chip* and *cheap*. Ask students to repeat the words several times.
- Tell them to write the numbers 1 to 5 in their notebooks. Play the tape and have them write *Group 1* or *Group 2* according to whether they hear the first or the second sound.
- Play the tape again so that you can correct the exercise with them.
- Finally have them repeat each word, first all together and then individually.

> **Answers:**
> 1 he's (group 1); 2 it (group 1); 3 leave (group 2); 4 these (group 2); 5 fit (group 1)

 TAPESCRIPT:

Module 6, Consolidation, Exercise E. Listen and repeat the sounds in these words. One.
READER: Chip.
NARRATOR: **Two.**
READER: Cheap.
Now listen and look at the words in your book. Which words do you hear?
NARRATOR: **One.**
READER: he's
NARRATOR: **Two**
READER: it
NARRATOR: **Three**
READER: leave
NARRATOR: **Four**
READER: these
NARRATOR: **Five**
READER: fit

Teacher's notes

Consolidation

Grammar

A

Complete the description with these words:

there is, any, there are (x2), there isn't, some

Alastair lives in a village. ¹ ... three or four shops and ² ... a small supermarket, but the village is small and ³ ... a cinema or a disco. Alastair sometimes goes to town on Saturday with his dad. ⁴ ... some good shops near the main square. Alastair doesn't buy ⁵ ... clothes, but he sometimes buys ⁶ ... cassettes or books.

B

VILLAGE GAME

- Draw two copies of the grid below. On one copy draw five buildings in different squares.
- In pairs, find out where your partner's buildings are. Draw them on the second grid.
- The first one to find all their partner's buildings is the winner!

Example:

A: Is there a building on C2?
B: Yes, there is a house.

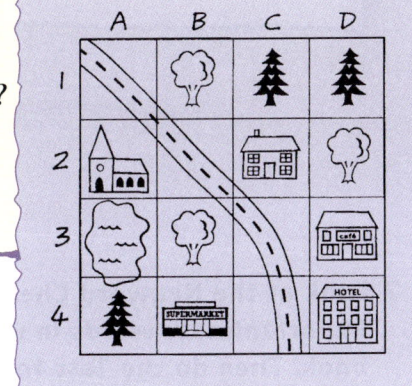

Vocabulary

C

What are these places?

Example: 1 art gallery

1 You can see famous paintings here.
2 You go here to get or change money.
3 You can have lunch or dinner here.
4 You buy food here.
5 You go here if you like music and dancing.
6 You go here if you are ill.
7 You go here to learn and see friends.

D

PERSONAL SPELLING TEST

- Look through the module and write ten words that are difficult for you to spell.
- Learn the spellings at home.
- In the next class, give your spelling list to a partner and test each other.

Pronunciation

E

Listen and repeat the sounds in these words:

Group 1 (/ɪ/): chip **Group 2** (/iː/): cheap

Listen. Which word do you hear?

1 his / he's
2 it / eat
3 live / leave
4 this / these
5 fit / feet

Module check

Grammar Reference

11 There is / there are

- We use **there is / there are** to indicate **what is present**:

  There's a very old church in my village.
  There are many churches in the city.

- We use **there is not (isn't)** and **there are not (aren't)** to indicate what is **not present**:

  There isn't a park and there aren't many hotels

- **There is / there isn't** is for **singular** things.

  There is a harbour but there isn't a boat club.

- **There are / there aren't** is for **plural** things.

  There aren't any shops but there are two hotels.

12 Some / any

	Affirmative	Negative	Questions
singular	a	a	a
plural + uncountable	some	any	any

- We use **a** for singular nouns.

  I have a cat, a dog and a fish.

- We use **some** in affirmative sentences and **any** in negatives and questions.

  I'd like some crisps and some lemonade, please.
  We haven't got any crisps or any lemonade.
  Is there any lemonade? Are there any crisps?

Keyword Check

Buildings: art gallery, bank, bar, beach, castle, church, cinema, disco, golf course, harbour, health centre, hotel, market, park, restaurant, school, shop, supermarket

Adjectives: beautiful, busy, excellent, famou historic, interesting, marvellous, pretty, unusual

Activities: dancing, fishing, horse riding, sailing, singing, surfing

Jobs: businessman/woman, dentist, doctor, journalist, lawyer, mechanic, police officer, teacher, waiter

Shopping: cakes, can (of cola/lemonade), cassettes, clothes, comics, computer games, crisps, fizzy drinks, ice-cream, packet (of sweets/crisps), sweets

Shopping expressions: Good morning. Can I help you? / I'd like some..., please. / I'm sorry, we haven't got any. / How much that, please? / That's three pounds, please. / Here you are. / Thank you very much. Goodbye.

Villages

1 Look at Grammar References 11-12 above and complete Grammar Files 11-12 in the Activity Book. Then do the *Test Yourself: Grammar* on page 46 of the Activity Book.

2 Look at the Keyword Check. Write important new words in your vocabulary book. Then do the *Test Yourself: Vocabulary* on page 46 of the Activity Book.

- This check should help students to reflect on several aspects of their learning and to assess their progress themselves.

- First, ask them to choose their favourite activity in this module (eg: the village game).

- Ask them to think about what they do when they write a composition. In what order do they do the following?
  Write their composition / Write a plan and notes / Think of ideas for writing / Check for mistakes

- Ask students to look at the *Grammar Reference* and the *Grammar File* and then do the *Test Yourself: Grammar* exercises.

- Ask them to look at the *Keyword Check* and write the important new words in their vocabulary books and then do the *Test Yourself: Vocabulary* exercises.

- Remind them that these activities should be done **by** themselves and **for** themselves. However, also make it clear that you are always willing to revise problem areas in class.

- It is a good idea to spot check their work so you can get a better idea of each student's general attitude and progress.

7 The Wild West

Objectives

Talk about life in the Wild West and about one's own life; read about Native Americans; listen to a story and two songs, and write a short biography.

Contents

Language Aims

Functions:

- Describing actions in the past
- Describing states and conditions in the past
- Indicating location or position in the past
- Saying where people came from
- Expressing age in the past
- Expressing the time with half hours and quarters
- Using linking words to form coherent paragraphs
- Discussing speaking strategies

Target language:

- *The Plains Indians lived in teepees.*
- *They were not rich but they were happy.*
- *There was an attic upstairs.*
- *My grandparents were from Ecuador.*
- *Billy the Kid was 21 when he died.*
- *They lived in a log cabin. Then her father died.*

Vocabulary:

Animals: *bear, bird, buffalo, horse, rabbit, wild cat, wolf*
People: *chief, gang, guard, gunman, judge, sheriff*
House: *bedroom, cooker, door, downstairs, fire, lamp, log cabin, rocking chair, table, teepee (tent), upstairs, window*
Weapons: *bow and arrow, gun, knife, spear*
Verbs: *carry (babies), follow (a person), join (a gang), live (in a place), hunt (animals), look after (children), make (clothes), marry (a man/woman), paint (pictures), pull out (a gun), ride (horses), rob (a bank), sentence (to hanging / prison), shoot (a gun / animals), use (animal skins)*
Verbs with no object: *arrive, be born, die, escape, return, travel*
Adjectives: *comfortable, dead, famous, incredible, little, poor, sad, satisfied, wild*
Times: *six o'clock (in the morning - 6:00 am / in the evening - 6:00 pm) half past six (6:30), a quarter past six (6:15), a quarter to seven (6:45)*
Linking words: *after that, then*
(Irregular) plurals, *next, babies, buffaloes, children, knives, people, wolves*

Pronunciation:

- Recognising and producing the regular past endings
- Marking the main stress in verbs in the regular past

Activity types

- Matching words and drawings
- Reading a text about the Plains Indians and completing a table
- Writing sentences about the life of an Indian woman
- Playing a true/false game in pairs
- Reading a text about Billy the Kid and ordering the paragraphs
- Listening to the text to check the answers
- Retelling the story in pairs
- Listening to a song about Billy the Kid and completing the lyrics
- Doing the activities in the *World Club Magazine*
- Reading a text about 'The Little House' and completing the information
- Asking and answering questions in pairs to practise saying the time
- Playing a memory game in groups
- Writing a short biography of Annie Oakley
- Listening to a cowboy song and completing the chorus
- Playing word games in teams to revise vocabulary
- Completing lexical sets
- Completing the *Module Check*
- Organising the new vocabulary in a notebook
- Carrying out self-evaluation tasks

Attitudes to learning

- Showing respect for different cultures and ethics
- Showing interest in finding out about the origins of The Wild West legends
- Understanding the importance of developing adequate speaking skills in order to improve communication
- Understanding the importance of developing learner autonomy and good study habits
- Accepting and viewing errors as a natural part of the learning process

Moral and Social Values

- Protection of the Environment
Encouraging students to reflect on the respectful attitude of aboriginal peoples towards their environment (Lesson 19: B and E).
- Peace Studies
Encouraging students to become aware of the rights of aboriginal peoples to their own land and culture (Lesson 19: B and E).

Lead-in

Module Objectives

Read and explain the module objectives to your students and make sure that they understand them.

Topic focus

- This lesson introduces the theme of the American West which, as Standing Bear, the Indian chief said, was not *wild* until Europeans arrived.

- Encourage environmental awareness by discussing in the students' own language the effects of the traditional Indian lifestyle on the ecosystem.

a Keywords/Individual

- Students look at the words in the box and match them with the drawings. Check orally with the whole class.

Answers:

chief, sheriff, bow and arrow, gun, log cabin, tepee, wolf, buffalo

b Reading/Pairs

- Divide the class into pairs. Students read the sentences and decide which one is false. Remind them to use the mini-dictionary if they need help with the vocabulary.

- Go over the answers with the class. Ask for a show of hands to check which pairs were correct.

Answer:

1T; 2F; 3T; 4T; 5T

The Wild West

ODULE OBJECTIVES

THIS MODULE YOU WILL ...

ead	about Native Americans and a literature extract.
alk	about life in the Wild West and your own life.
Listen	to a story and two songs.
Write	a short biography.
Practise	the past simple tense.

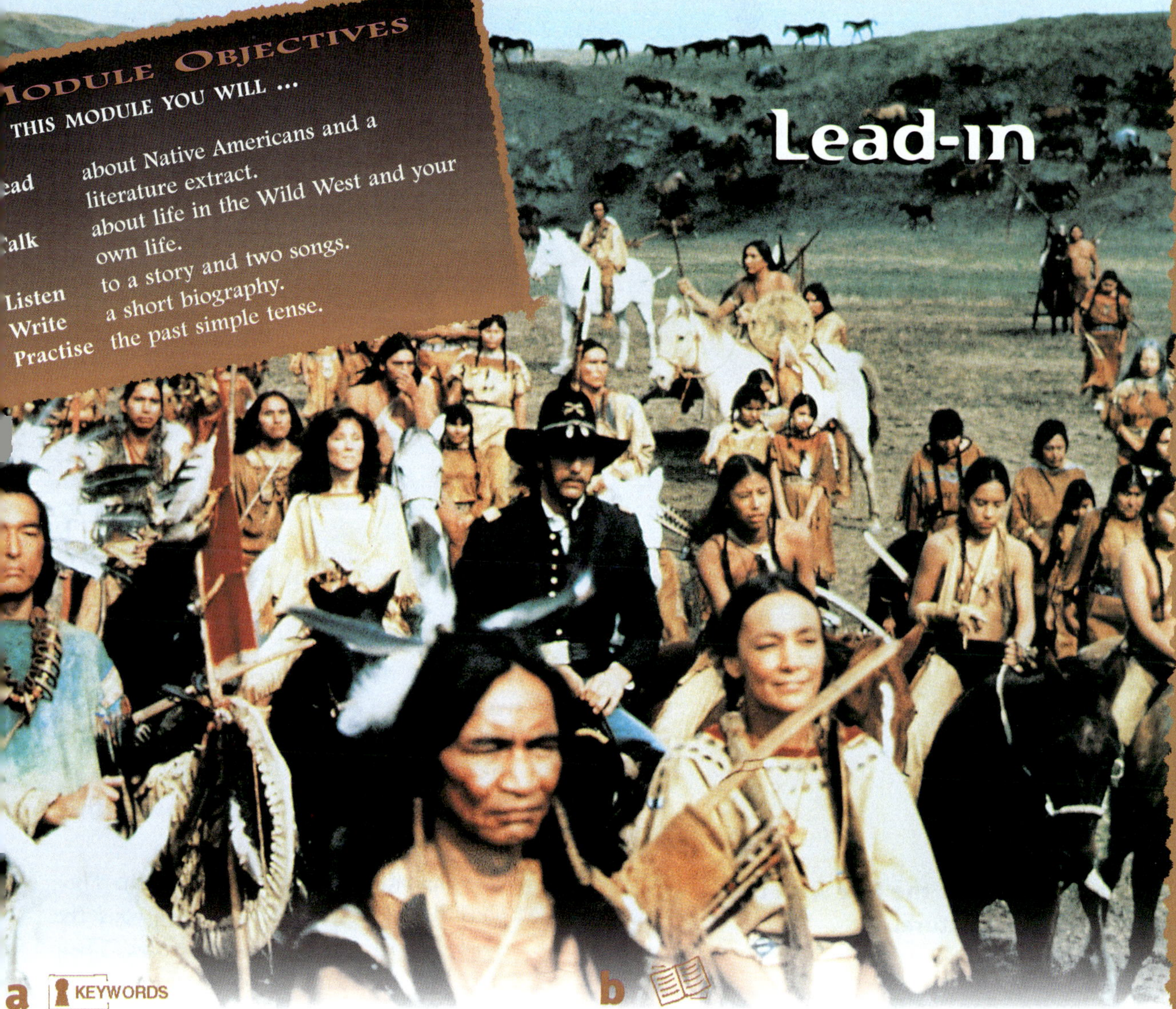

Lead-in

a KEYWORDS

Which of these things can you see in Wild West films?

chief police officer sheriff bow and arrow gun log cabin tepee wolf rocket castle buffalo tiger

b

In pairs, read these sentences. Decide which one is false.

1 Native American people originated in Asia.
2 All North American Indians lived in tepees.
3 Europeans killed all the buffaloes by the 1880s.
4 Many Indians live on reservations in the USA today.
5 The Indians didn't have horses before the Spanish arrived.

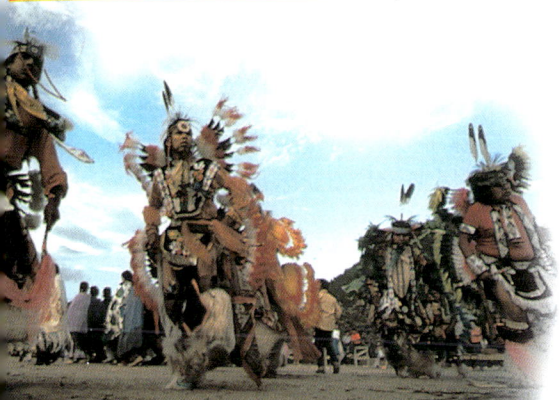

19 Native Americans

The Plains Indians

The Plains Indians didn't live in one place. When they travelled, dogs carried and pulled their things. They didn't have horses until the Spanish arrived in America. Some of their horses escaped. The Indians learned to ride the horses and used them when they hunted buffaloes.

The Indians cooked the buffalo meat. They used the skins for clothes. They used the bones for knives, arrows and spears. They lived in tepees (tents made of buffalo skins) and they painted pictures on them .

Indians loved their children. Mothers carried babies on their backs. Children didn't go to school! They learned everything from their parents. They played with dolls and organised fighting competitions. They played in rivers in the summer and in snow in the winter.

Life for the Indians changed when Europeans arrived. Standing Bear, an Indian chief, said "The plains were not wild for us. Then people arrived from the East and the 'Wild West' started."

A  KEYWORDS

Match the words in the box with the numbers in the picture.

buffalo   horse   dog   knife   spear   animal skins

B

Read about the Plains Indians. Copy and complete the table.

weapons:	bow and arrow, spear
transport:	
food:	
homes:	
education:	
children's games:	

The Wild West

68

A Keywords/Individual

- Students read the words in the box and match them with the numbers in the illustration. Give them a few minutes to look up the ones they don't know in the mini-dictionary.
- Correct orally with the whole class.

Answers:

buffalo 3; horse 4; dog 1; knife 6; spear 5; animal skins 2

B Reading/Individual

- Ask students to copy the table in their notebooks.
- Ask them to skim the text on the Plains Indians (remind them that it is not necessary to understand every single word) and complete the table.
- Check the answers orally with the whole class.

Answers:

horses; buffalo meat; tepees; the parents; dolls, fighting competitions, swimming

Language Focus: Past simple (regular verbs)

The past simple tense is used to express completed actions. The negative is formed using the auxiliary *didn't*. The pronunciation of the different endings is practised in the next lesson.

The form of the verb is the same for all persons but some verbs double the final consonant. At this level it is probably better to allow students to learn the common verbs by usage rather than explaining the spelling rules.

C Writing/Individual

- Students copy the table and complete it. While they are doing this, draw the headings on the board yourself.
- Have one or two volunteers come to the board and complete the table with the help of the other students.

Answers:

Affirmative: 1 changed, arrived, escaped, used, organised; 2 pulled, learned, cooked, painted, played, started; 3 carried
Negative: didn't live, didn't have

- Focus students' attention on the completed boxes and ask the following questions:
  - how do regular verbs end?
  - how do we form the negative?
  - is *didn't* used for all persons?

D Writing/Individual

- Ask students to read the sentences and fill in the gaps with a suitable verb in the past.
- Correct the exercise on the board with the whole class.

Answers:

2 didn't live; 3 painted; 4 didn't go; 5 used; 6 learned

E Writing/Individual

- Students use the notes to write sentences about the life of an Indian woman. They can work in pairs if you wish.
- Ask them to read out their sentences to the rest of the class.

F Writing/Speaking/Pairs

- Ask students to write three sentences about the Plains Indians with the verbs in the box. One or two sentences should be false.
- Divide the class into pairs and read the example. One student says a sentence and his or her partner must say if it is true or false.
- Wrap up the activity by asking individual students to say their sentences to the whole class.

Extra Time!

- Students turn to *World Club Magazine* and do Activity 19 on page 95.

Answers:

1 bone; 2 hunted; 3 fighting; 4 Chief; 5 carried; 6 wild; 7 clothes; 8 tent; 9 reservations
Mystery word: buffaloes

Reinforcement activity

Anagrams: Writing/Individual/ Pairs

- Students look through their vocabulary books and write down anagrams of words (words with the letters jumbled up).

- In pairs, they exchange lists. The first one to solve all the anagrams is the winner.

Activity Book Key

A (answers may be affirmative or negative)
1 walked / didn't walk;
2 played / didn't play;
3 cooked / didn't cook;
4 travelled / didn't travel;
5 used / didn't use;
6 arrived / didn't arrive

B 2 lived; 3 didn't travel; 4 didn't have; 5 walked; 6 travelled; 7 didn't hunt; 8 hunted; 9 used; 10 didn't have

C 2 They didn't hunt elephants. They hunted buffaloes.
3 They didn't use metal for knives and spears. They used bones.
4 The fathers didn't carry the babies on their backs. The mothers carried the babies.
5 The children didn't learn at school. They learned with their parents.
6 Europeans didn't arrive from the west. They arrived from the east.

D 1 helped; 2 arrived; 3 cooked; 4 talked; 5 walked; 6 travelled; 7 carried; 8 studied; 9 played

E 2 d; 3 f; 4 e; 5 c; 6 a

F 1 in; 2 on; 3 on; 4 in; 5 at; 6 from; 7 at/in; 8 from

Extension Activity Key

They travelled by horse, cart and sailed on the rivers in boats. They cooked meat, vegetables and bread. They made houses from wood and the rich lived in big halls. There weren't any schools and the only people with an education were the monks.

D

Complete the sentences.

Example: 1 hunted

1 The Indians ... buffaloes.
2 They ... in houses.
3 They ... pictures on the tents.
4 The children ... to school.
5 They ... skins to make clothes.
6 They ... to ride horses.

E

Use the notes to write sentences about the life of an Indian woman.

Example: She lived in a tepee.

> live in a tepee / work at home / cook for family /
> look after her children / not hunt buffaloes / then
> Europeans arrive in her area / her life change /
> live on a reservation / not like her new life

F

TRUE/FALSE GAME

> • Write sentences about the Plains Indians.
>   Use these verbs:
>   play / travel / cook / hunt / use / live
> • In pairs, take turns to say your sentences.
>   Say if they are true or false.
>
> *Example:* A: They hunted crocodiles.
>   B: False!

Language Focus: Past Simple (regular verbs)

C

Copy and complete the table with these verbs:

changed / pulled / didn't live / didn't have /
arrived / escaped / learned / cooked / used /
painted / carried / played / organised / started

Affirmative		
infinitive + d		change**d**
+ ed		pull**ed**
infinitive ~~y~~ + ied		carr**ied**

Negative	
did not + infinitive (didn't)	**didn't** live

EXTRA TIME

Look at World Club magazine on page 95.
Do activity 19.

The Wild West

20 Billy the Kid

Pat Garrett discovered that Billy was at a friend's house. Pat arrived at the house. Next, he pulled out his gun and killed Billy. Billy died on July 14th 1881.

At the age of fifteen, Billy killed a man in a gunfight. After that he joined a gang of gunmen and started to live a life of crime.

Billy the Kid was born in 1859 in the east of the United States. Then Billy and his mother travelled west by train.

Sheriff Pat Garrett captured Billy and put him in prison. But Billy killed two guards and escaped from the prison.

A

Find these things in the pictures.

prison guard   gunman   prison
gunfight   sheriff   gun

B

Read the story and put it in the correct order.

C

Listen to the story and check your answers.

The Wild West

70

Topic focus

- Billy the Kid is one of the best known characters to emerge from The Wild West. This lesson looks at his life and adventures.
- Explain the meaning of the word *Kid* (a colloquial word meaning a child or a young person).

A Keywords/Individual

- Students look at the words in the box and find them in the drawings. Go through the activity orally with the whole class.

B Reading/Writing/Individual

- Ask students to read the story of Billy the Kid and reorder the four paragraphs. Remind them to use the mini-dictionary if they need help with the vocabulary.

Answers:

3, 2, 4, 1

C Cassette/Individual

- Tell students they are going to hear the story so they can check their answers.
- Play the tape, more than once if necessary.

TAPESCRIPT:

Module 7, Lesson 20, Exercise C. Listen to the story and check your answers.

Billy the Kid was born in 1859 in the east of the United States. Then Billy and his mother travelled west by train. At the age of fifteen, Billy killed a man in a gunfight. After that he joined a gang of gunmen and started to live a life of crime.
Sheriff Pat Garrett captured Billy and put him in prison. But Billy killed two guards and escaped from the prison.
Pat Garrett discovered that Billy was at a friend's house. Pat arrived at the house. Next, he pulled out his gun and killed Billy. Billy died on July 14th 1881.

Pronunciation: *ed* endings

D Cassette/Individual/Whole class

- Write *moved, liked* and *hunted* on the board and ask students to focus on the sound at the end of the verbs as you say them. Which three sounds do they hear? Elicit the answers /d/, /t/ and /ɪd/.
- Ask them to look at the three lists. Play the tape, pausing between words for the class to repeat in chorus.
- Divide the class into pairs and ask partners to practise the words and correct each other.
- Play the tape again.

TAPESCRIPT:

Module 7, Lesson 20, Exercise D. Listen and repeat the verbs. One.

READER: moved, travelled, arrived, used, pulled
NARRATOR: Two.
READER: liked, cooked, escaped, helped
NARRATOR: Three.
READER: hunted, painted, carried, started

E Writing/Individual

- Explain to the students that to transform a series of sentences into a coherent paragraph, we use linking words such as *then, after that* and *next*.
- Read the example with them and ask them to translate it.
- Ask them to copy the sentences and add the necessary linking words to produce a paragraph. They can work in pairs if you wish.
- Correct the exercise by having different students read out the paragraph a sentence at a time.

Answers:

2 Then; 3 Next; 4 but

F Speaking/Pairs

- Divide the class into pairs. Students close their books and retell the story of Billy the Kid. Read out the example first.

G Cassette/Individual

- Tell students they are going to hear a song about Billy the Kid. Ask them to write the numbers 1 to 8 in their notebooks. The task is to listen to the song and write the missing words.

- Read through the song with the class and check they understand the vocabulary and the gist of the story.

- Play the tape, more than once if necessary. Pause between verses.

- You may wish students to compare their answers with another pair or group.

- Correct the exercise orally with the whole class.

Answers:
1 lived; 2 liked; 3 escaped; 4 started; 5 died; 6 killed; 7 walked; 8 pulled

 TAPESCRIPT:

Module 7, Lesson 20, Exercise G. Listen and complete the song about Billy the Kid.

This is a song about Billy the Kid,
This is the story of things that he did
In the Wild West a long time ago
He lived and he died down in old Mexico.
Billy the Kid, Billy the Kid, poor Billy the Kid!
Pat Garrett, the Sheriff, liked Billy the Kid,
But he put him in prison for the things that he did.
But Billy escaped and he started to run,
He said: "No-one can catch me now, I'm number one!"
Billy the Kid, Billy the Kid, poor Billy the Kid!
Now on the sad night when poor Billy died
He said to his friends: "I'm not satisfied.
Twenty-one men I killed, that is true,
Now sheriff Pat Garrett is number twenty-two.
Billy the Kid, Billy the Kid, poor Billy the Kid!
Now this is how Billy's life came to an end,
He stayed one night at the house of a friend,
Pat Garrett walked in, saw Billy in bed,
He pulled out his gun and poor Billy was dead.
Billy the Kid, Billy the Kid, poor Billy the Kid!

Extra Time!

- Students turn to *World Club Magazine* and do Activity 20 on page 95.

Answers:
1 T; 2 T; 3 T; 4 F; 5 T; 6 F; 7 T; 8 F

Reinforcement activity

Memory game: Speaking/groups

- In small groups, students can play this accumulative memory game using past tenses.

A: 'Yesterday, I had an interesting day. I went to the cinema.'

B: 'Yesterday, I had an interesting day. I went to the cinema and I bought some popcorn.' etc.

Activity Book Key

A 2 No, he didn't. He killed a man with a gun.
3 No he didn't. He sentenced him to hanging.
4 No he didn't. He killed the guards.
5 No he didn't. He was at a friend's house.
6 No he didn't. He killed him on July 14, 1881.

B 2 f; 3 d; 4 c; 5 e; 6 a

C judge, escaped, died, discover, buffaloes, skins, sheriff, friend, song, gang, gunfight, tent, travel, life, end, dead, guard, doll, lived

Extension Activity Key
1B; 2C; 3A

WANTED
DEAD OR ALIVE

BILLY THE KID

Reward $5,000

Billy the Kid

This is a song about Billy the Kid,
This is the story of things that he did.
In the Wild West a long time ago
He [1] ... and he died down in old Mexico.
Billy the Kid, Billy the Kid, poor Billy the Kid!

Pat Garrett, the Sheriff, [2] ... Billy the Kid,
But he put him in prison for the things that
he did.
But Billy [3] ... and he [4] ... to run,
He said "No one can catch me now,
I'm number one!"
Billy the Kid, Billy the Kid, poor Billy the Kid!

Now on the sad night when poor Billy [5] ...
He said to his friends, I'm not satisfied.
Twenty-one men I [6] .., that is true,
Now sheriff Pat Garrett is number twenty-two."
Billy the Kid, Billy the Kid, poor Billy the Kid!

Now this is how Billy's life came to an end,
He stayed one night at the house
of a friend,
Pat Garrett [7] ... in, saw Billy in bed,
He [8] ... out his gun and poor Billy was dead.
Billy the Kid, Billy the Kid, poor Billy the Kid!

D

PRONUNCIATION: 'ED' ENDINGS

Listen and repeat these verbs.

1 mov**ed** travell**ed** arriv**ed** us**ed** pull**ed**
2 lik**ed** cook**ed** escap**ed** help**ed**
3 hunt**ed** paint**ed** start**ed**

E

Choose the correct words.

Example: 1 After that

We moved to New Mexico in 1870. (¹*After/*
After that), my mother died. I killed a man
in a gunfight. (²*When/Then*) I escaped from the
town. (³*Next/Before*) I joined a gang. Pat Garret
captured me, (⁴*but/after*) I escaped.

F

**Close your books. In pairs, what can you
remember about the story?**

Example: A: Billy the Kid moved to the west.
  B: Then his mother ...

EXTRA TIME

**Look at World Club magazine on page 95.
Do activity 20.**

The Wild West

21 The Little House

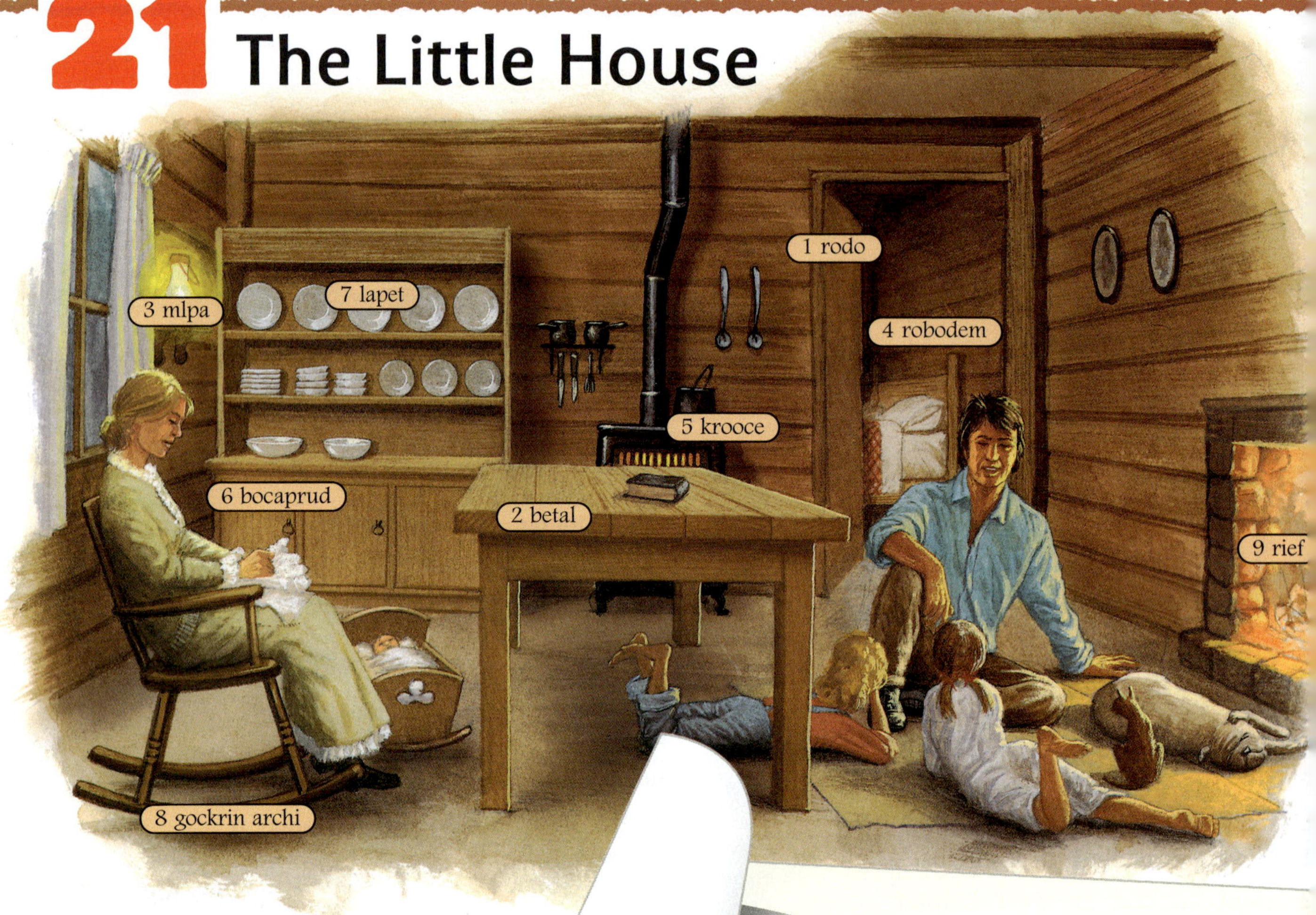

The picture shows a log cabin interior with the following labels:
- 3 mlpa
- 7 lapet
- 1 rodo
- 4 robodem
- 6 bocaprud
- 5 krooce
- 2 betal
- 9 rief
- 8 gockrin archi

A 🔑 KEYWORDS

Name the things in the picture.

Example: 1 door

B 📖

Read about the girl and complete this information.

Name: Laura

House:

Number of rooms:

People in family:

Pets:

Likes:

The Little House in the Big Woods

Once upon a time, a girl called Laura lived in a little grey log cabin in the Big Woods of Wisconsin. There weren't other houses or roads and there weren't any people. There were only trees and wild animals. Wolves, bears and wild cats lived in the Big Woods.

The house wasn't very big, but it was a comfortable house. Upstairs there was an attic and downstairs there was a small bedroom and a big room. In the big room there were two windows and two doors, a front door and a back door. There was a cooker, a cupboard with plates in it, and a big table.

One winter evening, when it was cold and there was snow outside, the family were warm and comfortable in their little house. Laura, her father and her sister Mary were in front of the fire. Her mother was in her rocking chair next to baby Carrie. The cat and the dog were asleep in front of the fire. Laura was very happy. She loved her father's stories.

The Wild West

Topic focus

- 'The Little House' books by Laura Ingalls Wilder are very popular with children all over the world.
- If students have read the books or seen the series on television, ask them to tell their classmates what they know about the family and setting.

A Keywords/Individual

- Students look at the illustration and name the items they know. Ask a volunteer to write the words on the board.

Answers:

1 door; 2 table; 3 lamp; 4 bedroom; 5 cooker; 6 cupboard; 7 plate; 8 rocking chair; 9 fire

B Reading/Individual

- Students read the text and complete the information about Laura. Tell them that it isn't necessary to understand every word to do the task and remind them to use the mini-dictionary if they need help with the vocabulary.
- Have one or two volunteers come to the board and complete the list with the help of the other students.

Answers:

House: log cabin; Number of rooms: three; People in the family: five; Pets: a cat and a dog; Likes: her father's stories

Language Focus: Past simple of *to be*

C Learning to Learn/Individual

- Ask students to look at the example sentences from the text and say whether the verbs are in the singular or in the plural form. Call their attention to the fact that in the past the first and third persons singular are the same.

Answers:

Singular: was, wasn't, Was

Plural: were, weren't, were

D Writing/Individual

- Read out the example. Ask students to reorder the words to make sentences. Remind them to use capitals and full stops.
- Check the exercise orally with the whole class.

Answers:

2 There were wild animals in the woods.
3 The house wasn't very big.
4 Was there a bedroom upstairs?

E Writing/Individual

- Students complete the sentences with the appropriate word. To give them additional writing practice, you can ask them to copy out the whole paragraph.
- Correct the exercise orally.

Answers:

1 was; 2 were; 3 were, 4 was; 5 wasn't; 6 was; 7 Were; 8 weren't

F Speaking/Pairs

- Before doing the exercise, review the time by drawing a clock face on the board and showing different hours. The whole class can say: *It's half past nine; It's a quarter past seven*, etc.
- Read the example dialogue with a student, then divide the class into pairs. Partners ask each other the questions. Encourage early finishers to ask more questions with different times.

G Dictionary work

- Look together at the two entries *sleep* and *sleepy* in the mini-dictionary. Elicit that one is a verb and one is an adjective.
- Students continue on their own.
- Check orally.

Answers:

1 sleepy (adj); 2 player (noun); 3 fun (noun); 4 life (noun)

Extra Time!

- Students turn to *World Club Magazine* and do Activity 21 on page 96.

MODULE 7 The Wild West

Answers:

Llamas were important for their wool.
The quipa was a bundle of knotted strings.
The Inca ruler was the head of the army.
The Inca noblemen used spears for fighting.
The centre of the Inca Empire was in Cuzco.

Extension activity

Different kinds of dwellings: Speaking/Pairs

- Divide the class into pairs or small groups. Students decide what kind of dwelling they want to describe, think of the necessary vocabulary and then draw the dwelling on poster paper. They label as many rooms and as much furniture as they can.

- If necessary, suggest some of the following: an igloo, a tepee, a mountain hut, a space station, a tree house, etc.

Activity Book Key

A There wasn't a fridge. There wasn't a television. There wasn't a computer. There wasn't a telephone. There wasn't a model aeroplane.

C 1 In the house there was an attic, a small bedroom and a big room.
2 In the big room there was a cooker, a big table, a rocking chair and a fire.
3 In the cupboard there were some plates, some knives and some bottles.
4 In the bedroom there was a bed, a chair and a picture.

D Across: kitchen, bath, lamp, toilet, bedroom, fire, cooker;
Down: table, chair

E 2 f; 3 d; 4 h; 5 a/g; 6 a/g; 7 b/e; 8 b/e

F 2 quarter past twelve;
3 quarter to six;
4 seven o'clock;
5 twenty past four;
6 ten to ten

Time to Read:

A He was 35.

B 1866 started to rob trains
1873 James gang started to rob trains
1875 railway police killed his mother
1876 failed to rob bank in Minnesota
1879 formed a new group
1882 died - killed by a member of the gang

C 2 they didn't want a railway across their land
3 he robbed railway trains
4 the people of the town stopped them
5 the railway people offered a reward for Jesse 'Dead or Alive'.

Language Focus: Past Simple *to be*

C

Which examples are singular and which are plural?

> ### AFFIRMATIVE
> Mother **was** in her rocking chair.
> There **were** two windows.

> ### NEGATIVE
> There **wasn't** a TV.
> The children **weren't** asleep.

> ### QUESTIONS
> Where **were** the children?
> **Was** there a lamp in the room?

D

Use the words to write sentences.

Example: 1 The little house was grey.

1 house / the / little / grey / was
2 there / animals / wild / were / woods / the / in
3 the / house / very / big / wasn't
4 bedroom / was / upstairs / there / a / ?

E

Complete with *was/wasn't* or *were/weren't*.

Yesterday at seven o'clock I [1] ... at home. My little sisters and I [2] ... in the living room in front of the TV. The dog and the cat [3] ... in the garden. My father [4] ... in the kitchen but my mother [5] ... (not) at home. She [6] ... at work. When she returned, she asked, " [7] ... your little sisters good?" "No, they [8] ...," I said.

F

In pairs, ask your partner questions like this:

Example: A: Where were you at 6 o'clock in the morning yesterday?
B: I was in bed!

1 six o'clock in the morning (6.00 a.m.)
2 half past nine in the morning (9.30 a.m.)
3 two o'clock in the afternoon (2.00 p.m.)
4 a quarter past seven in the evening (7.15 p.m.)
5 a quarter to twelve at night (11.45 p.m.)

G  DICTIONARY SKILLS

Choose the correct word to complete the sentences. Look them up in the mini-dictionary. Do you need a noun, a verb or an adjective?

1 The room was warm and she was ...
  sleep / sleepy
2 He wants to be a famous badminton ...
  play / player
3 We always have a lot of ... in the holidays.
  fun / funny
4 Billy the Kid's ... was very exciting.
  life / live

(EXTRA TIME)

Look at World Club magazine on page 96. Do activity 21.

The Wild West

 # Fluency

Writing: A Biography

 A

Write a short biography of the life of Annie Oakley, *The Greatest Shot in the West.*

Stage 1: Preparation

Read the notes:

- is born in Ohio - family poor - lives log cabin
- father dies - Annie nine years old
- starts shooting animals (rabbits, birds) for family to eat
- enters shooting competition - receives prize
- performs incredible shooting tricks
- is very famous - dies in 1926

Stage 2: Writing

Write your notes in sentences in the past simple. Use *then, after that, next, and* and *but.*

Example: She was born in Ohio. Her family was poor and they lived in a log cabin. Then her father died.

Stage 3: Checking

Check your writing for spelling and punctuation.

Speaking: My Life

B

In pairs, tell your partner about your life.

Stage 1: Preparation

Think about your life. Here are some ideas:

~ was born in ...
~ liked/didn't like my first day at school
~ my first teacher was called ...
~ she/he was very ...
~ my best friend was ...
~ started ... when I was ...

Example: I was born in 1990 in Mar del Plata.

Stage 2: Speaking

Tell your partner about your life. Include one piece of *false* information. At the end, your partner guesses what was false.

Listening: A Song

C

Listen to the song. Complete the chorus.

Oh! Susana! ^{1} ... you cry for ^{2} ... I ^{3} ... from Alabama ^{4} ... my banjo on ^{5} ... knee.

The Wild West

Writing: A biography

A Writing/Individual

Stage 1: Preparation

- Explain to students that they are going to write a short biography of the life of Annie Oakley. Go through the different stages in the exercise with the whole class and make sure that they understand each one.

- Ask students to read the notes about Annie Oakley's life. Remind them to check the mini-dictionary if they need help with the vocabulary.

Stage 2: Writing

- Students use their notes to write the biography. They should use linking words such as *then, after that, next, and, but,* to join the information.

Stage 3: Checking

- Students check their spelling with the help of their vocabulary books and mini-dictionary. If they have doubts about structures, they can also look at the Grammar Reference on page 76.

- After checking the language, they copy the text in their notebooks.

Speaking: My life

B Speaking/Pairs

Stage 1: Preparation

- Students look at the suggestions and make notes about the important or interesting events in their life.

Stage 2: Speaking

- Divide the class into pairs. Partners tell each other about their life.

- They must include one piece of false information. At the end of the conversation, each partner guesses what was false.

Listening: A song

C Cassette/Individual

- Tell students they are going to hear a popular American song about cowboys. The task is to complete the chorus. Ask them to write the numbers 1 to 5 in their notebooks.

- Play the tape, more than once if necessary and pause between verses.

- You may want them to compare their answers with another pair or group.

- Play the song again and then give students the correct answer.

Answers:

1 oh! don't; 2 me; 3 come; 4 with; 5 my

TAPESCRIPT:

Module 7, Fluency, Exercise C. Listen to the song. Complete the chorus.

I come from Alabama with my banjo on my knee,
I'm going to Louisiana my true love to see,
It rained all night the day I left,
The weather it was dry,
The sun was hot and I froze to death,
Susanna don't you cry.

Oh! Susanna, oh! don't you cry for me,
I come from Alabama with my banjo on my knee.
I had a dream the other night,
When everything was still,
I thought I saw Susanna
Coming down the hill,
A cake was in her mouth,
A tear was in her eye,
But I'm coming from the South,
So Susanna don't you cry.

Oh! Susanna, oh! don't you cry for me,
I come from Alabama with my banjo on my knee.

Consolidation

Grammar

A Writing/Individual

- Students complete the text with the past simple. To give them additional writing practice, you can ask them to copy out the whole paragraph.
- Correct the exercise by asking different students to write the verbs on the board.

Answers:

2 called; 3 wanted; 4 decided; 5 travelled;
6 didn't stop; 7 followed; 8 returned;
9 didn't escape; 10 killed

B Speaking/Whole class

- Divide the class into two teams. Each team has a number of words from which it is possible to make simple sentences in the past simple tense.
- Teams take turns to 'fire' sentences at each other. If the sentence is correct, the team gets a point.
- When you think the students have exhausted the possible number of sentences, finish the game and add up the score.
- You can also create possibilities of more sentences (and practise more verbs) by putting more of your own 'word bullets' on the board.

Vocabulary

C Keywords/Individual

- Students write the three headings *Animals, Weapons* and *Person* in their notebooks and complete the table with the plural of the words in the box.
- While they are doing this, put these same headings on the board and ask students who know more words to come up and write them.

Answers:

Animals: buffaloes, bears, wolves
Weapons: knives, spears
Persons: children, babies, gunmen, people

Pronunciation: Word stress

D Cassette/Individual

- Write the two examples on the board and say the words, exaggerating the main stress and marking it with a small box (as in the book).
- Explain to the students that they will hear the words from the list and have to mark the main stress with a similar box. Ask them to copy the words in their notebooks.
- Play the tape. While it is playing, write the words on the board.
- Check the answers by asking individual students to come out and mark the stress above the words on the board. The rest of the class agrees or corrects.
- Play the tape again and ask students to repeat the verbs.

Answers:

1st syllable: carried, travelled, started, painted; 2nd syllable: escaped, arrived, recovered, returned, continued, performed

 TAPESCRIPT:

Module 7, Consolidation, Exercise D. Listen to the words. Copy and mark the main stress.

READER: carried / escaped / arrived / travelled / started / recovered / returned / continued / performed / painted

Consolidation

A

Complete the text with the past simple.

Example: 1 robbed

Butch Cassidy [1] ... *(rob)* banks and trains with the 'Sundance Kid'. People [2] ... *(call)* them the Wild Bunch. The sheriffs [3] ... *(want)* to catch them. So Butch and the Sundance Kid [4] ... *(decide)* to go to South America. They [5] ... *(travel)* to Bolivia, but they [6] ... *(not stop)* robbing banks. The Bolivian army [7] ... *(follow)* them. Butch [8] ... *(return)* to the United States. People think the Sundance Kid [9] ... *(not escape)* and the army [10] ... *(kill)* him.

B

TEAM GAME

- Make sentences using words from your cowboy's gun. You can use a word more than once.
- Take turns to say a sentence.
- The team with the most correct sentences is the winner. The teacher is the referee.

Example: He walked to school.

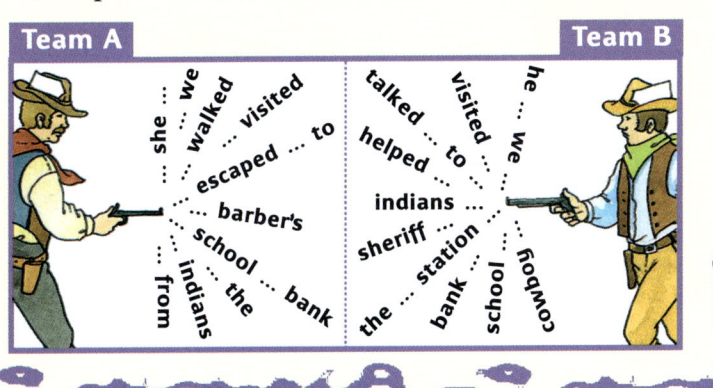

Vocabulary

C  KEYWORDS

Write the plural of these words and classify them in these groups.

> buffalo knife bear child
> baby cook person wolf
> gunman spear

Animals	Weapons	Person
buffaloes	Knives	children

Pronunciation: Stress

D

Listen to the words. Copy and mark the main stress.

Examples: carried, escaped

carried / escaped / arrived / travelled / started / recovered / returned / continued / performed / painted

Module check

Grammar Reference

13 Past simple: affirmative and negative (regular verbs)

	Affirmative	Negative
I/you/he/she/it/we/they	hunted	didn't hunt

- The **past simple** describes a finished action in the past:
- Regular affirmative verbs end in **d** or **ed**:

The Indians lived in tepees and they hunted buffaloes.

- We use **didn't + infinitive** to form the negative (don't add d or ed to the main verb):

The Spanish didn't hunt horses in America.
Billy the Kid didn't die in a prison.

14 Past simple: *to be*

	Affirmative	Negative
there/I/he/she/it	was	was not (wasn't)
there/you/we/they	were	were not (weren't)

Questions	
Was	there/I/he/she/it?
Were	there/you/we/they?

We use **was / were** to:
- Describe a state or a condition in the past:

The Indians were not rich but they were happy.

- Indicate things that were/weren't present:

There was a table. There weren't any chairs outside.

- Express age in the past:

Billy the Kid was 21 years old when he died.

- Say where people were from in the past.

My grandmother was from Kentucky.

Keyword Check 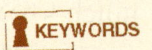 KEYWORDS

Animals: bear, birds, buffalo, dog, horse, rabbit, wildcat, wolf

People: chief, gang, guard, gunman, sheriff

House: bedroom, cooker, door, downstairs, fire, lamp, log cabin, rocking chair, table, tepee, upstairs, window

Irregular Plurals: babies, buffaloes, childre knives, people, wolves

Weapons: bow and arrow, gun, knife, spea

Verbs: carry, join (a gang), live, hunt, look after, make (clothes), marry, paint, pull out gun), ride, rob, shoot, use

Verbs with no object: arrive, be born, die escape, return, travel

Adjectives: comfortable, dead, famous, wil incredible, little, poor, sad, satisfied, warm,

Times: six o'clock (6.00), half past six (6.3 a quarter past six (6.15), a quarter to seve (6.45)

Linking words: after that, next, then

1 **Look at Grammar References 13-14 above and complete Grammar Files 13-14 in the Activity Book. Then do the *Test Yourself: Grammar* on page 53 of the Activity Book.**

2 **Look at the Keyword Check. Write important new words in your vocabulary book. Then do the *Test Yourself: Vocabulary* on page 53 of the Activity Book.**

The Wild West

- This check should help students to reflect on several aspects of their learning and to assess their progress themselves.

- First, ask them to choose their favourite activity in this module (eg: Billy the Kid song).

- Ask them to think about what they do when they are doing the final speaking tasks. Do they prepare vocabulary before they start? Ask their partner to repeat when they don't understand? Look at their partner while he/she is speaking?

- Ask students to look at the *Grammar Reference* and the *Grammar File* and then do the *Test Yourself: Grammar* exercises.

- Ask them to look at the *Keyword Check* and write the important new words in their vocabulary books and then do the *Test Yourself: Vocabulary* exercises.

- Remind them that these activities should be done **by** themselves and **for** themselves. However, also make it clear that you are always willing to revise problem areas in class.

- It is a good idea to spot check their work so you can get a better idea of each student's general attitude and progress.

8 Travel

Objectives

Read about explorers and airships; talk about journeys; tell a story and write an adventure story.

Contents

Language Aims

Functions:

- Asking and answering questions about past events
- Describing actions in the past
- Describing climates
- Using linking words to form coherent paragraphs
- Reviewing means of transport
- Discussing end of year results

Target language:

- *Did Erik the Red live in Iceland?*
- *Yes, he did.*
- *Gulliver swam to an island; he didn't swim to England.*
- *Leif Erikson discovered a very green and wet place.*
- *Erik killed two men; after that, he decided to leave Iceland.*

Vocabulary:

Transport: *airship, bicycle, boat, bus, car, motorbike, plane, train*
Travel: *cabin, destination, flight, journey, passenger, trip*
Places: *Canada, Greenland, Germany, Iceland, North America, Norway*
Weather: *cold, icy, rainy, snowy, warm, wet*
Verbs (present / past): *eat/ate, drink/drank, go/went, hurt/hurt, leave/left, meet/met, sail/sailed, sit/sat, sleep/slept, swim/swam*
Adjectives: *afraid, beautiful, comfortable, enormous, friendly, happy, hard, horrible, hungry, nice, pretty, tired*
Linkers: *after that, later, two days later, the next day*

Pronunciation:

- Pronouncing dates
- Contrasting and producing the diphthongs in *day* /deɪ/ and *night* /naɪt/

Activity types

- Talking about travelling and means of transport
- Matching words and drawings
- Classifying positive and negative adjectives
- Listening to a story and ordering the pictures
- Listening and matching questions with their answers
- Reordering words to make questions
- Writing questions about Gulliver's adventures
- Playing a guessing game with the whole class
- Doing the activities in the World Club Magazine
- Brainstorming for the titles of other popular adventure books
- Reading a text and listening to the tape
- Listening to and repeating dates
- Looking at four drawings and finding specific items
- Reading a text and matching the paragraphs with the pictures
- Finding the past tenses of a given list of verbs in the text
- Writing an adventure story
- Drawing a map and illustrating the story
- Telling the story in small groups
- Completing the Module Check
- Organising the new vocabulary in a notebook
- Carrying out self-evaluation tasks
- Carrying out the yearly assessment task

Attitudes to learning

- Showing interest in past and present history
- Showing interest in finding out about innovations in transport
- Appreciating the importance of reflection as an aid to language learning
- Showing interest in achieving accuracy in English
- Considering assessment and self-assessment important tools to measure progress
- Reflecting on one's achievements and looking forward to the next course

Moral and Social Values

- Road Safety

Discussing with students the relative dangers and merits of modern means of transport (Lesson 24: A, B and C).

- Peace Studies

Helping students realise that Europe and America are linked by common cultures (Lesson 23: B, C and E).

Lead-in

Module Objectives

Read and explain the module objectives to your students and make sure that they understand them.

Topic focus

- Focus on the title of the module *Travel* and explain the meaning. Elicit different ways of travelling (let students look through the module) and write them up on the board: *car/bus/plane/train/on foot/airship/ship.*

a Keywords/Individual

- Students look at the words in the box and say which of the things are in the photo. Check orally with the whole class.

Answers:

Can't see an airship or a motorbike

b Speaking/Pairs

- Divide the class into pairs and go through the dialogue with a student. Partners ask and answer the three questions.

Travel
Lead-in

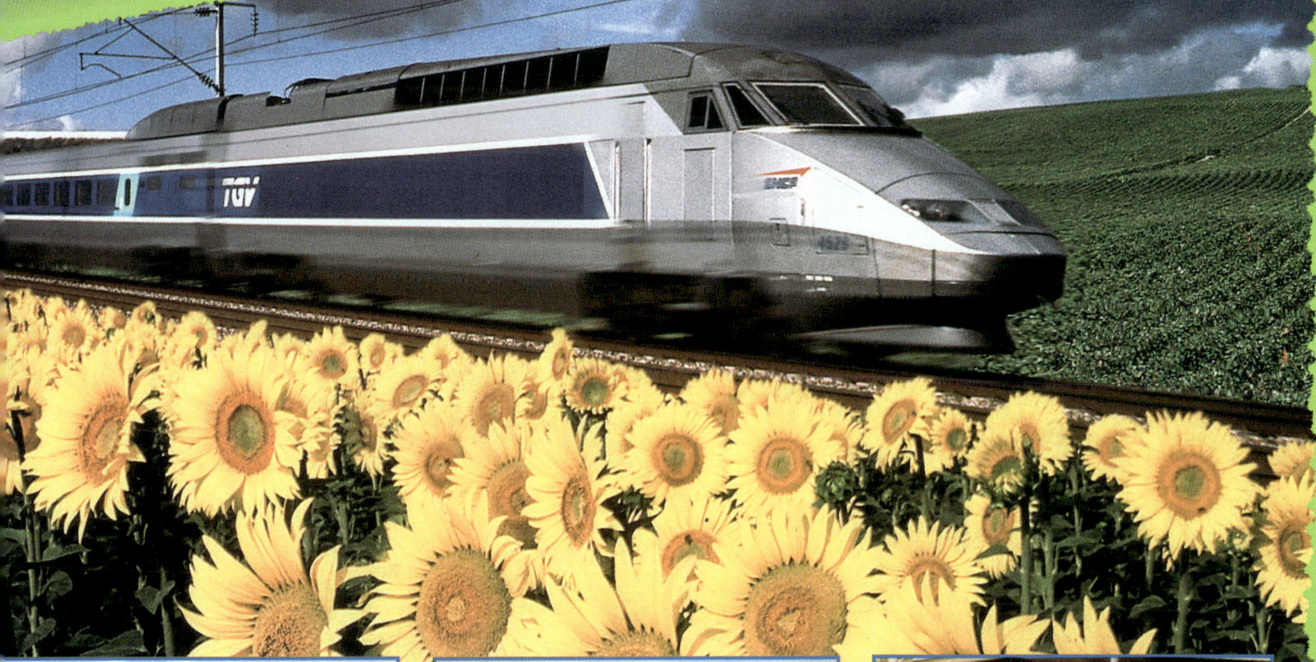

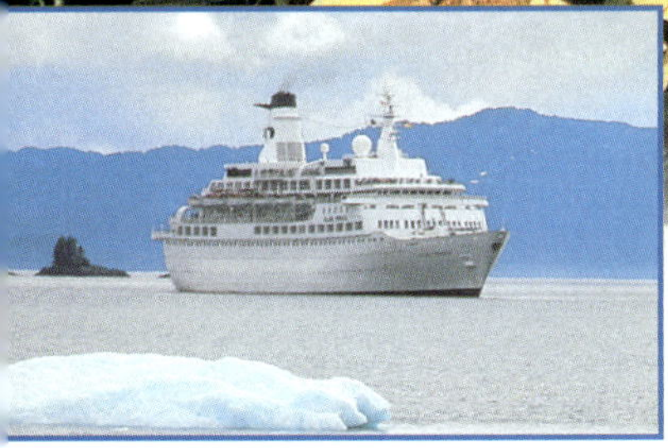

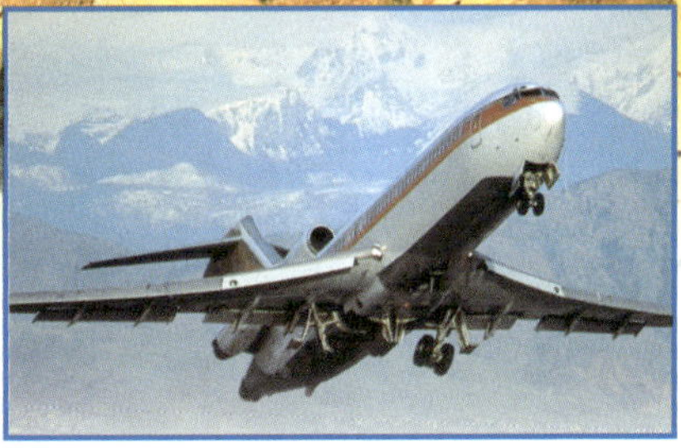

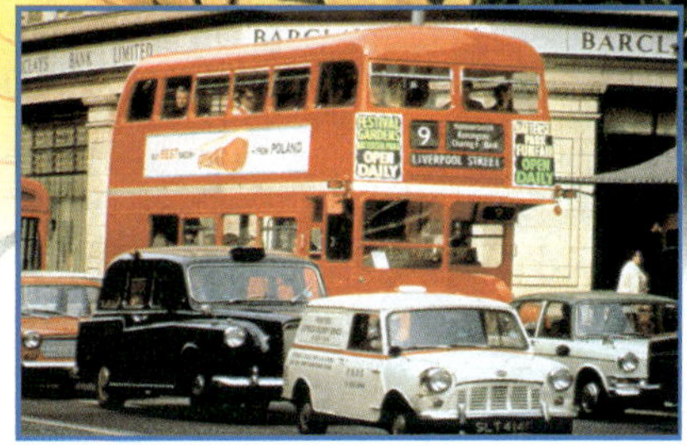

a KEYWORDS

Which of these things are in the pictures?

aeroplane taxi bicycle car train boat airship motorbike bus

b

In pairs, ask and answer these questions.

Example: A: How do you get to school?

B: By bus. And you?

A: I come on foot.

1 How do you get to school?

2 How do your parents get to work?

3 How do you normally travel on holiday?

22 Gulliver's Travels

A

Are these adjectives positive (+) or negative (−)?

Examples: tired (−) happy (+)

> tired happy terrible hungry pretty afraid
> fantastic horrible nice friendly

B

A father is telling his daughter a story. Listen and put the pictures in the correct order.
Example: 1 B

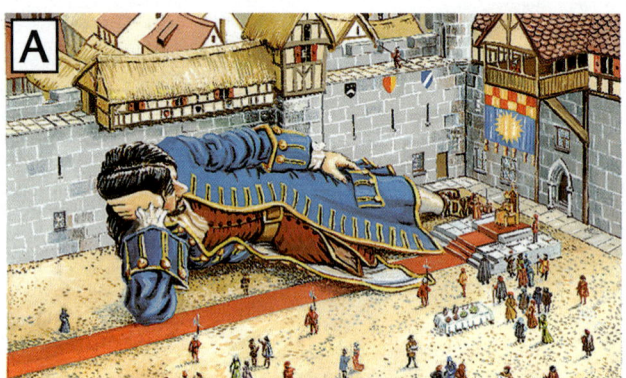

Topic focus

- Ask students if they have heard of Gulliver and elicit anything about his adventures.

A Keywords/Individual

- Students decide whether the adjectives are positive or negative. Remind them to use the mini-dictionary if they need help.
- Correct the exercise.

Answers:
terrible (-); hungry (-); pretty (+); afraid (-); fantastic (+); horrible (-); nice (+); friendly (+)

B Cassette/Individual

- Write up the key vocabulary on the board. Explain the words using the pictures. Tell students that they are going to hear a father telling his daughter a story.
- Play the tape. Students try to put the pictures in order. Remind them that it is not necessary to understand every word.
- Check the answers orally with the whole class.

Answers:
2d; 3e; 4c; 5a

TAPESCRIPT:

Module 8, Lesson 22, Exercise B. Listen and put the pictures in your book in the correct order.

FATHER: This story is about the adventures of a man called Gulliver. One day he was on a boat and there was a terrible storm. Gulliver was very afraid. All the people died, except Gulliver.

DAUGHTER: Did he stay on the boat?

FATHER: No, he didn't. The boat started to go down. Gulliver started to swim...

DAUGHTER: Where did he swim to?

FATHER: He swam to an island. He felt happy, but he was really tired, and he went to sleep on the beach, for many hours. When he woke up, he tried to move, but it was impossible. There were ropes around his arms and legs. Then, suddenly, he noticed lots of little people, about ten centimetres tall.

DAUGHTER: What did they do?

FATHER: They shouted and attacked him with spears and bows and arrows.

DAUGHTER: Did they hurt him?

FATHER: Yes, they did. It was horrible. And then they decided he was a friend. Gulliver walked to their city. Everything was small and very pretty. The houses were like dolls'

houses. Gulliver was hungry. The food was really small but was fantastic.

DAUGHTER: What did he have?

FATHER: Well.. for dinner, he had twenty chickens, fifty plates of rice and a hundred apples! After that he was very tired again.

DAUGHTER: Where did he sleep?

FATHER: He slept on seventy of their little beds! The next day, Gulliver talked with the king of the little people. He was very nice and was friendly to Gulliver. The king asked questions about England.

DAUGHTER: When did Gulliver go home?

FATHER: Well, he went to another place after his visit to Lilliput. In fact, this was only the beginning of his adventures.

Language Focus: Past and simple questions

C Cassette/Individual

- Tell students to complete the girl's questions about Gulliver.
- Play the tape, more than once if necessary.
- Students say whether the verbs are in the past or the infinitive.

Answers:
1 Did (past); 2 swim (infinitive); 3 did (past); 4 hurt (infinitive); 5 did (past); 6 sleep (infinitive); 7 did (past), go (infinitive)

TAPESCRIPT:

Module 8, Lesson 22, Exercise C. Listen and complete the questions.

1 DAUGHTER: Did he stay on the boat?
  FATHER: No, he didn't.
2 DAUGHTER: Where did he swim to?
  FATHER: He swam to an island.
3 DAUGHTER: What did they do?
  FATHER: They shouted and attacked him.
4 DAUGHTER: Did they hurt him?
  FATHER: Yes, they did.
5 DAUGHTER: What did he have?
  FATHER: Well.. for dinner, he had twenty chickens..
6 DAUGHTER: Where did he sleep?
  FATHER: He slept on seventy of their little beds!
7 DAUGHTER: When did Gulliver go home?
  FATHER: Well, he went to another place

D Writing/Individual

- In their notebooks, students reorder the words to make sentences. Remind them to use capitals.
- Check the exercise orally with the whole class.

Answers:

2 What did Gulliver try to do?
3 How did they attack him?
4 Did Gulliver talk with the king?
5 Did Gulliver have more adventures?

E Writing/Individual

- Write the example question and answer on the board. Point out the use of the auxiliary *did* for questions in the past. Students use the cues to write eight questions which they match with the answers.
- Ask them to exchange notebooks with another student and correct his or her sentences.
- Correct orally with the whole class. One student asks a question and another gives the answer.

Answers:

2 Where did Gulliver swim to? (f)
3 Where did he sleep after the storm? (a)
4 Did the little people attack him? (b)
5 Where did he go with them? (h)
6 What did he have for dinner? (c)
7 Who did he talk to? (g)
8 Did Gulliver go home? (e)

F Speaking/Whole class

- Divide the class into two teams, team O and team X. Ask a student to copy the grid with the nine verbs on the board twice.
- Players on each teams take turns to choose a verb and make a question. If the question is correct, the scorekeeper puts an O or an X in the corresponding box.
- The winner is the first to complete a line.
- Ask students to choose different verbs and play the game in pairs. Monitor the activity to make sure that they are using the auxiliary and the infinitive in the questions.

Extension activity

More adventure stories: Speaking/Groups

- Divide the class into small groups. Ask students to name as many adventure books and tales as possible.
- They can write the titles in their own language if they don't know the English names.
- Ask one student from each group to read out the list. Pick out the English books and write the titles on the board.

Extra Time!

- Students turn to *World Club Magazine* and do Activity 22 on page 96.

Answers:

1 c; 2 b; 3 b; 4 b

Activity Book Key:

A 2 When did you go to school?
  3 How did you go to school?
  4 Who did you talk to in the first lesson?
  5 What did you do in the lesson?
  6 Where did you have lunch?

B 2 Did he sleep in a tree? No, he didn't.
  3 Did little men attack him? Yes, they did.
  4 Did he visit their city? Yes, he did.
  5 Did he talk to the President? No, he didn't.
  6 Did he go home after that? No, he didn't.

C 2 went; 3 didn't like; 4 had; 5 stayed;
  6 swam; 7 didn't sleep; 8 didn't want

D 2 ship; 3 by car; 4 bicycle; 5 April;
  6 summer

E 1a; 2d; 3e; 4f; 5b; 6c

F 2 what; 3 where; 4 which; 5 when; 6 why

G 2 Where/What places did you visit?
  3 Why did you have problems?
  4 What did you do in Lilliput?
  5 When did you return to England?
  6 Which place did you like best?

anguage Focus: Past mple Questions

mplete the questions.

. he stay on the boat?
Where did he ... to?
What ... they do?
Did they ... him?
What ... he have?
Where did he ...?
When ... Gulliver ... home?

the main verb in the past or e infinitive?

the words in the correct der to make questions.

ample: 1 Did Gulliver sleep
for a long time?

Gulliver / did / for a long time / sleep?

what / did / try to do / Gulliver?

how / they / did / attack him?

did / talk with the king / Gulliver?

more adventures / did / Gulliver / have?

E

Write questions about Gulliver's adventure and match them with the answers.

Example: 1: Why did the boat go down?

d: There was a storm.

1 why / the boat go down?
2 where / Gulliver swim to?
3 where / he sleep after the storm?
4 the little people attack him?
5 where / he go with them?
6 what / he have for dinner?
7 who / he talk to?
8 Gulliver go home?

a On the beach.
b Yes, they did.
c Chickens, rice and apples.
d There was a storm.
e No, he didn't.
f To an island.
g The king.
h To their city.

F

TEAM GAME

• Play in two teams – team O and team X.
• Take turns to choose a box (e.g. box 2).
• Make a question using the verb.

Example: What did you study in maths yesterday?

• If the question is correct, put O or X in that box.
• You win when you complete a line.
• Choose different verbs and play the game in pairs.

play?	study?	watch?
have?	start?	live?
listen to?	do?	go?

Look at **World Club** magazine on page 96. Do activity 22.

Travel

79

23 Father and son

A 🔑 KEYWORDS

Match the weather words with the pictures.

warm and sunny icy and snowy
rainy and wet

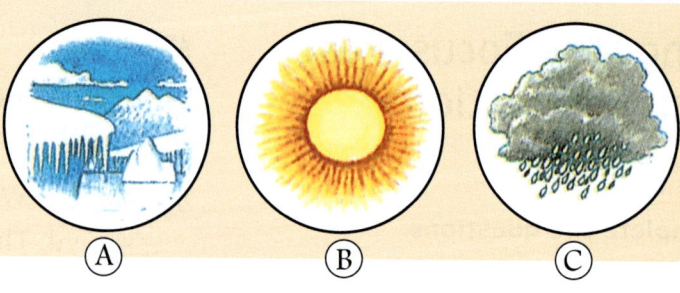

Ⓐ Ⓑ Ⓒ

B 📖 📼

Read the text and listen. Match the pictures with the countries.

Example: Picture A – Iceland

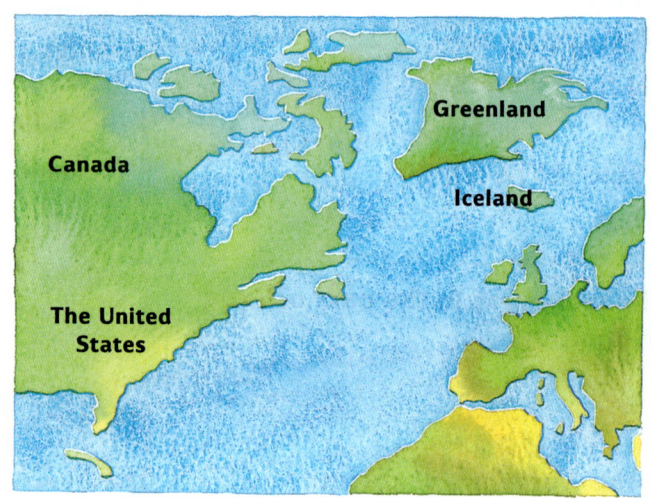

Canada

Greenland

Iceland

The United States

The Adventures of Erik and Leif

Erik the Red was born in Norway in 950, but he moved to Iceland when he was a boy. People called him 'the Red' because of his red hair. Life in Iceland was hard and it was a very cold place. Erik had many enemies, and he killed two men. After that, he decided to leave Iceland to escape from his enemies.

In 982, Erik sailed west and discovered a new country. was cold, icy and snowy, but Erik wanted people to com to this new country, so he called it Greenland. Later, h returned to Greenland with more people in 986. Th boats were very small, but they had cows, pigs, sheep an hens with them!

Topic focus

- Write the names *Eric the Red* and *Leif the Lucky* on the board. Explain to the students that Eric was Leif's father and that they were famous Viking explorers. Tell them that archaeological evidence shows that the Vikings discovered America nearly five hundred years before Christopher Columbus.

- Ask students to name other famous explorers and travellers, and write them up on the board, for example *Marco Polo, Livingstone, Cook, Orellana,* etc.

A Keywords/Individual

- Students look at the weather words in the box and match them with the pictures. Check orally with the whole class.

Answers:

warm and sunny: B; icy and snowy: A; cold: D; rainy and wet: C

B Reading/Cassette/Individual

- Ask students to look at the map and identify the countries.

- Focus their attention on the question and on the four drawings. Ask them to read the text and look up the new words in the mini-dictionary.

- Play the tape, more than once if necessary, stopping after every paragraph. Remind students that at this stage it is more important to get the general idea than to understand every word.

- Check orally with the whole class.

Answers:

Picture B: Greenland: cold, icy and snowy
Picture C: Canada: wet
Picture D: North America: warm and sunny

 TAPESCRIPT:

Module 8, Lesson 23, Exercise B. Read the text and listen. Match the pictures with the countries and the weather.

Erik the Red was born in Norway in 950, but he moved to Iceland when he was a boy. People called him 'the Red' because of his red hair. Life in Iceland was hard and it was a very cold place. Erik had many enemies, and he killed two men. After that, he decided to leave Iceland to escape from his enemies.

In 982, Erik sailed west and discovered a new country. It was cold, icy and snowy, but Erik wanted people to come to this new country, so he called it 'Greenland'. Later, he returned to Greenland with more people in 986. The boats were very small, but they had cows, pigs, sheep and hens with them!

Leif, Erik's son, was born in 975 and lived with his father in Greenland. Like his father, he wanted to travel. In the summer of 1002, Leif sailed west to look for another country. He discovered a very green and wet place. It had trees and rivers with lots of salmon. This was Canada. Later, Leif continued his travels south. He discovered another green and beautiful place. It was warm and sunny and there were different fruits, including grapes. This was part of the modern United States. Leif and his men were probably the first Europeans to visit North America.

C Reading/Individual

- Look at the sentences with the students and teach the new vocabulary. Explain what a time line is.

- Ask students to read the text again and to match the sentences with the years.

- Correct the exercise orally with the whole class.

Answers:

1 Eric discovered Greenland – 982; 2 Leif was born – 975; 3 Leif sailed to America – 1002; 4 Eric returned to Greenland – 986; 5 Eric was born – 950

Pronunciation: Years

D Cassette/Individual/Whole class

- Focus on the years and how they are said in English.

- Play the tape and point out that the last number is stressed.

- Play the tape again. This time students write down the year. They can work in pairs to check each other's answers. Correct the exercise by having different students write the years on the board and say them.

- Play the tape again for the class to repeat in chorus.

Answers:

2: 1968; 3: 2001; 4: 2012; 5: 1999

TAPESCRIPT:

Module 8, Lesson 23, Exercise D. Listen to the pronunciation of these years.

READER: 1002; 1994

Now listen and write the years you hear. One.
READER: 1998
NARRATOR: Two.
READER: 1968
NARRATOR: Three.
READER: 2001
NARRATOR: Four.
READER: 2012
NARRATOR: Five.
READER: 1999

E Speaking/Pairs

- Divide the class into pairs and read the example with a student. Partners ask each other questions with the sentences in Exercise C. Go round the class and monitor use of past simple regular and irregular forms.

Extra Time!

- Students turn to *World Club Magazine* and do Activity 23 on page 97.

Answers:
1 He was a scientist.
2 Four and a half years.
3 Brazil, Argentina, Uruguay, Chile.
4 He was fifty.

Reinforcement activity

Dates: Speaking/groups

- One student says a date and, for example, 'plus four'. The next student must add four years and say the new date. He/she then says, for example, 'minus seven'.
- Go round encouraging students not to complicate the arithmetic too much and to change centuries every five or six turns.

Activity Book Key

A 2 Where did Erik sail to? To Greenland.
3 What did he take to Greenland? Cows, pigs, hens and sheep.
4 When was Leif born? In 975.
5 Which countries did he visit? Canada and the USA.
6 What fruit did he discover there? Grapes.

B **Weather:** sunny, snowy, rainy, cold, hot;
Animals: cows, pigs, hens, sheep, buffaloes;
Food: apples, rice, meat, sandwiches, sausages

C 2 eighteen fifteen;
3 fifteen eighty-eight;
4 fourteen ninety-two;
5 nineteen sixty-nine

D 2 people; 3 chicken; 4 friendly; 5 different;
6 European

Teacher's notes

C

Match the sentences with the years.

Example: Eric was born – 950

1	Eric discovered Greenland.	950
2	Leif was born.	975
3	Leif sailed to America.	982
4	Eric returned to Greenland.	986
5	Eric was born.	1002

D  PRONUNCIATION: YEARS

Listen to the pronunciation of these years.

1002 = ten-oh-two   1994 = nineteen-ninety-four

Now listen and write the years you hear.

Example: 1 = 1998

Listen again and repeat the years.

E

Look at exercise C. Ask and answer questions with *when*.

Example: A: When was Eric born?

B: He was born in the year 950.

Did you know?

Vikings, like Leif Eriksson, traded with North American Indians 500 years before Columbus 'discovered' America.

EXTRA TIME

Look at World Club magazine on page 97. Do activity 23.

if, Erik's son, was born in 975 and lived with his father
Greenland. Like his father, he wanted to travel. In the
summer of 1002, Leif sailed west to look for another
country. He discovered a very green and wet place. It had
ees and rivers with lots of salmon. This was Canada.

Later, Leif continued his travels south. He discovered another green and beautiful place. It was warm and sunny and there were different fruits, including grapes. This was part of the modern United States. Leif and his men were probably the first Europeans to visit North America.

Travel

24 Airships

A  KEYWORDS

Find these things in the pictures.

> passengers lounge explosion
> cabins grand piano

B

Read the text and match the paragraphs with the pictures.

Example: 1 B

The Hindenburg

(1) The Zeppelin Company made enormous airships. They were like big ships with dining rooms, lounges and cabins, but they crossed the Atlantic in two days. They were fast; in 1929, an airship called the Graf Zeppelin went round the world in twenty-one days!

(2) On 4th May, 1937, an airship called the Hindenburg began its last flight. It left Germany for the USA. The airship had thirty-five passengers on board.

(3) The passengers on the Hindenburg were very comfortable. They slept in cabins, sat and played cards in a lounge, and ate and drank in a big dining room. In the evenings they listened to music from a grand piano and danced!

(4) On 6th May, the Hindenburg got to the USA, but the passengers did not arrive at their destination. Suddenly, there was an enormous explosion! All the passengers died.

Topic focus

- This lesson is about airships, which were developed in Germany in the 1920s and 1930s. At the time, they seemed to open up great possibilities for fast and comfortable intercontinental travel but a series of disasters (in which the airships exploded) forced the companies involved to abandon the idea.

- Focus on the title and explain the meaning of *airships*. Ask: *Do people travel on airships now?*

A Keywords/Individual

- Students read the words in the box and find the items in the illustrations.
- Go through the exercise orally with the whole class.

Answers:

passenger: A; lounge: A; explosion: D; cabins: B; grand piano: A

B Reading/Individual

- Students read the text and match the paragraphs with the pictures. Tell them that it isn't necessary to understand every word to do the task, and remind them to use the mini-dictionary if they need help with the vocabulary.
- Correct orally with the whole class.

Answers:

2c; 3a; 4d

C Reading/Individual

- Students read the text again and give short answers to the questions.
- Correct orally with the whole class.

Answers:

2 On 4th May, 1937. 3 They listened to music and danced. 4 In cabins. 5 Thirty-five.

Language Focus: Past simple (irregular verbs)

- The most common verbs tend to be irregular in the past simple, and it is important for students to learn them properly from the beginning. This is the moment to call their attention to the

list of irregular verbs on page 96. The most common error is the use of regular instead of irregular forms, for example: *he comed.*

D Reading/Individual

- Ask students to find and write down the past tense of the verbs in the text.
- Check the exercise orally with the whole class.

Answers:

got; made; began; went; left; had; slept; sat; ate; drank

E Learning to learn/Individual

- Look at the title of the *Language Focus* section: *Past simple: irregular verbs.* Ask students what the regular form of the past simple is and write up three or four examples on the board: *played, arrived, lived,* etc.
- Students then look at the verbs in the boxes and say which one is irregular. Ask them to justify their answer.

Answer:

leave

F Writing/Individual

- Students complete the text in the past simple. To give them additional writing practice, you can ask them to copy out the whole paragraph.
- Go through the answers with the whole class.

Answers:

2 began; 3 were; 4 had; 5 listened; 6 didn't sleep; 7 got up; 8 didn't eat; 9 sat; 10 was; 11 got

G Speaking/Pairs

- Divide the class into pairs. Partners take turns asking and answering questions about their journey to school.
- Monitor the activity and note any problems. If necessary, review the past simple again and give more examples on the board.

MODULE 8 Travel

H Dictionary work

- Point students to the list of irregular verbs on page 87. Look together at a few more examples in the mini-dictionary

- Ask students to do the exercise on their own or in pairs.

- Check orally.

Answers:

caught chose drew fought gave hid kept knew said sang spoke threw

Extra Time!

- Students turn to *World Club Magazine* and do Activity 24 on page 97.

Answers:

1 He looked after his father's sheep.
2 'Wolf! Wolf! Help! A wolf is killing our sheep.
3 Because there was no wolf.
4 Because they thought that there wasn't a wolf.

Reinforcement activity

Verb Bingo: Speaking/Whole class

- In their notebooks, students draw a grid with nine squares. They write one of the following irregular verbs in each square: *make, take, go, leave, have, sleep, eat, drink, come.* Tell them to cover any three squares.

- Explain that you are going to read out the past form of the verbs. Write these on small pieces of paper and draw them out of a bag or box. As they hear the verbs, students cover them up. The first person to cover all the squares wins.

- Play the game again, with the winner calling out the verbs.

Activity Book Key

A 2 I slept very well last night.
   3 I didn't make my bed yesterday.
   4 She began classes last week.
   5 We didn't eat the meat.
   6 Did you have breakfast this morning?

B 2 I had breakfast with my mother.
   3 Tina left home after lunch.
   4 We went to school by bus.
   5 They begin classes at nine o'clock.

C 2 left; 3 had; 4 were; 5 listened; 6 drank; 7 ate; 8 slept; 9 escaped; 10 didn't stop; 11 died

D 1 train; 2 boat; 3 airship; 4 bicycle; 5 plane; 6 bus; 7 car; 8 motorbike

F 2 in; 3 in; 4 on; 5 at, on, 6 in; 7 on; 8 in

Time to Read:

A c

B 1 Venice.
   2 Yes.
   3 On horseback or by camel.
   4 Because the Kublai Khan asked him to work for him.
   5 Marco Polo's friend.

C 2 Who did he go with?
   3 Who was the Emperor of China?
   4 Where did Kublai Khan live?
   5 Why didn't people believe Marco Polo's stories?

C

Read the text again and answer these questions.

Example: 1 airships

1 What did the Zeppelin Company make?
2 When did the *Hindenburg* leave Germany?
3 What did the passengers do in the evenings?
4 Where did the passengers sleep?
5 How many passengers died in the explosion?

Language Focus: Past Simple (irregular verbs)

D  KEYWORDS

Find the past tense of these verbs in the text.

> get make begin go leave have
> sleep sit eat drink

E

Look at the verbs *play* and *leave* in the boxes. Which verb is irregular?

AFFIRMATIVE

They **played** cards.
It **left** on 4th May.

NEGATIVE

They **didn't play** tennis.
They **didn't leave** on 3rd May.

QUESTIONS

Did they **play** cards?
Did it **leave** on 4th May?

F

Complete the text in the past simple. There is a list of irregular verbs on page 111.

Example: 1 left

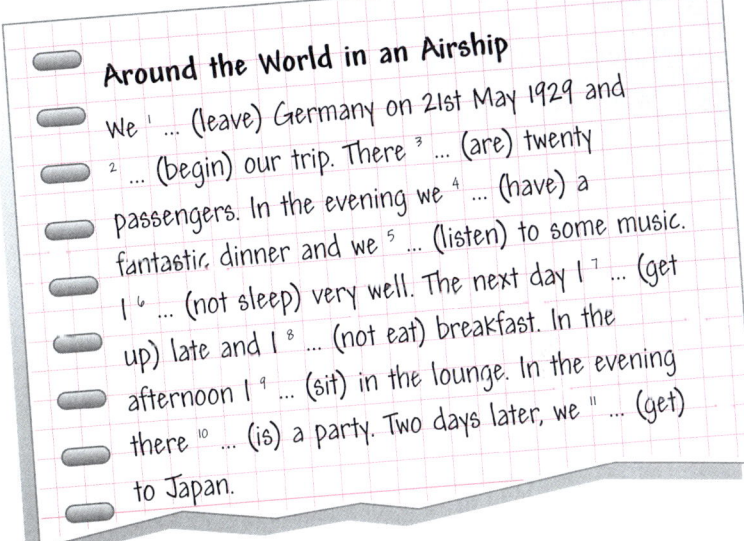

Around the World in an Airship

We ¹ ... (leave) Germany on 21st May 1929 and ² ... (begin) our trip. There ³ ... (are) twenty passengers. In the evening we ⁴ ... (have) a fantastic dinner and we ⁵ ... (listen) to some music. I ⁶ ... (not sleep) very well. The next day I ⁷ ... (get up) late and I ⁸ ... (not eat) breakfast. In the afternoon I ⁹ ... (sit) in the lounge. In the evening there ¹⁰ ... (is) a party. Two days later, we ¹¹ ... (get) to Japan.

G

In pairs, ask and answer questions about coming to school today.

1 What time did you get up?
2 What did you have for breakfast?
3 How did you travel?
4 Who did you come with?
5 What time did you get to school?

H  DICTIONARY SKILLS

Use the mini-dictionary to find the past simple of these irregular verbs.

catch choose draw fight give hide keep
know say sing speak throw

 EXTRA TIME

Look at World Club magazine on page 97. Do activity 24.

Travel

83

Fluency

Writing: A Story

A

Write an adventure story.

Stage 1: Preparation

Invent a character who went to a strange place. Write notes about the story.

Example:

The trip – Paula goes to visit Aunt in Peru for summer holidays

What happened – plane crashes – Paula alone on island – sees strange animals (describe) – meets people in village – frightened

What happened in the end – Paula builds boat – leaves island

Stage 2: Writing

Use your notes to write the story in the past tense. Include these words: *after that, later, then, next, in the end.*

Example: The plane crashed. Paula got out and saw she was alone. After that she...

Stage 3: Checking

Check your writing for irregular verbs. Draw a map and illustrate your story.

Speaking: Telling Your Story

B

Tell the group your story.

Stage 1: Preparation

Look at your notes from the writing task. Practise telling the story to yourself.

Stage 2: Speaking

Tell the other students your story. You can look at your notes, but don't read out your final story.

Listening: Discovery Quiz

C

Try to answer these questions. Then listen to the quiz and check your answers.

1 Where did Columbus first arrive in America?
   a) the Bahamas b) Venezuela

2 Who was the first person to go around the world?
   a) Drake b) Magellan

3 Who was the first European to arrive in Peru?
   a) Cortes b) Pizarro

4 What country did Erik the Red discover in 982?
   a) Iceland b) Greenland

5 Who was the first man to walk on the moon?
   a) Aldrin b) Armstrong

6 Where did the North American Indians originate?
   a) Asia b) Africa

Who won - Sian or James?

Travel

84

Writing: A story

A Writing/Individual

Stage 1: Preparation

- Explain to students that they are going to write an adventure story. Go through the different stages in the exercise with the whole class and make sure that they understand each one.

- Ask students to read the notes about Paula's adventures and to write notes in preparation for their story. Remind them to check the mini-dictionary if they need help with the vocabulary.

Stage 2: Writing

- Students use their notes to write the story in the past tense. They should use linking words such as *after that, later, then, next, in the end* to join the information.

Stage 3: Checking

- Students check their spelling with the help of their vocabulary books and mini-dictionary. If they have doubts about structures, they can also look at the *Grammar Reference* on page 86.

- After checking the language, they copy the text on a sheet of paper, draw a map of the region and illustrate their story.

- You may want to display the finished compositions on the walls around the room. Make comments, ask questions, and encourage students to do the same about the productions of all the groups.

Speaking: Telling your story

B Speaking/Groups

Stage 1: Preparation

- Students look at their notes from the writing task and practise telling the story to themselves.

Stage 2: Speaking

- Students tell the rest of the class or group their story. They can look at their notes but reading is out!

Listening: Discovery quiz

C Cassette/Individual

- Tell students they are going to hear a quiz about explorers. The task is to listen to the questions and choose the correct answer.

- Play the tape, more than once if necessary. Pause between questions. Students write a, b or c in their notebooks.

- You may want them to compare their answers with another pair or group.

- Read or play each question again and give students the correct answer.

Answers:

1a; 2b; 3b; 4b; 5b; 6a; Sian won (4 points, James had 2)

 TAPESCRIPT:

Module 8, Fluency, Exercise C. Listen and check your answers.

QUIZMASTER: Hello and welcome to Discovery Quiz.

QUIZMASTER: Today we have Sian Stephens and James Dodds from St. Marys secondary school in Kent.

JAMES AND SIAN: Hello

QUIZMASTER: Round 1- questions about discoveries. Question one for James. Where did Columbus first arrive in America? What country is it now?

JAMES: The Dominican Republic.

QUIZMASTER: Sian?

SIAN: The Bahamas.

QUIZMASTER: Yes it was the sunny Bahamas. Second question. Sian again. Who was the first person to go around the world?

SIAN: Magellan

QUIZMASTER: Very good. Now question three for James. Who was the first European to arrive in Peru?

JAMES: Was it Pizarro?

QUIZMASTER: Yes. Fourth question for Sian. What country did Erik the Red discover in 982?

SIAN: Iceland

JAMES: Greenland

QUIZMASTER: Yes James it was Greenland. Fifth question. Sian. Who was the first man to walk on the moon?

SIAN: Uh. I think it was Armstrong. Yes Armstrong

QUIZMASTER: Sixth question James. Where did the North American Indians originate?

JAMES: Africa

SIAN: Asia

QUIZMASTER: At the end of round one, the scores are …

MODULE 8 Travel

Consolidation

Grammar

A Writing/Individual

- Students complete the text in the past simple.
- Correct the exercise by asking different students to write the verbs on the board.

> **Answers:**
> 1 went; 2 had; 3 stayed; 4 slept; 5 had;
> 6 began; 7 got; 8 was; 9 sat; 10 got off;
> 11 had; 12 ate; 13 drank; 14 visited; 15 left;
> 16 got; 17 went

B Writing/Individual

- Students use the cues to write questions about the trip in exercise A.
- They exchange notebooks and write the answers to the questions.

> **Answers:**
> 2 Where did they stay? In a little hotel near Hyde Park.
> 3 What did they do after breakfast? They toured London in an open-top bus.
> 4 How did they travel around London? By bus and taxi.
> 5 What did the girl have for lunch? A hamburger and a coke.
> 6 What did they do after lunch? They went to the National Gallery and the British Museum.

C Writing/Individual

- Ask students to write six sentences about themselves.
- Divide the class into pairs. Students exchange notebooks and formulate questions in the past. For example: *When were you born?*

D Speaking/Groups

- Students exchange their sentences from the preceding exercise.
- They take turns to read sentences from another notebook. The rest of the group must guess who the person is.

Vocabulary

E Keywords/Individual

- Students match the verbs and the nouns.
- Correct the exercise and ask individual students questions with these expressions. For example: *Can you ride a motorbike?*

> **Answers:**
> 2a; 3d; 4e; 5b

Pronunciation

F Cassette/Individual

- First contrast the two vowel sounds in *day* and *night*. Ask students to repeat the words several times.
- Tell them to draw two columns in their notebooks. Play the tape and have them write each word in the correct column.

> **Answers:**
> Group 1: ride, bike, drive, fly, time
> Group 2: train, plane, sail, take, stay

 TAPESCRIPT:

Module 8, Consolidation, Exercise F. Listen to these words.

READER: Group 1: day. Group 2: night
NARRATOR: **Now listen and write these words into the correct group.**
READER: ride, train, plane, bike, drive, sail, fly, take, stay, time

Consolidation

Grammar

A

Complete the text in the past simple.

Last year my parents, sister and I ^{1} ... (go) on holiday to London and we ^{2} ... (have) a great time. We ^{3} ... (stay) in a little hotel near Hyde Park. I ^{4} ... (sleep) in a room with my big sister. The first morning we ^{5} ... (have) a big English breakfast. After that, we ^{6} ... (begin) our trip around London. First, we ^{7} ... (get) tickets for a tour on an open-top London bus. It ^{8} ... (be) fantastic and we ^{9} ... (sit) upstairs. We ^{10} ... (get off) the bus in Trafalgar Square and ^{11} ... (have) lunch – I ^{12} ... (eat) a hamburger and ^{13} ... (drink) a coke. Then we ^{14} ... (visit) the National Gallery and the British Museum. I was very tired when we ^{15} ... (leave) the museum. We ^{16} ... (get) a taxi back to the hotel. That night we ^{17} ... (go) to bed early!

B

Write questions about the trip in exercise A.

Example: 1 Where did they go?

1 Where / family / go?
2 Where / they / stay?
3 What / they do / after breakfast?
4 How / they travel / around London?
5 What / the girl / have for lunch?
6 What / they do / after lunch?

Now, answer the questions.

C

Write six sentences about your life.

go / begin / make / eat / be born / have / play

Example: I was born in 1988. In 1993 I ...

D

In groups, exchange your sentences from exercise C. Read the sentences and the others guess who it is.

Vocabulary

E  KEYWORDS

Match the verbs with the transport.

1 ride   a a boat
2 sail   b a bus
3 fly   c a motorbike
4 drive   d a plane
5 catch   e a car

Pronunciation

F

Listen to these words.

Group 1 (/eɪ/): day
Group 2 (/aɪ/): night

Now listen and write the words you hear in the correct group.

Travel

Module check

Grammar Reference

15 Past simple: questions

Questions			
	Did		
Where When Why	**did**	I/you/he/she/it/we/they	**stay?**

- We use the auxiliary **did** + infinitive and we don't add **d** or **ed** to the main verb:

Did Erik live in Iceland? Where did Gulliver stay?

16 Past simple: irregular verbs

- Verbs that **do not** end in **ed** in the past are **irregular**. (See irregular verb list on page 96.)
- **Affirmative:** use the **irregular** form:

Gulliver **swam** to an island. He **drank** a lot of beer.
- **Negative:** use **didn't** + infinitive:

He **didn't swim** to England. He **didn't win** the cup.
- **Questions:** use **did** + infinitive:

Did he **swim** to Lilliput? What **did** he **eat** there?

Keyword Check 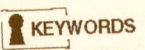 KEYWORDS

Transport: airship, bicycle, boat, bus, car, motorbike, plane, train

Travel: cabin, destination, flight, journey, passenger, trip

Places: Canada, Greenland, Germany, Iceland, North America, Norway

Weather: cold, icy, rainy, snowy, warm, w

Verbs: (present/past): eat/ate, drink/dran go/went, hurt/hurt, leave/left, meet/met, sail/sailed, sit/sat, sleep/slept, swim/swan

Adjectives: afraid (–), beautiful (+), comfortable (+), enormous (+), friendly (happy (+), hard (life) (–), horrible (–), hungry (–), nice (+), pretty (+), tired (–)

Linkers: after that, later, two days later, the next day

Mark your progress in these areas this year. Be honest!

speaking
grammar
reading
writing
pronunciation
vocabulary
listening

key
9–10 = excellent
7–8 = very good
5–6 = good
3–4 = unsatisfactory
1–2 = very poor

1 Look at Grammar References 15-16 above and complete Grammar Files 15-16 in the Activity Book. Then do the *Test Yourself: Grammar* on page 60 of the Activity Book.

2 Look at the Keyword Check. Write important new words in your vocabulary book. Then do the *Test Yourself: Vocabulary* on page 60 of the Activity Book.

Travel

86

- This check should help students to reflect on several aspects of their learning and to assess their progress themselves.
- First, ask students to choose their favourite activity in this module (eg: reading about Gulliver).
- Ask students to look at the *Grammar Reference* and the *Grammar File* and then do the *Test Yourself: Grammar* exercises.
- Ask them to look at the *Keyword Check* and write the important new words in their vocabulary books and then do the *Test Yourself: Vocabulary* exercises.
- Ask them to evaluate their progress by filling in the tables. Make sure that you have a look at everyone's answers.

Extension activity

Evaluation of the course: Speaking/Groups

- Divide the class into groups. Students discuss the following aspects of the course: best points/worst point; favourite activities/activities they didn't like; most difficult things/easiest things; areas they feel they have improved in; how they intend to get even better!; resolutions for the summer as far as English is concerned.

It would be a good idea to make notes and consider modifying the activities the following year where there seems to be a consensus.

Module 8 Travel

WELCOME TO

WORLD CLUB MAGAZINE!

In this magazine you can: read stories, do puzzles, play games and have fun!
You can also make your own magazine. This symbol  means:
Add this to your magazine! Good luck!!

PLANET DARG

Story Time

Animal Quiz

THE INCAS

Puzzle time

WORLD CLUB MAGAZINE!

1 Puzzle time

Can you find the words in the circles?

N D
A
F
R
A T
G
R E H

N D
A H
B U
S

R I
U T
E
O
F
A

D A
R U
G
E
T H

✏ **Write three more word circles.
Can your friend find the words?**

2 READ THE PICTURES

Look at the picture description. Can you use the pictures to write the description?

I AM FROM 🗼 IN 🇫🇷 . MY FATHER IS A

🛡 . MY 👩 IS A DOCTOR. MY 🐟 IS FIVE.

MY FAVOURITE SPORT IS 🏀 AND I AM IN

THE SCHOOL TEAM. MY FAVOURITE SUBJECTS ARE 🧪

AND √⨯= . MY FAVOURITE COLOURS ARE 🔵

AND 🟡 .

✏ **Write your own picture description!**

3 Good Parents

Animals are very good parents. Here are some examples.

A female hippo is a good baby-sitter! She looks after the babies of other hippos.

Mother elephants look after baby elephants very carefully. The babies walk under them.

Baby polar bears think cold water is horrible! Their mothers teach them to swim. When they are six months old they are excellent swimmers.

The male penguin has got a difficult job! He sits on the egg for two months. He is cold and hungry. When the baby is born, the mother returns and looks after it.

True or false?

1 Hippos are good babysitters.
2 Elephants are good mothers.
3 Polar bears are good teachers
4 The male penguin is a good father.

Look at the animals on page 106 of the picture dictionary. Choose three or four animals for each of these headings:

These animals are small.
These animals are dangerous.
These animals are big.
These animals are friendly.

 Make a poster with the four groups. Draw the animals.

Animal Quiz

1 Which animal can climb trees?
  a camel / a monkey / a sheep
2 Which animal can swim underwater?
  a dog / a tiger / an alligator
3 Which bird can't fly?
  a parrot / a penguin / a duck
4 Which animal can't jump?
  a snake / a dolphin / a kangaroo
5 Which animal can eat other animals?
  a cow / a rabbit / a lion

 Write your own Quiz! Write three questions.

5 Who is it?

Who is Steve: a, b or c? Read the conversation and find out!

Jane: This is a picture of my brother, Steve.
Sarah: His hair is very short!
Jane: Yes. It's very short and dark.
Sarah: And his nose is very big!

Jane: Steve's nose is big and his eyes are big.
Sarah: Can he play football?
Jane: No, he can't. But he can read. He's very intelligent.

**Read about the Swiss Family Robinson.
Can you match the texts to the paragraphs?**

THE SWISS FAMILY ROBINSON

1 This story is about a family from Switzerland – the mother, father and their four children – Fritz, Ernest, Jack and little Francis. They are on a ship and suddenly there is a terrible storm. The other people get in a boat and leave the family on the ship!

2 The next morning the storm is finished. The family see an island. They make a boat and go to the island. They take a lot of things and these animals – a cow, some hens, two ducks, two dogs and a very intelligent monkey.

3 They make their new home on the beach. They stay on the island for a long time. They make a tree house and explore. They call the island 'New Switzerland'. They have many adventures. Finally, a ship comes and rescues them.

Find the odd one out.

1 a) model cars b) model tigers c) model ships

2 a) Japanese b) Holland c) Spain

3 a) basketball b) table tennis c) computer games

4 a) make models b) collect dolls c) study English

5 a) magazines b) stamps c) comics

 Write two more odd-one-outs!

8 WHAT'S THE GAME?

Look at the picture. Can you find these games?

cards   Trivial Pursuit
dominoes   computer game
Game Boy   word puzzle

c

e

f

9 From you to us!

Read the e-mail message from a World Club fan. Now write your e-mail to World Club magazine.

New Message - 1

Send Address Attach Reply Reply All Forward Draft Print Delete   Normal ▼   ☒ Log ☐ Receipt

My name is Meral. I'm from Turkey. I'm thirteen years old. I've got two brothers- Ahmet and Umut. We've got two goldfish called Skully and Mulder.

My favourite sport is basketball. I play in my school team. In the summer we go to the mountains. I go swimming in the lake.

I like World Club Magazine - it's very interesting. Can we have articles about Leonardo DiCaprio?

Meral

10 Puzzle time

Find out about Carol's likes and dislikes. Follow the strings to the balloons. Then write sentences

She likes …
She …
She …

dancing   Playing Games   Singing

likes   hates   doesn't mind

WORLD CLUB MAGAZINE!

11

Find the jobs in these anagrams.

1 trawie
2 rai sstohes
3 meafrr
4 nuotsjialr
5 yarwle
6 sneru

 Write three more anagrams. Use page 109 in the Picture Dictionary.

12

Guess the festivals.

❖ You can see fantastic processions. People dance the samba in the streets. It happens in Rio de Janeiro.

❖ It happens on 14th February. People send cards with hearts and flowers to people they love. Usually they don't write their name on the card!

❖ We burn candles and give our friends presents. It is the beginning of a new year in India.

❖ It happens in Britain on November 5th. People have fireworks parties and burn a large doll called a 'guy'.

Answers: 1- Carnival 2- Valentine's Day 3- Diwali 4- Guy Fawkes (Bonfire) Night

 Write about a festival *you* know!

13

Look at the picture. What are the Zorgons doing?

Example: Zizi is drinking.

14

Find the words and write the description.

TheZorgonfamilyarevisitingahuman,Mrs Smith,atherhouse.MrsSmithistalkingtoZed butheiswatchingtelevision.Hiswife,Zeeta,is sittingonthetelevision.Zigislisteningtomusic andeatingrocks.Hissister,Zizi,isdrinking petrolandsleeping.MrsSmithisnotveryhappy.

Write advice for the Zorgons.

Example: Don't sit on the TV.

Story Time

PLANET DARG

A. Yin and Yanda escape to the desert of Yarga. They don't have any water and it is very hot. Then hundreds of Dargans attack them. The Dargans take them to their village.

B. Suddenly, a big spaceship arrives. The Dargans disappear and a group of Zorgon tourists come out. The Zorgons are very friendly and they take Yind and Yanda back to planet Alpha.

C. Their spaceship crashes on the planet Darg in the horrible forests. There are enormous trees, snakes and giant insects.

D. A brother and sister called Yind and Yanda live on planet Alpha. One day they decide to explore space in their parent's spaceship.

Read the story carefully. Can you put the paragraphs into the correct order?

English or British?

Do you know the difference between English and British? Read and check if you are right. Then write the names of the countries and capitals on the map.

'You speak English. You live in England, in the capital, London. You're English!'

'No, I'm not. I'm studying in London but I'm from Scotland. My family live in Edinburgh, the capital of Scotland. I'm Scottish.'

'OK, you're not English, you're Scottish. So you're not British?'

'I am British! People from England, Scotland, Wales and also Northern Ireland are all British because they live in the British Isles.'

'So people from Cardiff, the capital of Wales, are Welsh and also British?'

'That's right. And people from Belfast, the capital of Northern Ireland, are both Irish and British. It's very simple, you see!'

17 Tiddlehampton

Read Sam's, Daphne's and Captain Darnley-Smith's descriptions. Can you find the houses and cars for each family in the picture? How many jobs can you list?

Example: The Boggis family
house: number 5
Mr Boggis – job: waiter; car: number 1
Mrs Boggis – job: doctor; car: number 8

Sam Boggis

Hi!
Welcome to the fantastic village of Tiddlehampton. My mum's the village doctor and my dad's a wa in the Slugg Arms Hotel. Can you that big white house with a big ga near the church? That's our house we've got two cars! My mum's ca that yellow sports car and m dad's car is white and it's very small.

Captain Darnley-Smith

Good morning. My name's Darnley-Smith, Captain Darnley Smith. I'm a businessman and my wife is a policewoman. Can you see our cars? My car is very big and it's red. My wife's car is new and it's green. And Rupert, my son, loves cars. That old blue car is his car and the big black car is his wife's car. Our family has two houses in the village. We live in one and Rupert and Celia live in the other. The green house with big, red garage doors is our house and the small white house near the river is their house.

Daphne Stott

Hello.
I'm Daphne. Daphne Stott. I'm the teacher at Tiddlehampton School and my husband Eric is a dentist. Can you see my car? That small yellow car is my car. Where do we live? Well, we love colours and our house is blue, with a red door and pink windows. Pink's my favourite colour, you know! And my daughter Lavinia has got a house in the village. That green house, with the blue door and yellow windows, is her house.

Shopping puzzle

How much money has Sammy got in the end?

Sammy has got £10. He goes to the village shop. He meets his grandmother. She gives him £5 for his birthday. He buys a comic for £1.75 and a cassette for £5.00. Then he goes by bus to the town. The bus costs 50p. He goes to a café and has a lemonade for £1.25 and a hamburger for £3.00. In the street he finds £5.00! He goes to a shop and buys a computer game for £8. Then he walks home.

Write your own shopping puzzle.

20 True or false Quiz

How much do *you* know about Native Americans and the Inuit? Test your knowledge in this quiz.

1 The Native Americans arrived in America from Siberia.
2 The Sioux Indians lived on the plains.
3 The Sioux Indians were nomadic.
4 The 'Pueblo' Indians lived in Alaska.
5 They constructed houses and villages.
6 The Inuit hunted penguins.
7 The Inuit travelled in kayaks (canoes).
8 The Pacific Coast Indians hunted buffaloes.

Answers: 1- T; 2- T; 3- T; 4 - F; 5 - T; 6 - F; 7 - T; 8 - F

Scores   1~3: Oh dear, you don't know much!
4~6: Not bad
7~8: Amazing! You're an expert!

19 Crossword

Do the crossword and find the mystery word.

Mystery word clue: These were very important for the Plains Indians

The Plains Indians made spears and arrows out of …

They also … with spears.

Sometimes the children organised … competitions.

The leader was called the … .

The women … their babies on their backs.

The plains were not … until the Europeans arrived.

They used animal skins to make …

A tepee is the name of an American Indian …

The Europeans put the Indians in …

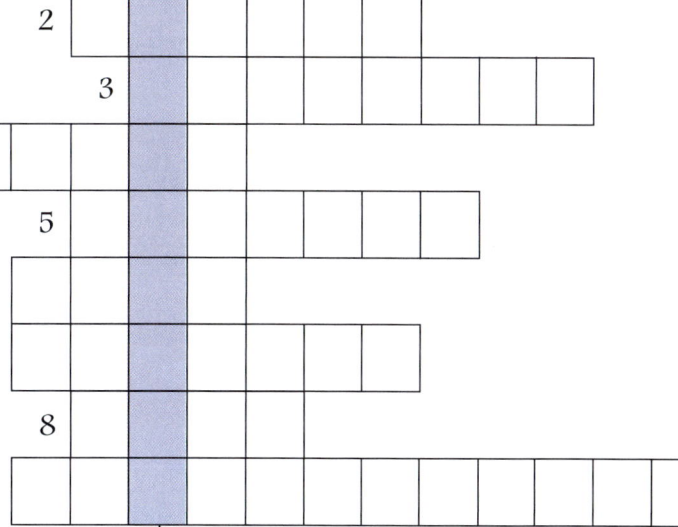

Mystery word

WORLD CLUB MAGAZINE!

21 What do you know about the early American civilisations? Read about the Incas.

THE INCAS

500 years ago, there was a great empire in the high Andes mountains of South America. The city of Cuzco was the centre of this Inca Empire. In Cuzco, the great Inca rulers built roads and conquered other peoples around them.

The Inca ruler was called 'Son of the Sun'. He was the leader of the empire and the leader of the army. The soldiers used short wooden clubs for fighting. The Inca noblemen had spears and bright helmets.

Llamas were very important for the Incas. These animals carried loads on the mountain roads and provided wool for clothes and blankets. The Incas did not write, but they counted and kept records using a quipu – a bundle of knotted strings. The Inca Empire ended very suddenly when soldiers from Spain arrived. Today we can still see the ruined city of Machu Picchu, high up in the mountains. And in parts of Peru, we can still hear the language of the Incas.

Match these sentence halves.

Llamas	used spears for fighting.
The quipu	was in Cuzco.
The Inca ruler	were important for their wool.
The Inca noblemen	was a bundle of knotted strings.
The centre of the Inca Empire	was the head of the army.

22 History Quiz

Answer these quiz questions.

1 What did Columbus discover?
  a) India b) North America c) America

2 Where did Marco Polo go?
  a) America b) China c) Australia

3 Who sailed around the world first?
  a) Francis Drake b) Magellan c) Pizarro

4 Who was the first person to go to the moon?
  a) David Bowie b) Neil Armstrong
  c) Yuri Gagarin

Answers: 1- c, 2- b, 3- b, 4- b

 Write your own history quiz.

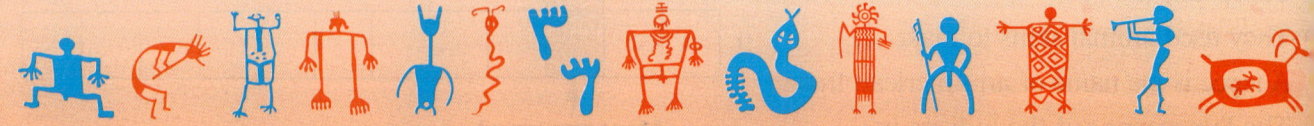

23

Read about the travels of Charles Darwin and trace his voyage on the map.

Charles Darwin was born in 1809 in a small town in England. When he was young, he decided that he wanted to study botany and geology. In 1831, he joined an expedition to Patagonia in South America. Darwin sailed on the British ship, the Beagle, as a scientist. It was his job to collect and record information about the rocks, plants and animals in South America.

The Beagle sailed across the Atlantic and reached Bahia (now Salvador) in Brazil in spring 1832. Darwin was amazed by the brilliant colours of the flowers and birds he saw. Then they sailed south along the coast. They stopped at places like Montevideo and Buenos Aires. Darwin travelled to the pampas of Argentina and lived among the gauchos. In Patagonia he found fossils of animals which are now extinct.

They sailed to Tierra del Fuego at the southern tip of South America and then north along the coast of Chile. Darwin always wrote his notes and collected rocks, fossils, plants, bird, animals and shells everywhere.

In September 1835, the Beagle reached the Galapagos Islands in the Pacific Ocean, 1000 kilometres west of Ecuador. Darwin was excited to find very different plants and animals on these Islands.

Darwin arrived home in October 1836. During his long voyage he saw many exciting things. He had a lot of questions in his mind. For twenty years he thought and wrote. He finally published his book 'The Origin of Species' in 1859. His ideas of evolution changed our world.

Answer the questions.

1 What was Darwin's job?

2 How long was Darwin's voyage on the Beagle?

3 Which South American countries did Darwin visit?

4 How old was he when he published 'The Origin of Species'?

24 Story Time

THE BOY WHO CRIED WOLF

This story is about a boy from a small village in the mountains. He didn't go to school – he looked after his father's sheep. But the job was very boring.

One day the boy had an idea for a joke to play on the people of the village. He shouted "Wolf! Wolf! Help! A wolf is killing our sheep".

The people of the village ran to the place. The boy laughed and the people saw there was no wolf. They were very angry.

Then, one day, the boy was with the sheep. He saw a big wolf. He shouted "Wolf! Wolf! Help! Come and help me, please." But the people in the village thought, "Oh yes, it's him again. There isn't a wolf". And so they didn't go to help the boy. The wolf killed all the sheep.

Answer these questions:

What job did the boy do?

What did he shout?

3 Why were the village people angry?

4 Why didn't the people come in the end?

Mini-dictionary

We recommend that you refer to the **Longman New Junior English Dictionary** (published 1993) for words not included here. Remember that this mini-dictionary is not a substitute for a complete dictionary.

A

adventure /əd'ventʃə/ *noun* an exciting story or journey. *adjective* an **adventure** *story;* an **adventure** *holiday.*

afraid /ə'freɪd/ *adjective* feeling fear: *Are you* **afraid** *of the dark?*

after /'ɑːftə/ *preposition* later than; following: *Tomorrow is the day* **after** *today.*

airport /'eəpɔːt/ *noun* a place where planes arrive and leave.

airship
/'eəʃɪp/ *noun*

album /'ælbəm/ *noun* a book with empty pages where you can put stamps, photographs, etc.

alphabet /'ælfəbet/ *noun* the letters of a language in a special order: *The English* **alphabet** *begins with A and ends with Z.*

amphibious /æm'fɪbɪəs/ *adjective* of an animal that can live both on land and in water.

arrive /ə'raɪv/ *verb* to get to a place: *They* **arrived** *at the hotel.*

arrow /'ærəʊ/ *noun* a weapon.

art /ɑːt/ *noun* drawing and painting: *He's very good at* **art**.

art gallery /'ɑːt ˌgæləri/ *noun* a building where you can see paintings.

article /'ɑːtɪkəl/ *noun* a piece of writing in a newspaper: *an* **article** *about ships.*

ask /ɑːsk/ *verb* to say something that is a question: *"Who are you?" she* **asked**.

atlas /'ætləs/ *noun* a book of maps, showing countries, rivers, mountains, etc.

attack /ə'tæk/ *verb* to start to fight somebody: *The cowboys* **attacked** *the Indians.*

attractive /ə'træktɪv/ *adjective* pleasing, especially to look at.

axe /æks/ *noun* a weapon.

B

baby /'beɪbi/ *noun* a very young child (or animal).

babysitter /'beɪbiˌsɪtə/ *noun* a person who looks after the children when the parents are not at home.

bad /bæd/ *adjective* not good.

badge /bædʒ/ *noun* something that you wear on your clothes to show yourname, your job, the name of your school, etc.

badminton /'bædmɪntən/ *noun* a game like tennis.

bag /bæg/ *noun* something you use for carrying things.

bank /bæŋk/ *noun* a building where you put and keep money.

bar /bɑː/ *noun* a place where you can buy and drink drinks.

baseball /'beɪsbɔːl/ *noun* a sport where you hit a ball and run.

basketball /'bɑːskɪtbɔːl/ *noun* a sport where you throw a ball into a net.

beach /biːtʃ/ *noun* the place next to the sea: *We play football on the* **beach**.

beautiful /'bjuːtɪfəl/ *adjective* good-looking; attractive.

believe /bɪ'liːv/ *verb* to think that somebody is telling the truth: *Don't you* **believe** *me?*

bicycle /'baɪsɪkəl/ *noun*

big /bɪg/ *adjective* of great size, height or weight; large; not small.

bite /baɪt/ (*past:* **bit** /bɪt/) *verb* to cut or wound something with the teeth: *Does your dog* **bite**?

blond /blɒnd/ *adjective* (used of hair) light yellow in colour.

blood /blʌd/ *noun* the red liquid that flows through your body.

board game /'bɔːd geɪm/ *noun* a game like Ludo or Snakes and Ladders.

boat /bəʊt/ *noun*

boring /'bɔːrɪŋ/ *adjective* not interesting: *The film was* **boring** *and I fell asleep.*

born /bɔːn/ *adjective* given life: *She was* **born** *in 1991.*

bow /bəʊ/ *noun* a weapon.

bowl /bəʊl/ *noun* a deep round dish: *Fill the* **bowl** *with water.*

box /bɒks/ *noun* a container with straight sides.

brain /breɪn/ *noun* **1** the part inside your head that you think with. **2** your intelligence.

brilliant /'brɪljənt/ *adjective* very good: *I saw a* **brilliant** *film.*

broomstick /'bruːmˌstɪk, 'brʊm-/ *noun* a long brush used by a witch.

brush /brʌʃ/ *noun*

burn /bɜːn/ *verb* to destroy something with fire: *He **burned** the wood.*

bus /bʌs/ *noun*

bus station /ˈbʌs ˌsteɪʃən/ *noun* the place where buses start and finish.

busy /ˈbɪzi/ *adjective* working; not free; having a lot to do: *He's **busy** now. He's **busy** writing letters.*

buy /baɪ/ (*past:* **bought** /bɔːt/) *verb* to give money for something. *He **buys** a newspaper every day.*

cabin /ˈkæbɪn/ *noun* a small house made of wood.

café /ˈkæfeɪ/ *noun* a place where you can buy drinks and simple meals.

can /kæn/ *noun* a metal container with food or drink in it: *A **can** of lemonade.*

canoeing /kəˈnuːɪŋ/ *noun* a sport using a canoe.

cap /kæp/ *noun* a soft hat

car /kaː/ *noun*

car park /ˈkaː ˌpaːk/ *noun* a place where you can leave a car.

card /kaːd/ *noun* a piece of stiff paper with a picture on the front and a message inside: *a birthday **card**.*

cards /kaːdz/ *noun* a game

carnival /ˈkaːnɪvəl/ *noun* a public celebration with processions and dancing.

carry /ˈkæri/ *verb* to hold something and take it somewhere: *I **carry** my bag to school.*

cart /kaːt/ *noun* a wooden vehicle pulled by horses.

cartoon /kaːˈtuːn/ *noun* drawings which tell a story: *A Disney **cartoon**.*

cassette /kəˈset/ *noun*

castle /ˈkaːsəl/ *noun* a large strong building made so that nobody can attack the people inside.

catch /ˈkætʃ/ (*past:* **caught** /kɔːt/) *verb* to run after something and take hold of it.

celebration /ˌseləˈbreɪʃən/ *noun* a special meal or party that you have because something good has happened.

change /tʃeɪndʒ/ *verb* to become or make different: *He **changed** the pictures in his room.*

cheap /tʃiːp/ *adjective* costing little money: *I bought a **cheap** T-shirt.*

chess /tʃes/ *noun* a game played by moving different shaped pieces on a board of black and white squares.

chief /tʃiːf/ *noun* the leader of a tribe of Indians.

child /tʃaɪld/ (plural **children** /ˈtʃɪldrən/) *noun* **1** a young person. **2** a son or daughter.

choose /tʃuːz/ (*past:* **chose** /tʃəʊz/) *verb* to decide from a number of things or people the one you want: *She **chose** to study art.*

church /tʃɜːtʃ/ *noun* a building where Christians meet and pray.

cinema /ˈsɪnəmə/ *noun* a place where you pay to watch a film.

city /ˈsɪti/ *noun* a large town, e.g. London, New York.

climb /klaɪm/ *verb* to go up: *We **climbed** a mountain.*

close /kləʊz/ *verb* to shut: ***Close** the door, please.*

clothes /kləʊðz, kləʊz/ *noun* what you wear, e.g. shirt, jeans, jacket.

cloudy /ˈklaʊdi/ *adjective* (of the sky) grey; not clear blue.

club /klʌb/ *noun* **1** a place where you can go to enjoy yourself, e.g. a yacht club. **2** a long stick used to hit a ball in golf.

coast /kəʊst/ *noun* the land next to the sea: *a town on the **coast**.*

coin /kɔɪn/ *noun* a piece of money made of metal.

cold /kəʊld/ *adjective* not hot: *Snow is very **cold**.*

collect /kəˈlekt/ *verb* to keep lots of things: *He **collects** stamps.*

comfortable /ˈkʌmftəbəl, ˈkʌmfət-/ *adjective* nice, pleasant: *I sat in a **comfortable** chair.*

comic /ˈkɒmɪk/ *noun* something you read with funny stories and pictures.

communicate /kəˈmjuːnɪkeɪt/ *verb* to speak or write to somebody: *If you know English, you can **communicate** with a lot of people.*

computer /kəmˈpjuːtə/ *noun* a machine that stores information.

continent /ˈkɒntɪnənt/ *noun* a large area of land, e.g. Europe, Africa.

cook /kʊk/ *verb* to make food ready to eat by heating it: *He's **cooking** sausages for lunch.*

costume /ˈkɒstjuːm/ *noun* clothes worn for a special reason: *She's wearing a witch's **costume**.*

cottage /ˈkɒtɪdʒ/ *noun* a small attractive house in the country.

count /kaʊnt/ *verb* **1** to say numbers in the right order: *to **count** from 1 to 100.* **2** to find out how many there are: *I **counted** the books - there were 14 of them.*

country /ˈkʌntri/ *noun* **1** a nation with a government, e.g. Argentina, Uruguay. **2** rural areas; not the city.

countryside /ˈkʌntrisaɪd/ *noun* land outside towns and cities.

crash /kræʃ/ *verb* to move into another object with force: *The car **crashed** into the wall.*

creative /kriˈeɪtɪv/ *adjective* having new and original ideas.

crime /kraɪm/ *noun* an action that is wrong and can be punished by the law: *Killing people is a **crime**.*

criminal /ˈkrɪmɪnəl/ *noun* a person who has does something wrong and against the law.

cross /krɒs/ *verb* to travel to the other side of something: *She **crossed** the street.*

cut down /ˌkʌt ˈdaʊn/ *verb* to make something fall to the ground by cutting it: *cut down a tree.*

cycle /ˈsaɪkəl/ *verb* to go by bicycle: *She **cycles** to school.*

D

dance /daːns/ *verb* to move to music: *We **danced** at the party.*

dangerous /ˈdeɪndʒərəs/ *adjective* something that can hurt you: *Don't play with fire - it's **dangerous**.*

dark /daːk/ *adjective* **1** like night; not light or bright: *It was dark, so we hurried home.* **2** of a deep colour: *She has **dark** hair.*

dead /ded/ *adjective* not living: *My grandfather is **dead**.*

decide /dɪˈsaɪd/ *verb* to choose to do something: *We **decided** to have a party.*

desert /ˈdezət/ *noun* a very dry area with not many plants or animals.

Mini-dictionary

destination /ˌdestɪˈneɪʃən/ *noun* the place at the end of your journey.

destruction /dɪˈstrʌkʃən/ *noun* the breaking of something completely.

dictionary /ˈdɪkʃənəri/ *noun* a book that tells you what words mean and how to spell them.

die /daɪ/ *verb* to stop living: *He died in 1956.*

different /ˈdɪfərənt/ *adjective* not the same: *French and Spanish are different languages.*

difficult /ˈdɪfɪkəlt/ *adjective* not easy; hard: *This maths problem is difficult.*

disappear /ˌdɪsəˈpɪə/ *verb* to go away; be no longer seen: *The boy disappeared round the corner.*

disco /ˈdɪskəʊ/ *noun* (**discotheque**) a place where you dance to loud pop music.

discover /dɪˈskʌvə/ *verb* to find or learn about something for the first time: *Did Columbus discover America?*

dive /daɪv/ *verb* to jump into water with you head first.

doll /dɒl/ *noun* a toy made to look like a person, especially a baby, girl or woman.

dominoes /ˈdɒmɪnəʊz/ *noun* a game played with small flat pieces of wood with spots on.

downstairs /ˌdaʊnˈsteəz/ *adverb* in or towards the part of the house which is on ground level: *He came downstairs. The kitchen is downstairs.*

draughts /drɑːfts/ *noun* a game played on a board using 24 round pieces.

draw /drɔː/ (*past:* **drew** /druː/) *verb* to make a picture: *He likes drawing pictures.*

drink /drɪŋk/ (*past:* **drank** /dræŋk/) *verb* to take liquid in the mouth: *He drinks tea for breakfast.*

drive /draɪv/ (*past:* **drove** /drəʊv/) *verb* to make a vehicle move in the direction you want: *to drive a car.*

dry /draɪ/ *adjective* not wet; with no water.

E

earring /ˈɪərɪŋ/ *noun* a piece of jewellery you wear on your ear.

Earth /ɜːθ/ *noun* the world we live in: *The Earth goes round the sun once a year.*

east /iːst/ *noun* the direction from which the sun comes up in the morning.

eat /iːt/ (*past:* **ate** /et, eɪt/) *verb* to take food in the mouth: *She eats a lot of fruit.*

educational /ˌedjʊˈkeɪʃənəl/ *adjective* helping you to learn.

emperor /ˈempərə/ *noun* a ruler of a big country or several countries.

end /end/ *verb* to finish: *The party ended at 9 o'clock.*

enjoy /ɪnˈdʒɔɪ/ *verb* to get pleasure from something: *She enjoys listening to music.*

enormous /ɪˈnɔːməs/ *adjective* very big.

escape /ɪˈskeɪp/ *verb* to run away from a person or place: *He escaped from the police.*

evening /ˈiːvnɪŋ/ *noun* the time from the end of the afternoon to when you go to bed.

event /ɪˈvent/ *noun* something that happens, often something important or unusual.

excellent /ˈeksələnt/ *adjective* very good.

excited /ɪkˈsaɪtɪd/ *adjective* having strong feelings of pleasure; not calm: *I was very excited when I got the letter.*

exciting /ɪkˈsaɪtɪŋ/ *adjective* causing strong emotions: *I saw an exciting football match.*

expensive /ɪkˈspensɪv/ *adjective* costing a lot of money: *A Mercedes is an expensive car.*

expedition /ˌekspəˈdɪʃən/ *noun* a journey with a specific purpose, usually scientific or military.

explosion /ɪkˈspləʊʒən/ *noun* a sudden loud noise caused, for example, by a bomb.

F

fabulous /ˈfæbjʊləs/ *adjective* very good; wonderful: *a fabulous holiday.*

factory /ˈfæktəri/ *noun* a place where people work and make things: *a car factory.*

fair /feə/ *adjective* (of hair) light-coloured; not dark.

family /ˈfæməli/ *noun* a group of relatives including parents and their children, grandparents, etc.

famous /ˈfeɪməs/ *adjective* well-known: *Prince is a famous singer.*

fancy dress /ˌfænsi ˈdres/ *noun* strange clothes that you wear for fun at a party.

fantastic /fænˈtæstɪk/ *adjective* very good.

fashion show /ˈfæʃən ʃəʊ/ *noun* an event where you can see smart clothes.

fast /fɑːst/ *adjective* quick; not slow.

fat /fæt/ *adjective* having a wide round body: *I think he's too fat.*

favourite /ˈfeɪvərɪt/ *adjective* what you like a lot: *Prince is my favourite singer.*

feather /ˈfeðə/ *noun*

female /ˈfiːmeɪl/ *adjective* belonging to the sex that has young ones: *The female lion protects her young.*

fight /faɪt/ (*past:* **fought** /fɔːt/) *verb* to use your body or weapons against somebody in a violent way.

figure /ˈfɪgə/ *noun* a shape, especially the shape of a human body: *I saw a tall figure near the door.*

film /fɪlm/ *noun* what you watch at the cinema.

find out /faɪnd ˈaʊt/ (*past:* **found out** /faʊnd ˈaʊt/) *verb* to discover the facts about something.

fire /faɪə/ *noun* **1** heat and flames that burn and destroy things. **2** burning coal or wood used to make a room warm: *to sit in front of the fire.*

fishing /ˈfɪʃɪŋ/ *noun* an activity when you try to catch fish.

fizzy /ˈfɪzi/ *adjective* containing gas: *a fizzy drink.*

flight /flaɪt/ *noun* a journey on a plane.

flower /ˈflaʊə/ *noun*

fly /flaɪ/ (*past:* **flew** /fluː/) *verb* **1** how a bird travels in the air. **2** to travel in a plane, airship, etc.

follow /ˈfɒləʊ/ *verb* to go or come after somebody: *He went out and I followed.*

food /fuːd/ *noun* things you eat.

football /ˈfʊtbɔːl/ *noun* a sport where two teams kick a ball into a goal.

form /fɔːm/ *verb* to make or produce something: *They formed a group.*

friend /frend/ *noun* a person you know and like.

friendly /ˈfrendli/ *adjective* kind and helpful.

fuel /ˈfjuːəl/ *noun* something that burns to give heat, light or power.

fun /fʌn/ *noun* amusement; a good time: *Parties are fun.*

funfair /ˈfʌnfeə/ *noun* a place where people go to have fun by riding on special machines.

funny /ˈfʌni/ *adjective* amusing; something or someone that makes you laugh: *He told a funny story.*

G

game /geɪm/ *noun* something you play for fun: *Let's have a game of chess.*

gang /gæŋ/ *noun* a group of people working together, e.g. criminals.

garden /ˈgɑːdn/ *noun* a place with grass and flowers.

geography /dʒɪ'ɒgrəfi, 'dʒɒgrəfi/ *noun* the study of the countries of the world and things like seas, mountains and weather.

ghost /gəʊst/ *noun* the form of a dead, person that some people believe can be seen.

give /gɪv/ (*past:* **gave** /geɪv/) *verb* to hand or pass something to someone for them to use, or as a present.

glasses /glɑːsɪz/ *noun*

go /gəʊ/ (*past:* **went** /went/) *verb* to move or travel: *I go to school by bus.*

gold /gəʊld/ *noun* a yellow metal that costs a lot of money.

golf /gɒlf/ *noun* a game where you hit a small ball into holes in the ground.

golf course /gɒlf kɔːs/ *noun* the place where you play golf.

good /gʊd/ *adjective* **1** of a high standard: *a good school.* **2** pleasant: *a good party.* **3** skilful at something: *She's good at languages.*

grand piano /ˌgrænd pi'ænəʊ/ *noun* a large flat piano.

great /greɪt/ *adjective* very good: *The party was great.*

group /gruːp/ *noun* **1** a number of people or things together: *a group of girls.* **2** a number of people who sing and play popular music together.

guard /gɑːd/ *noun* a person who watches over someone or something to prevent danger or escape.

guess /ges/ *verb* to give an answer that you feel may be right, although you are not sure: *If you don't know the answer, guess.*

guitar /gɪ'tɑː/ *noun*

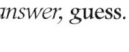

gun /gʌn/ *noun* a weapon.

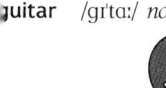

gunfight /gʌnfaɪt/ *noun* an act of fighting when guns are used.

gunman /gʌnmən/ *noun* a criminal armed with a gun.

H

happy /'hæpi/ *adjective* very pleased: *I am happy to see you again.*

harbour /'hɑːbə/ *noun* a place on the shore where ships and boats can shelter safely.

hard /hɑːd/ *adjective* **1** not moving or soft when touched: *This ground is too hard to dig.* **2** difficult: *a hard exam.*

harm /hɑːm/ *verb* to hurt someone or something.

hate /heɪt/ *verb* not to like someone or something at all: *I hate snakes.*

have /hæv/ (*past:* **had** /hæd/) *verb* **1** to own; to hold; to keep: *He has a good job. Have you got a car?* **2** to do something: *We have tea for breakfast.*

health centre /helθ ˌsentə/ *noun* a place where you go to see a doctor or a nurse.

heart /hɑːt/ *noun* **1** the part of your body that pumps blood. **2** your feelings: *He has a kind heart.*

help /help/ *verb* to do something for somebody.

hide /haɪd/ (*past:* **hid** /hɪd/) *verb* to put in a place other people don't know: *Where did you hide the money?*

historic /hɪ'stɒrɪk/ *adjective* important in the past.

history /'hɪstəri/ *noun* the study of things that happened in the past.

holiday /'hɒlɪdi/ *noun* a time when you don't work or go to school: *Next Friday is a holiday.*

home /həʊm/ *noun* the place where you live or are from.

horrible /'hɒrɪbəl/ *adjective* not good; not nice.

horse riding /hɔːs ˌraɪdɪŋ/ *noun* the sport of going on a horse.

hospital /'hɒspɪtl/ *noun* a building where doctors and nurses care for people who are ill.

hotel /həʊ'tel/ *noun* a place you pay to sleep in: *She stayed at the Ritz Hotel.*

hungry /'hʌngri/ *adjective* how you feel when you want something to eat.

hunt /hʌnt/ *verb* to look for and kill animals.

hurt /hɜːt/ (*past:* **hurt** /hɜːt/) *verb* to damage part of someone's body and cause pain.

hurt /hɜːt/ *adjective* feeling pain.

I

icy /'aɪsi/ *adjective* very cold.

idea /aɪ'dɪə/ *noun* a thought or plan that you form in your mind: *What a good idea!*

ideal /aɪ'dɪəl/ *adjective* the best possible.

identical /aɪ'dentɪkəl/ *adjective* exactly the same.

ill /ɪl/ *adjective* not feeling healthy; unwell.

incredible /ɪn'kredɪbəl/ *adjective* something you can't believe.

indoors /ˌɪn'dɔːz/ *adverb* inside a building: *Let's stay indoors today.*

informal /ɪn'fɔːməl/ *adjective* in an easy friendly way and not according to rules.

insect /'ɪnsekt/ *noun* a very small animal that has six legs: *Bees and ants are insects.*

interesting /'ɪntrəstɪŋ/ *adjective* something that gets your attention: *I like this book - it's interesting.*

invite /ɪn'vaɪt/ *verb* to ask somebody to do something nice with you: *I invited him to my party.*

island /'aɪlənd/ *noun* a piece of land surrounded by water.

J

join /dʒɔɪn/ *verb* to become a member of something: *He joined the gang.*

journey /'dʒɜːni/ *noun* when you go from one place to another: *I'm going on a journey to India.*

jump /dʒʌmp/ *verb* to push yourself up in the air or over something: *He jumped over the wall.*

jungle /'dʒʌŋgəl/ *noun* a thick forest in hot countries.

K

keep /kiːp/ (*past:* **kept** /kept/) *verb* to store in a particular place: *I keep my stamps in an album.*

keyring /'kiːrɪŋ/ *noun* a ring on which you keep keys.

kill /kɪl/ *verb* to make a person or animal die.

king /kɪŋ/ *noun* a male ruler of a country: *the King of Spain.*

kiss /kɪs/ *verb* to touch someone with your lips, as a sign of love or greeting.

Mini-dictionary

kit /kɪt/ *noun* the things you need for doing a particular sport: *Where's my football* **kit***?*

knife /naɪf/ *noun*

know /nəʊ/ (*past:* **knew** /njuː/) *verb* **1** to have something in your mind which you are sure is true: *I don't* **know** *his name.* **2** to be familiar with a person or place: *Do you* **know** *London?*

L

lake /leɪk/ *noun* a big pool of water with land all round it.

lamp /læmp/ *noun* a small light which you have on a table, etc.

lantern /ˈlæntən/ *noun* a lamp which you can carry.

later /ˈleɪtə/ *adverb* after some time.

leader /ˈliːdə/ *noun* the chief person doing something.

leave /liːv/ (*past:* **left** /left/) *verb* to go away from a place: *The train leaves in five minutes.*

left /left/ *adverb* the opposite direction to right: *Turn left at the corner.*

letter /ˈletə/ *noun* something you write to or receive from another person: *I got a* **letter** *from my penfriend today.*

life /laɪf/ *noun* the time during which someone is alive: *He had a happy* **life***.*

light /laɪt/ *noun* something that helps you to see: *He put off the* **light** *and went to sleep.*

like /laɪk/ *verb* to find pleasant; to enjoy: *I like ice-cream.*

little /ˈlɪtl/ *adjective* small: *The mother was carrying her* **little** *girl.*

live /lɪv/ *verb* **1** to exist: *Kangaroos* **live** *in Australia.* **2** to spend your life: *She* **lives** *in Argentina.*

local /ˈləʊkəl/ *adjective* a place near where you live: *a* **local** *cinema.*

log cabin /ˌlɒg ˈkæbɪn/ *noun* a small house made of wood.

look after /lʊk ˈɑːftə/ *verb* to care for: *I* **looked after** *my baby brother.*

look at /lʊk ət, æt/ *verb* to point your eyes towards something: **Look at** *the blackboard.*

look for /lʊk fə, fɔː/ *verb* to try to find someone or something: *I'm* **looking for** *my key.*

lounge /laʊndʒ/ *noun* a room you can relax in.

ludo /ˈluːdəʊ/ *noun* a board game.

lunch /lʌntʃ/ *noun* a meal you eat in the middle of the day.

M

magazine /ˌmægəˈziːn/ *noun* a book with paper covers, containing stories, articles and pictures, which you buy every week or month.

magic /ˈmædʒɪk/ *noun* clever or strange tricks somebody does to amuse people.

main /meɪn/ *adjective* most important: *the* **main** *street.*

make /meɪk/ (*past:* **made** /meɪd/) *verb* to produce or create: *He* **makes** *model aeroplanes.*

male /meɪl/ *adjective* belonging to the sex which does not give birth to young: *The* **male** *bird is brightly coloured.*

mammal /ˈmæməl/ *noun* an animal that is fed on its mother's milk when young, e.g. a cow.

market /ˈmɑːkɪt/ *noun* a place, often outside, where people come to buy and sell.

marry /ˈmæri/ *verb* to become husband and wife.

married /ˈmærid/ *adjective* having a husband or wife: *a* **married** *man.*

marvellous /ˈmɑːvələs/ *adjective* wonderful; great: *a* **marvellous** *film.*

mask /mɑːsk/ *noun* a covering over all or part of someone's face.

match /mætʃ/ *verb* to be like something else in size, shape, colour, etc: *These shoes don't* **match** *my dress.*

maths /mæθs/ (**mathematics** /ˌmæθəˈmætɪks/) *noun* the study of numbers, shapes, etc.

meet /miːt/ (*past:* **met** /met/) *verb* **1** to see and talk to somebody for the first time: *I* **met** *John at a party.* **2** to see somebody at a fixed time or place: **Meet** *me outside the cinema.*

melt /melt/ *verb* to become a liquid by heating: *The ice is* **melting** *in the sun.*

merchant /ˈmɜːtʃənt/ *noun* a person who buys and sells goods, often buying them in one country and selling them in another.

model /ˈmɒdl/ *noun* a small version of something: *a* **model** *car.*

modern /ˈmɒdən/ *adjective* new, and in the style that is popular now: **modern** *fashion.*

monk /mʌŋk/ *noun* one of a group of men who live together and have given their lives to religion.

monster /ˈmɒnstə/ *noun* a big, frightening animal, usually invented.

motorbike /ˈməʊtəbaɪk/ *noun* a large heavy bicycle worked by an engine.

mountain /ˈmaʊntən/ *noun* a very high hill: *Mount Everest is a* **mountain***.*

moustache /məˈstɑːʃ/ *noun* the hair that grows above a man's mouth.

N

nasty /ˈnɑːsti/ *adjective* not nice; bad.

national /ˈnæʃənəl/ *adjective* of or belonging to a country: *a* **national** *doll.*

near /nɪə/ *preposition* not far from; close to: *I live* **near** *the school.*

new /njuː/ *adjective* not old: *I've got a* **new** *bicycle.*

newspaper /ˈnjuːsˌpeɪpə/ *noun* a set of sheets of paper containing news, which is sold every day.

next to /ˈnekst tə, tʊ/ *preposition* beside: *Come and sit* **next to** *me.*

nice /naɪs/ *adjective* good: *This apple is* **nice***.*

normal /ˈnɔːməl/ *adjective* usual or expected.

north /nɔːθ/ *noun* the direction that is on the left when you look towards the rising sun: *Manchester is in the* **north** *of England.*

notebook /ˈnəʊtbʊk/ *noun* a book in which you write things that you need to remember.

O

ocean /ˈəʊʃən/ *noun* a very large area of water: *the Atlantic* **Ocean***.*

offer /ˈɒfə/ *verb* to show someone that you want to give them something: *I* **offered** *her a chocolate.*

office /ˈɒfɪs/ *noun* a place where people do written work and business.

oil /ɔɪl/ *noun* thick liquid that comes from under the ground or sea, used for making machines run smoothly.

old /əʊld/ *adjective* **1** not new: *I live in an* **old** *house.* **2** not young: *My grandmother is very* **old***.* **3** your age: *How* **old** *are you?*

organise /ˈɔːgənaɪz/ *verb* to put things in order: *You must* **organise** *your ideas.*

original /əˈrɪdʒɪnəl, -dʒənəl/ *adjective* new and different: *an* **original** *idea.*

originate /əˈrɪdʒɪneɪt/ *verb* to begin to happen or exist: *This festival* **originated** *in Spain.*

outdoors /ˌaʊtˈdɔːz/ *adverb* outside; in the open air: *It's a nice day; let's play* **outdoors**.

P

packet /ˈpækɪt/ *noun* a small paper or plastic container: *I ate a* **packet** *of crisps.*

paint /peɪnt/ *verb* to put colour on something: *We* **painted** *the room blue.*

pair /peə/ *noun* two things of the same kind that are usually used together: *a* **pair** *of shoes.*

paper /ˈpeɪpə/ *noun* thin material used for writing on: *I haven't got any* **paper**.

parents /ˈpeərənts/ *noun* mother and father.

park /pɑːk/ *noun* a large open space in a town with grass and trees and sometimes a play area for children.

partner /ˈpɑːtnə/ *noun* a person you work or play with.

party /ˈpɑːti/ *noun* a meeting of friends to have fun, dance, play games, etc.

passenger /ˈpæsɪndʒə/ *noun* a person who travels on a bus, train, etc.

pen /pen/ *noun*

pencil /ˈpensəl/ *noun*

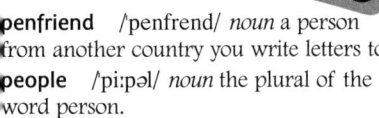

penfriend /ˈpenfrend/ *noun* a person from another country you write letters to.

people /ˈpiːpəl/ *noun* the plural of the word person.

person /ˈpɜːsən/ *noun* a man, woman or child.

personal /ˈpɜːsənəl/ *adjective* about a particular person: *a* **personal** *letter.*

pet /pet/ *noun* an animal that lives in your house.

petrol /ˈpetrəl/ *noun* liquid used to work car engines.

piano /piˈænəʊ/ *noun*

picture /ˈpɪktʃə/ *noun* something represented on paper as a drawing, painting or photograph.

picturesque /ˌpɪktʃəˈresk/ *adjective* pretty; like a picture.

piece /piːs/ *noun* one item of something: *a piece of paper.*

plain /pleɪn/ *noun* a large flat piece of country.

plane (aeroplane) /pleɪn/ *noun*

plant /plɑːnt/ *noun* something living that is not an animal: *Trees and vegetables are* **plants**.

play /pleɪ/ *verb* **1** to take part in a game: *I* **play** *football every day.* **2** to use a musical instrument: *I* **play** *the piano.*

player /ˈpleɪə/ *noun* a person who plays a game or a sport: *a tennis* **player**.

poet /ˈpəʊɪt/ *noun* a person who writes poems.

pointed /ˈpɔɪntɪd/ *adjective* having a sharp end.

polar region /ˈpəʊlə ˌriːdʒən/ *noun* the area round the North or South Pole.

pollution /pəˈluːʃən/ *noun* the process of making the air, water or soil dirty and dangerous.

poor /pɔː/ *adjective* **1** not having much money: *She was too* **poor** *to buy new clothes.* **2** needing kindness or help: *Look at that* **poor** *cat. It's hungry.* **3** not of a good standard: *Your writing is* **poor**.

popular /ˈpɒpjʊlə/ *adjective* when lots of people like something: *Football is a* **popular** *sport.*

prefer /prɪˈfɜː/ *verb* to like one thing more than another: *I* **prefer** *swimming to cycling.*

present /ˈprezənt/ *noun* something somebody gives you: *My sister gave me a birthday* **present**.

pretty /ˈprɪti/ *adjective* attractive and nice to look at.

prison /ˈprɪzən/ *noun* a place where criminals are sent as a punishment.

private /ˈpraɪvət/ *adjective* belonging to one person or group; not public: *This garden is* **private**.

procession /prəˈseʃən/ *noun* a line of people or vehicles following one another as part of a ceremony.

pull /pʊl/ *verb* to move something towards you: *He* **pulled** *a book out of his bag.*

pupil /ˈpjuːpəl/ *noun* a person being taught, especially at a school.

puzzle /ˈpʌzəl/ *noun* a game which is difficult to do.

Q

quiet /ˈkwaɪət/ *adjective* having or making very little noise: *He has a* **quiet** *voice, so I can't hear him.*

quiz /kwɪz/ *noun* a competition where you test people by asking questions.

R

race /reɪs/ *noun* a competition to see who can run, swim, walk, etc. fastest.

racket /ˈrækɪt/ *noun* something used to hit the ball in tennis.

railway /ˈreɪlweɪ/ *noun* a track for trains to run on.

read /riːd/ (*past:* read /red/) *verb* to look at and understand words: *I* **read** *a book yesterday.*

realistic /ˌrɪəˈlɪstɪk/ *adjective* life-like: *The monsters in this game are very* **realistic**.

record /rɪˈkɔːd/ *verb* to write something down so that you can know about it later.

relay /ˈriːleɪ/ *noun* a race where each member of the team runs or swims part of the distance.

repair /rɪˈpeə/ *verb* to make something that is old or broken new again.

restaurant /ˈrestərɒnt/ *noun* a place where you can buy and eat food.

reward /rɪˈwɔːd/ *noun* something given in return for good work, kindness, bravery, etc.

rise /raɪz/ (*past:* rose /rəʊz/) *verb* to become higher.

river /ˈrɪvə/ *noun* a natural flow of water: *the River Nile.*

rob /rɒb/ *verb* to take something from a person, a bank or a shop when it is not yours: *They* **robbed** *a bank.*

rock /rɒk/ *noun* a large piece of stone that sticks up out of the ground or sea.

rocket /ˈrɒkɪt/ *noun*

rocking chair /ˈrɒkɪŋ tʃeə/ *noun* a chair that moves gently backwards and forwards.

round /raʊnd/ *adjective* like a ring or circle: *a large round plate.*

Mini-dictionary

rubber /ˈrʌbə/ *noun*

ruined /ˈruːɪnd/ *adjective* almost destroyed.

ruler /ˈruːlə/ *noun*

run /rʌn/ (*past:* **ran** /ræn/) *verb* to move very quickly on your feet: *I was late, so I ran to school.*

S

sad /sæd/ *adjective* not happy.

sail /seɪl/ *verb* to travel by boat or ship.

satisfied /ˈsætɪsfaɪd/ *adjective* pleased; contented.

say /seɪ/ (*past:* **said** /sed/) *verb* to speak something: *He said hello.*

school /skuːl/ *noun* a place where you study.

schoolmate /ˈskuːlmeɪt/ *noun* a person who is at school with you.

science /ˈsaɪəns/ *noun* the study of nature and how things in the world are made and behave.

screen /skriːn/ *noun* a flat square surface that shows pictures etc. at a cinema, on TV or on a computer.

season /ˈsiːzən/ *noun* one of the four parts of the year, e.g. summer.

sell /sel/ (*past:* **sold** /səʊld/) *verb* to change something for money: *They sell sweets in the shop.*

sentence /ˈsentəns/ *noun* a group of words making a statement or a question. It begins with a capital letter and ends with a full stop.

serve /sɜːv/ *verb* to help a customer in a shop, restaurant, etc.

shake /ʃeɪk/ (*past:* **shook** /ʃʊk/) *verb* to move quickly from side to side or up and down: *I said hello and we shook hands.*

sheet /ʃiːt/ *noun* a large thin piece of cloth, usually white, for putting on a bed.

shoot /ʃuːt/ (*past:* **shot** /ʃɒt/) *verb* to use a gun.

shop /ʃɒp/ *noun* a place where you can buy things: *a clothes shop.*

short /ʃɔːt/ *adjective* not tall; not long.

silly /ˈsɪli/ *adjective* not serious or sensible.

similar /ˈsɪmɪlə/ *adjective* alike: *Our T-shirts are similar.*

sing /sɪŋ/ (*past:* **sang** /sæŋ/) *verb* to make music with your voice.

sinister /ˈsɪnɪstə/ *adjective* something that looks frightening and dangerous.

sit /sɪt/ (*past:* **sat** /sæt/) *verb* to rest on the bottom of your back: *He sat on a chair.*

ski /skiː/ *verb* to travel on snow wearing long narrow pieces of wood on your feet.

skin /skɪn/ *noun* the outside of your body or an animal's body: *They used animal skins for clothes.*

sleep /sliːp/ (*past:* **slept** /slept/) *verb* to rest with your eyes closed: *I usually sleep for nine hours a night.*

sleepy /ˈsliːpi/ *adjective* wanting to sleep: *I felt sleepy, so I went to bed.*

slowly /ˈsləʊli/ *adverb* to do something in a slow manner: *He walks very slowly.*

small /smɔːl/ *adjective* not big.

smart /smɑːt/ *adjective* dressed in good, clean clothes: *She always wears smart clothes.*

smile /smaɪl/ *verb* to move your mouth to show you are happy.

snow /snəʊ/ *noun* very cold rain which is soft and white.

snowy /ˈsnəʊi/ *adjective* what the weather is like when it snows.

sociable /ˈsəʊʃəbəl/ *adjective* friendly.

soft drink /ˈsɒft drɪŋk/ *noun* a drink with no alcohol in it.

song /sɒŋ/ *noun* a piece of music with words that are sung.

soon /suːn/ *adverb* in a short time: *Come and see me soon.*

south /saʊθ/ *noun* the direction that is on the right when you look at the sun at the start of the morning.

speak /spiːk/ (*past:* **spoke** /spəʊk/) *verb* **1** to say words aloud: *Children learn to speak when they are very small.* **2** to be able to talk in a particular language: *She speaks Italian.*

spear /spɪə/ *noun* a weapon.

spell /spel/ *verb* to say the letters that make up a word: *You spell dog, D-O-G.*

spiky /ˈspaɪki/ *adjective* long and pointed: *He's got spiky hair.*

sports centre /ˈspɔːts ˌsentə/ *noun* a place where you can do different sports for pleasure.

sport /spɔːt/ *noun* games in general: *Football is a sport.*

sporty /ˈspɔːti/ *adjective* of a person who loves sports.

spring /sprɪŋ/ *noun* the season between winter and summer.

square /skweə/ *adjective* having four straight sides of equal length: *The window was square.*

stamp /stæmp/ *noun*

stand /stænd/ (*past:* **stood** /stʊd/) *verb* to be on your feet.

stick /stɪk/ (*past:* **stuck** /stʌk/) *verb* to fix something with glue: *I stuck a stamp on the letter.*

sticker /ˈstɪkə/ *noun* something you can stick somewhere.

stop /stɒp/ *verb* to finish doing something: *We stopped eating.*

storm /stɔːm/ *noun* a time of high winds and sometimes thunder and rain.

strange /streɪndʒ/ *adjective* unusual; not what you are accustomed to.

street /striːt/ *noun* a road with buildings at the side of it.

subject /ˈsʌbdʒɪkt/ *noun* something that you study: *English is one of our school subjects.*

suffer /ˈsʌfə/ *verb* to be in pain or trouble.

summer /ˈsʌmə/ *noun* the season between spring and autumn: *The weather is usually hot in summer.*

sunny /ˈsʌni/ *adjective* what the weather is like when it's hot and there are no clouds.

supermarket /ˈsuːpəmɑːkɪt, ˈsjuː-/ *noun* a large shop where you can buy different types of food and drink and things for the house.

surfing /ˈsɜːfɪŋ/ *noun* a sport where you ride on the waves of the sea.

surprised /səˈpraɪzd/ *adjective* what you feel when something unexpected happens: *I was surprised by the news.*

survive /səˈvaɪv/ *verb* to continue to live.

swim /swɪm/ (*past:* **swam** /swæm/) *verb* to move in water.

sword /sɔːd/ *noun* a weapon.

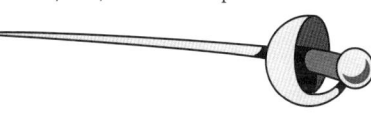

T

take turns to /ˌteɪk ˈtɜːnz tə, tʊ/ *verb* to do something one after another.

talk /tɔːk/ *verb* to speak: *I talk to my friends.*

tall /tɔːl/ *adjective* not short.

taxi /ˈtæksi/ *noun* a car which takes you on a journey which you pay for.

tea /tiː/ *noun* **1** a hot drink: *We drink tea for breakfast.* **2** a meal in the afternoon or evening: *We have tea at six o'clock.*

team /tiːm/ *noun* a group of two or more people who play a game.

tennis /ˈtenɪs/ *noun* a sport where two or four people hit a ball over a net.

tepee /ˈtiːpiː/ *noun* an American Indian tent.

terrible /ˈterɪbəl/ *adjective* very bad.

thin /θɪn/ *adjective* **1** not fat: *He's thin because he doesn't eat much.* **2** not thick: *This paper is too thin.*

think /θɪŋk/ *verb* **1** to use your mind: *Think before you speak.* **1** to have an opinion: *What do you think of my singing?*

throw /θrəʊ/ (*past:* **threw** /θruː/) *verb* to send something through the air with your arms.

ticket /ˈtɪkɪt/ *noun* a small piece of paper which shows you have paid to travel on a bus, see a film at the cinema, etc.

tired /ˈtaɪəd/ *adjective* needing rest or sleep: *I felt tired after school.*

town /taʊn/ *noun* a place with many houses and other buildings where people live and work.

toy /tɔɪ/ *noun* something a child plays with.

train /treɪn/ *noun*

travel /ˈtrævəl/ *verb* to go from one place to another.

trick /trɪk/ *noun* an amusing action done to make someone look silly: *Let's play a trick on him.*

treat /triːt/ *noun* something special which gives you pleasure: *Her birthday treat was a trip to London.*

trip /trɪp/ *noun* a short journey, usually for pleasure: *a trip to London.*

try /traɪ/ *verb* to attempt to do something: *He tried to climb the tree but it was too difficult.*

twin /twɪn/ *noun* one of two children born to the same mother at the same time.

typical /ˈtɪpɪkəl/ *adjective* the same as other people or things belonging to that group or kind.

U

understand /ˌʌndəˈstænd/ (*past:* **understood** /ˌʌndəˈstʊd/) *verb* to hear or read something and know what it means.

underwater /ˌʌndəˈwɔːtə/ *adverb* below the surface of the water: *He swam underwater.*

unhappy /ʌnˈhæpi/ *adjective* not happy.

unusual /ʌnˈjuːʒuəl, -ʒəl/ *adjective* not usual; strange.

upstairs /ʌpˈsteəz/ *adverb* on an upper floor in a building: *She went upstairs.*

use /juːz/ *verb* to employ something to do something else: *She used her new pen to write a story.*

useless /ˈjuːslɪs/ *adjective* having no good purpose; not helpful.

V

vegetable /ˈvedʒtəbəl/ *noun* a plant that you can eat: *Carrots and cabbages are vegetables.*

village /ˈvɪlɪdʒ/ *noun* a small town; a group of houses.

violin /ˌvaɪəˈlɪnt/ *noun* a musical instrument.

violent /ˈvaɪəlɪnt/ *adjective* aggressive; using force to hurt someone.

volleyball /ˈvɒlibɔːl/ *noun* a sport where you knock a large ball backwards and forwards across a net.

voyage /ˈvɔɪ-ɪdʒ/ *noun* a long journey by sea.

W

walk /wɔːk/ *verb* to move on your feet: *I walk to school every day.*

walkman /ˈwɔːkmən/ *noun* a small machine for playing music, which you can carry with you.

wall /wɔːl/ *noun* one of the sides of a building or a room.

war /wɔː/ *noun* a time of fighting between countries.

warm /wɔːm/ *adjective* a temperature between cold and hot.

watch /wɒtʃ/ *noun* a small clock that you wear on your arm.

watch /wɒtʃ/ *verb* to look at (usually with interest).

wear /weə/ (*past:* **wore** /wɔː/) *verb* to have clothes on.

weekend /ˌwiːkˈend/ *noun* the time from Friday evening to Sunday evening.

welcome /ˈwelkəm/ *verb* to meet and greet someone with pleasure.

west /west/ *noun* the direction in which the sun goes down.

wet /wet/ *adjective* **1** covered with or containing liquid: *My hair is wet.* **2** rainy: *a wet day.*

whirlpool /ˈwɜːlpuːl/ *noun* a place in a river or the sea where the water goes round and round.

wild /waɪld/ *adjective* not friendly or domesticated: *Lions are wild cats.*

Wild West /ˌwaɪld ˈwest/ *noun* the parts of the United States before people built towns.

winter /ˈwɪntə/ *noun* the season between autumn and spring: *The weather is usually cold in winter.*

wood /wʊd/ *noun* material from trees: *The cabin was made of wood.*

wool /wʊl/ *noun* the soft thick hair of sheep.

word /wɜːd/ *noun* a group of letters which mean something: *What's the Spanish word for 'mouse'?*

work /wɜːk/ *noun* a person's job: *to go to work.*

world /wɜːld/ *noun* everything on our planet: *There are a lot of countries in the world.*

write /raɪt/ (*past:* **wrote** /rəʊt/) *verb* to communicate using a pen and paper.

wrong /rɒŋ/ *adjective* not correct; not right: *This answer is wrong.*

Y

yacht /jɒt/ *noun* a boat with sails

young /jʌŋ/ *adjective* not old; of not many years: *She's three years old - she's very young.*

Picture dictionary

Food and drink

cabbage

cauliflower

sausages

hamburger

pumpkin

melon

chicken

orange

bread

cheese

apple

banana

hot dog

grape

cola

lemonade

tomato

potato

water

carrot

sweets

milk

crisps

cake

fizzy drink

sugar

ice cream

sandwich

rice

egg

House

plant · bathroom
ceiling
poster
door
bedroom · window
radio
toilet
back door · kitchen
cupboard · cooker
fire
sofa · television
table · rocking chair
lamp
dining room · front door

Picture dictionary

Families

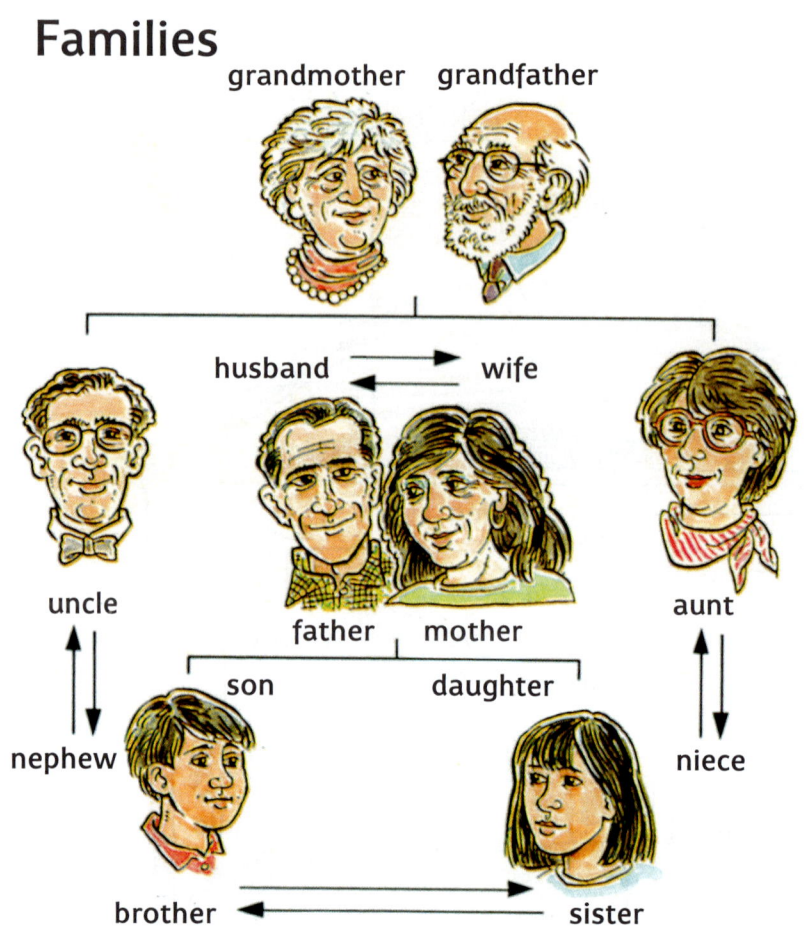

grandmother   grandfather

husband → wife

uncle

father   mother

nephew

son   daughter

aunt

niece

brother ← sister

Numbers

Number	Order	Number	Order
1 one	first	13 thirteen	thirteenth
2 two	second	14 fourteen	fourteenth
3 three	third	20 twenty	twentieth
4 four	fourth	21 twenty-one	twenty-first
5 five	fifth	30 thirty	thirtieth
6 six	sixth	40 forty	fortieth
7 seven	seventh	50 fifty	fiftieth
8 eight	eighth	60 sixty	sixtieth
9 nine	ninth	70 seventy	seventieth
10 ten	tenth	80 eighty	eightieth
11 eleven	eleventh	90 ninety	ninetieth
12 twelve	twelfth	100 a hundred	hundredth
		1000 a thousand	thousandth

Colours

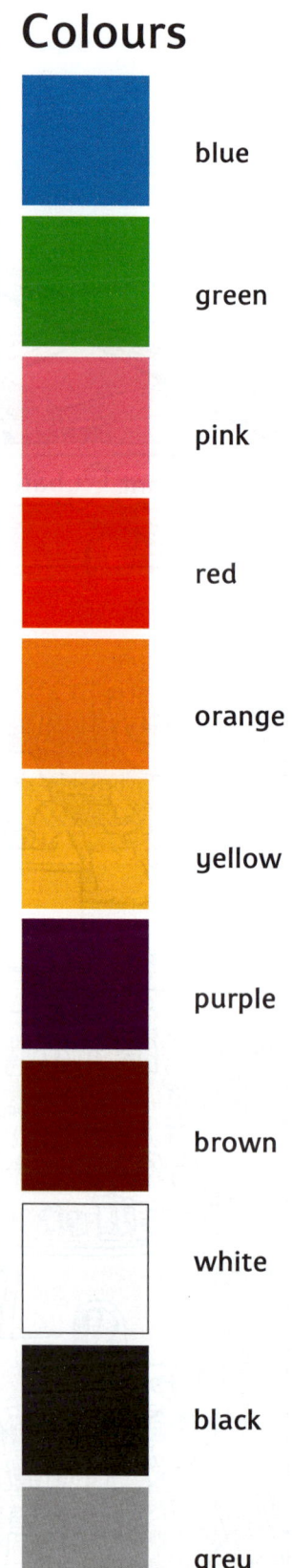

blue

green

pink

red

orange

yellow

purple

brown

white

black

grey

People

st

bus driver

farmer

jockey

gardener

riter

air hostess

lawyer

journalist

police officer

mechanic

teacher

cook

nurse

pilot

waiter

astronaut

soldier

vampire

secretary

doctor

businessman

designer

neer

sheriff

cowboy

businesswoman

Picture dictionary

Animals

whale

bear

rab

tarantula

buffalo

goldfish

piranha

polar bear

duck

leopard

zebra

scorpion

dog

camel

seal

crocodile

wolf

horse

lion

sheep

dolp

cow

tiger

panther

gorilla

kangaroo

spider

elephant

jaguar

hippo

pe

fox

snake

monkey

alligator

110

Irregular verb list

Infinitive	Past tense
egin	began
uild	built
uy	bought
ome	came
rink	drank
rive	drove
o	did
at	ate
nd	found
y	flew
et	got
o	went
ave	had
urt	hurt
ave	left
ake	made
eet	met
ut	put
ead	read
de	rode
un	ran
e	saw
ell	sold
t	sat
eep	slept
and	stood
wim	swam
ke	took
nderstand	understood
ear	wore
rite	wrote

End-of-year self-assessment

Assess yourself:

- [A] I have no problems.
- [B] I have some problems.
- [C] I have a lot of problems with this.

Speaking *Writing*

- ☐ ☐ Talking about you, your hobbies, your family, etc.
- ☐ ☐ Using English in the class.
- ☐ ☐ Describing people and places.
- ☐ ☐ Talking about likes and dislikes.
- ☐ ☐ Talking about the past.

Listening

- ☐ to your teacher
- ☐ to dialogues (on the cassette)
- ☐ to other students

Grammar

- ☐ *To be*
- ☐ *Can*
- ☐ *Have got*
- ☐ Present simple
- ☐ Present continuous
- ☐ Past tense
- ☐ Questions
- ☐ *Some /any*

Assessment

Introduction

In *World Club* comprehensive guidance is given on assessment:

- Some suggestions are given for when and how to carry out *informal assessment* (marking and correction of class and homework). These include projects, which are useful activities to assess as they usually combine more than one skill as well as opportunities for developing positive attitudes towards working together in a team, gaining self-confidence, etc.

- Suggestions are made for encouraging students to carry out their own *self-assessment*. This is closely linked with the important learner training element in the course.

- *Formal assessment* containing sixteen tasks, covering both skills and language input, is included. These assessment tasks (short tests) are completely integrated into the course. It is complemented by materials for formal oral assessment which can be carried out at the end of the year.

You have permission to photocopy the assessment tasks.

Evaluation criteria

Students should be assessed according to their ability to:

- Extract global and specific information from oral messages produced in 'face-to-face' situations about topics related to students' daily lives and to the sociocultural aspects of English-speaking countries.

- Extract relevant information from oral messages produced on audio cassettes about topics which do not require special knowledge.

- Participate in short conversations, using appropriate communicative strategies according to specific situations and purposes.

- Extract global and specific information from simple authentic written texts of limited length (descriptive, narrative), being able to predict the meaning of some of the elements through context and sociocultural elements.

- Read texts graded according to the students' level and interests, using the dictionary and visual support, demonstrating comprehension by carrying out specific tasks related to the text.

- Produce written texts on varying subjects, respecting the basic conventions of written language (function of sentences, discourse markers, etc.) and using the correct elements to ensure cohesion and coherence.

- Consciously use the knowledge acquired about the new linguistic system as a tool for controlling and correcting one's own productions and as a resource to improve understanding of other people's productions.

- Persevere in trying to understand and make oneself understood in 'face-to-face' situations using all available communicative strategies to overcome possible difficulties of communication and comprehension.

- Identify and interpret sociocultural information which appears in texts, using linguistic and non-linguistic resources as an aid to comprehension.

Assessment for diversity

Many teachers will find that amongst their students there is a wide diversity of level and ability. This must be taken into account when assessing. While there exists a series of minimum objectives, it is important in compulsory secondary education to be flexible, in order to encourage the students both at the bottom and the very top of the spectrum. If this does not happen and if a rigid pass/fail barometer based only on tests is used, the weaker students will inevitably give up as they will realise at the outset that they have no chance of passing and doing well. Also, if assessment is only based on test results, the better students in the class will probably realise that they have to make no effort in order to pass and may waste the year and even cause discipline problems because they are bored.

Possible ways of carrying out assessment and taking into account diversity are as follows:

- Balancing formal and informal assessment (for example, giving performance in tests 50% of the marks and giving class and homework the other 50%). This will mean that weaker students who make an effort and who actually make progress, can pass even if they do not do well in all the tests. It will also mean that the very best students cannot get away with doing nothing in class, knowing that they will easily be able to pass the tests.

- Awarding marks for group as well as for individual performance. This can be done for instance when assessing final written tasks. The finished task or project done by a pair or group is assessed, even though each member of the group will have contributed according to his/her own ability. However, it is important to make sure that the groups are working well and that one or two people are not doing the work for the rest of the group. One way of checking this is by giving students a peer assessment form, to assess the working of the group and that of its members.

- Giving a percentage of marks for attitude (effort, participation, co-operation in class). This can be done globally, over a whole term or year, or done when assessing performance (adding effort as one of the key criteria when assessing speaking or writing).

- Using graded tests that start off with easier and move on to more difficult tasks. This means that weaker students have a chance of passing and that better students are stretched if they are to get very good marks. The assessment tasks in this course have been worked out on this principle.

- Implementing self-assessment so that assessment becomes more individualised and that students have to think about how much progress they are making and what problems they are having. As well as increasing awareness, self-assessment can help the teacher by providing more individualised information about each student on which to make judgements (see the section on self-assessment).

Informal assessment

Each teacher has his/her own methods of carrying out informal assessment. However, here are some suggestions of when and how you can carry out continuous informal assessment when using this Coursebook.

Assessing written final tasks

When students have made an effort to produce a piece of written work, it is important for them to be given some kind of mark and feedback about it. This should not mean vast amounts of marking outside class. As students finish tasks in class you can assess what they have done. If it has been done by a group, give students a group mark.

Use the following criteria:

For tasks in the first three modules

Effort and presentation of final tasks: _/5
Message: the relevance of what they have written and its comprehensibility: _/5

For tasks in the rest of the book

Accuracy: in terms of grammatical structures, lexis, spelling and basic punctuation: _/5
Organisation: how well organised the material is: _/5

Assessing speaking

There are two ways of assessing speaking informally:

Over a period of time

Tell students that you will be giving them a mark for speaking throughout this module. Observe and assess four or five students during all of the speaking activities that you do in the module. Tell the students the criteria you are going to use beforehand.

During the speaking tasks in the fluency lessons

Some of the speaking tasks in the *Fluency* lessons can be used for informal assessment, with students making presentations to the rest of the class. It is vital to have something for the others to do, while groups are presenting. The best thing to do is to use a task sheet produced by the group of students.

The following assessment criteria can be used:

In the first term

Effort/participation: it is important that students are rewarded well for actually having a go at speaking in English: _/5
Comprehensibility: how well students can actually be understood despite problems with grammar, vocabulary and pronunciation: _/5

In the other terms you can also add these criteria

Accuracy: in terms of grammar and lexis: _/5
Pronunciation: both in terms of sound and intonation: _/5
Message: relevance of what students say to the context: _/5

Assessing listening and reading

The tasks below can be done and assessed. Remember, you do not always have to take in listening and reading tasks that you want to assess. You can get students to mark each other's work and then hand them to you. In addition to material you can use graded readers as a source of assessment for reading (see *Teacher's HELP 11* for ideas on tasks for graded readers).

Module 1. Families

Reading: Lesson 2. Exercises B and C. Take in students' answers to these and mark them (or students can correct each other's and then give them to you).

Listening: Lesson 3. Exercise C. Students write down the animals.

Module 2. Cartoons

Listening: Lesson 5. Exercise C. Take in students' drawings of the cartoon character and give a global mark out of ten for the accuracy of the drawing.

Reading: Lesson 6. Exercise B. Students write down the differences between the text and the picture.

Module 3. Hobbies

Reading: Lesson 7. Exercise B.
Listening: Lesson 9. Exercise B.

Module 4. Parties

Listening: Lesson 10. Exercise A.
Reading: Lesson 12. Exercises B and C.

Module 5. Planet Earth

Reading: Lesson 14. Exercise E.
Listening: Lesson 15. Exercise B.

Module 6. Villages

Reading: Lesson 17. Exercises B and C.
Listening: Lesson 18. Exercise C.

Module 7. The Wild West

Reading: Lesson 19. Exercise B.
Listening: Lesson 20. Exercise G.

Module 8. Travel

Listening: Lesson 22. Exercise B.
Listening and Reading: Lesson 23. Exercise B.

Assessing Attitudes

When assessing students' attitudes it is important to use clear indicators, or students can easily say that your assessment is based on personal factors.

Vocabulary books

Take these in from time to time and give students a mark out of ten for organisation (how well it is organised and how neat it is) and a mark out of ten for effort (that students have been really writing down new vocabulary).

Module Check

You can get students to write down their answers in their notebooks, and at the end of the term give them to you to assess for effort.

Class observation

Through observation you can note students who have been making an effort. It is important not only to think of oral activities. Many shy students may not like to speak in front of the whole class but they do participate in oral pairwork and groupwork and make an effort in written activities. It is important also to observe how well students work together in groups.

Homework

How often students do their homework and how much time they put into it is a very clear indicator of effort and maturity.

The following criteria for assessing attitudes can be used:

_/5 interest and effort (both in class and when doing homework)
_/5 ability to organise work and work independently
_/5 ability to co-operate and work with others

Self-assessment

The degree to which self-assessment is taken into consideration will depend very much on the individual teacher. However, self-assessment is a vital part of learner development, encouraging the learner to think about his/her own progress and problems rather than depending totally on the teacher. Self-assessment can also provide very useful information for the teacher and can form part of an overall assessment system.

Here are some suggestions for self-assessment:

Diagnosis

At the beginning of the course it can be useful to give a questionnaire in students' own L1, to find out about students' previous learning experiences: how long they have been learning, the topics, vocabulary and basic classroom language they know, etc.

Test Yourself

At the end of each module there are *Test Yourself* activities in the Activity Book. These aim to help students check their own learning of target structures and lexis in the module. When going over these activities it is possible to deal with any problems that crop up, and explain again any structures that students still do not understand. It is also possible to give students further practice and consolidation of areas that are causing difficulties (see *Language Work-out*). When such remedial work has been done students can go on to do the grammar assessment tasks.

Module Check

The *Module Check* aims to get students to reflect on their own learning throughout the preceding module as well as to evaluate the lessons. Give students time in class to complete them in their notebooks and then discuss the results with students. This discussion could be done in students' own language as such explicit reflection can prove linguistically and cognitively difficult. Students can keep the *Checks* to refer to later, at the end of the term or year when they are looking back over their learning.

Portfolios

It is possible to build up a portfolio of students' work throughout the year. As well as providing you with a corpus of material to assess over the three terms, it can be very useful to help students do end of term and end of year self-assessments. You can ask students to include the following pieces of work:

- final written tasks (these can be photocopied if they have been done in groups)
- examples of three or four tests
- vocabulary books
- module checks

This work can be kept in a file, and referred to when discussing students' progress with parents and with other teachers. It can finally be photocopied and passed on to the next teacher when working out the programme for the following year.

End of term

Having built up self-assessment through *Test Yourself* activities and the *Module Check*, it is possible to ask students to assess their own progress over the whole term, with the help of their portfolios. A report card, similar to the one your school uses, could be made for the student to assess him or herself. At the same time you do your own assessment using marks from all types of assessment tasks done throughout the year. Then you can compare the marks with your student's own assessment and discuss this together.

Formal Assessment

A comprehensive assessment package, containing sixteen tasks, covers both skills and language input. It is completely integrated into the course, as is the separate oral assessment (to be carried out at the end of the year).

You have permission to photocopy all of the assessment tasks in this book (and only these tasks). The tasks should be administered at specific points during the course, as follows:

1	Reading	(after module 1)
2	Writing	(after module 1)
3	Listening	(after module 2)
4	Grammar/Vocabulary	(after module 2)
5	Writing	(after module 3)
6	Reading	(after module 3)
7	Listening	(after module 4)
8	Grammar/Vocabulary	(after module 4)
9	Reading	(after module 5)
10	Writing	(after module 5)
11	Listening	(after module 6)
12	Grammar/Vocabulary	(after module 6)
13	Reading	(after module 7)
14	Writing	(after module 7)
15	Listening	(after module 8)
16	Grammar/Vocabulary	(after module 8)

Administration of tasks

- These are progress tests, and are constructive rather than punitive.

- The assessment should be linked to revision and self-assessment activities. The language items should be revised and the *Test Yourself* activities carried out before students are assessed.

- Tasks should be administered under formal conditions. This means that students should be working individually with no opportunity to help each other or to copy.

- Go through the instructions with students before they begin a task.

- Dictionaries may be used unless specifically forbidden.

- The listening texts should be repeated at least twice.

- The time needed for each task will vary between 10 minutes and 30 minutes. Give students more time rather than less.

- Answers and written marking criteria are provided. (Do not penalise for inaccuracy of language in reading and listening tasks.)

- Most students should get over 50% in all the tests. (If they do not you will have to consider why not and deal with any problems they may have.)

- Check the tests with students so that they see where they have gone wrong. (Do, however, collect the tests in afterwards, as black markets in tests can flourish in schools!)

- You may be able to discuss individual problems with students and differences between their results and their own evaluation of their progress.

- The recorded material for the *Assessment tasks* is found after each corresponding module on the cassette.

Name: _____ Class: _____ Date: _____ ___ /10

---

15 Cresswell Gardens, Flat B
LONDON NW 17
January 5

Dear Raymond,

Hi! My name is Charlie McEwan and I'm twelve years old. I am from London, but my family is from Scotland. The photo is of me and my twin brother Andrew. I've also got a sister – Kirsty. She's only three months old.

Andy and I look very similar but really we are different. We're both very sociable – but I'm very active and sporty and Andy is not.

My favourite sports are rugby and football. I'm in the under fourteen rugby team at school.

My favourite club is Glasgow Celtic and my favourite football player is Ronaldo.

I'm not a good student at school. My favourite subject is sport! Andy is different – his favourites are maths, history, science and English.

My favourite music is rock. My favourite group is Oasis – they're fantastic! My favourite colour for clothes is blue and green.

My dad's name is Craig. He's forty-five and he's a teacher. My mum's name is Julia and she's forty. She's from Edinburgh. She's an industrial engineer.

Write to me and tell me about you and your family.

Charlie

A (5 points)
Complete the McEwan family tree.

Mother: _____ Father: _____

age: _____ age: _____

Sons: _____ Daughter: _____

_____ Age: _____

Ages: _____

_____

B (5 points)
Read the letter again and answer these questions.

1 Where is Charlie from?

_____

2 What is his personality?

_____

3 What are his favourite sports?

_____

4 Who is a good student at school – Charlie or Andy?

_____

5 How old is their mum and what is her job?

_____

Assessment

Name: _____ Class: _____ Date: _____ ___ /10

Complete the form about you.

WORLD CLUB LANGUAGE SCHOOL

Name:
_____

Home:
_____

Family:
_____

Occupation(s) of parents:
_____

Telephone number:
_____

Favourite colour:
_____

Favourite hobby:
_____

Favourite sport:
_____

Favourite music:
_____

Favourite school subject:
_____

Favourite activities in class:
_____

Put photograph
here.

Name: _____ Class: _____ Date: _____ ___ /10

A (4 points)

Listen to the descriptions. Write the names of the students under the correct pictures.

Sam / Tom / Liz / Sally

B (6 points)

Listen again and complete the table.

	Favourite activity in class	Favourite animal	Favourite colour
Liz	listening to songs	kangaroo	yellow
Tom	reading		red
Sally			
Sam		piranha	

Assessment

task 4 Grammar/Vocabulary

Name: _____ Class: _____ Date: _____ ___ /20

Grammar

A (5 points)
Complete the sentences.

1 Trudy __*is*__ thirteen years old.

2 She _____ got a brother called Eric.

3 They _____ from New Zealand.

4 They (not) _____ got animals at home.

5 Trudy (not) _____ a good student.

6 Her favourite activity at school is sport – she _____ play tennis and swim very well.

B (5 points)
Use the words to write questions.

1 (you / play / chess?) *Can you play chess?*

2 (she / got / a computer?)

_____

3 (where / Tim / from?)

_____

4 (how old / Brian and Jean?)

_____

5 (they / ride / a bicycle?)

_____

6 (you / got / dark hair?)

_____

Vocabulary

A (5 points)
Classify these words:

mouth / nephew / panther / grandmother / nose / daughter / eyebrows / tiger / lion / eyes

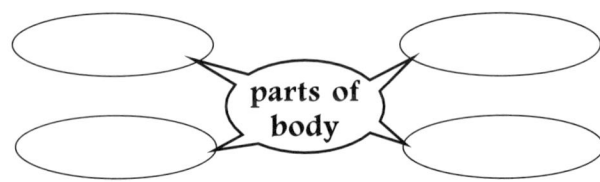

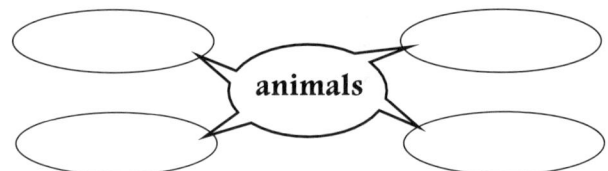

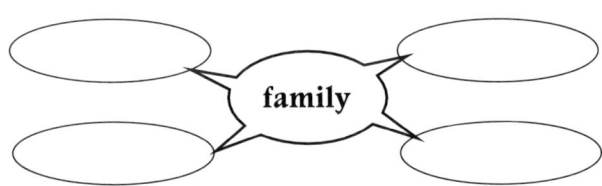

B (5 points)
Match the opposites.

1 blond   a thin
2 good   b small
3 fat   c tall
4 short   d dark
5 true   e bad
6 big   f false

Assessment

Name: _____ Class: _____ Date: _____ ___ /10

A (5 points)

Complete these notes about your free time.

My Free Time

Things I collect:
_____

Things I make:
_____

Sports I play:
_____

Favourite games (+ computer games):
_____

Outdoor activities: winter _____

                             summer _____

Music I like:
_____

B (5 points)

Use your notes. Write sentences about your free time.

_____

_____

_____

_____

_____

_____

_____

_____

_____

_____

_____

_____

Assessment

Name: _____ Class: _____ Date: _____ ___ /10

Hi!,

My name is Seb Simons and I'm from Australia. I live in Kimberly – a small village in Tasmania. It is very quiet but I like it – I like the outdoor life.

My favourite hobbies are swimming and surfing in the summer and horseriding in the winter. I love horses and we've got three at home. I sometimes go canoeing with my school.

I have also got other hobbies. I make and collect model ships. I make them from kits and paint them. Now I have got about twenty-five ships – old sailing ships and modern ones.

I've got a computer with some very good games. I like simulation games – I've got a fantastic flying programme. I also like chess. I play chess at school, with my dad and with people in other countries on the internet.

Write to me and tell me about your hobbies!

All the best,

Seb

A (10 points)

Answer these questions about Seb.

1 Where is he from?

_____

2 What are his favourite outdoor hobbies in summer?

_____

3 What is his favourite outdoor hobby in winter?

_____

4 What activity does he sometimes do with his school?

_____

5 What animals has he got at home?

_____

6 What does he make and collect?

_____

7 How many has he got in his collection?

_____

8 What computer games does he like?

_____

9 What is his favourite computer game?

_____

10 Who does he play chess with?

_____

Name: _____ Class: _____ Date: _____ ___ /10

A (3 points)

Listen to the survey. Where are the people from?

Tina: _____

Bobby: _____

Pam: _____

B (7 points)

Listen again and complete the table.

	Tina	**Bobby**	**Pam**
school clothes	*skirt / jacket*		
party clothes			
summer clothes		*shorts / T-shirts*	

Assessment

task 8 Grammar/Vocabulary

Name: _____ Class: _____ Date: _____ ____ /20

Grammar

A (7 points)
Complete the sentences.

1 I really _____ fancy dress parties-
  they're terrible!
2 Lucy (not) _____ play computer
  games.
3 _____ Terry like the festival?
4 When we go to parties _____
  parents take us.
5 Leonardo di Caprio is great. I really like
  _____
6 What sports _____ you play in
  the summer?
7 I _____ mind basketball, but I
  prefer football.

B (3 points)
Write questions for these answers:

1 (like chess?)

  _____

  No, I don't.
2 (collect / badges?)

  _____

  Yes, she does.
3 (where / live?)

  _____

  Tom? In Plymouth, in England.

Vocabulary

A (6 points)
Match the two parts of the sentences.

1 At parties you   a very well- she is in
  can meet   my class.
2 I know her   b canoeing in the
                            winter
3 In the winter   c my bag to school
  I play   every morning.
4 I sometimes wear   d new people.
5 I carry   f basketball.
6 I often go   e long dresses in the
                            winter.

B (4 points)
Classify these words.

badges / T-shirts / model planes / trainers
/ jackets / national dolls / shoes / coins

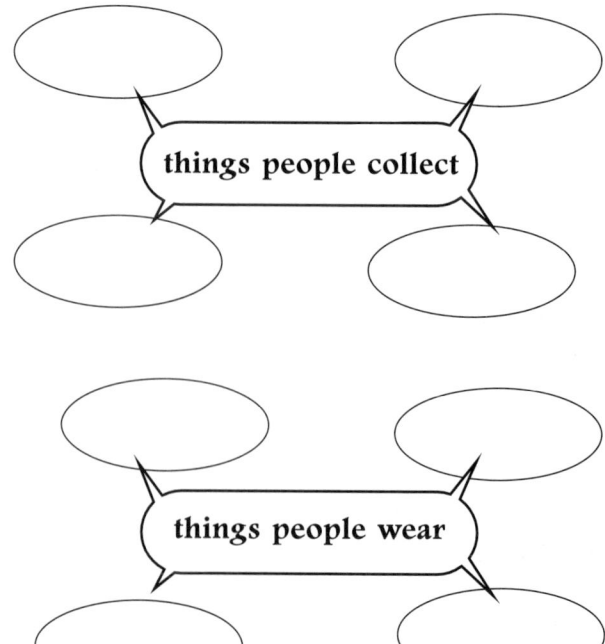

Assessment

Name: _____ Class: _____ Date: _____   ____ /10

RURITANIA

Ruritania is a small, but very strange country in the Ostrogovian Alps.

Places to visit

Walk in the beautiful gardens of Rurt city – see the famous collection of blue parrots.

Come and see the famous vampire cats in the mountains.

Look at the penguins in Rurt Zoo – they can fly!

Go to the summer festival in Rurt City – see the spectacular processions.

Go to the street parties – food, music and dancing for five days!

Things to do

In the summer, go canoeing in the rivers and go swimming in Lake Rurt.

Go walking or horse riding in the forests.

In the winter, go skiing in the mountains.

Learn Ruritanian dancing – a fantastic experience!

Advice for tourists

In winter bring warm clothes – a good jacket and a good pair of boots.

Wear a hat in the summer – it can be very hot.

When you meet Ruritanians, shake hands and say "Valevole" – (hello).

Don't watch Ruritanian television – it is terrible!

Don't go swimming in August in Lake Rurt – the piranhas are very dangerous.

A (5 points)

Read the information about Ruritania. Answer these questions.

1 Where can you see vampire cats?

  _____

2 Where is the collection of parrots?

  _____

3 Where can you see processions?

  _____

4 Where can you go horse riding?

  _____

5 Where can you go swimming?

  _____

B (5 points)

Read the information again and answer these questions.

1 What is special about the penguins in the zoo?

  _____

2 What can you do in the street parties in Rurt City?

  _____

3 What outdoor activities can you do in the summer?

  _____

4 What clothes do you need in the summer?

  _____

5 What is dangerous in August?

  _____

Assessment

task 10 Writing

Describe the picture above.

The park is very beautiful. Five children are playing football. _____

_____

_____

_____

_____

_____

_____

_____

_____

_____

_____

Assessment

Name: _____ Class: _____ Date: _____ ____ /10

A (4 points)

Listen to the description of Richard's Castle, a village in England. Underline the *eight* places in the village.

bank / bus station / castle / church / cinema / disco / doctor's / factory / hospital / hotel /
park / restaurant / school / swimming pool / shop / sports centre / supermarket

B (6 points)

Listen again and answer these questions.

1 Is Richard's Castle a big village?

_____

2 Where is the swimming pool?

_____

3 What day do the boy and his family eat at the hotel?

_____

4 Who works near the church?

_____

5 Where does the boy's mother work?

_____

6 Is there a festival in the village?

_____

Assessment

task 12 Grammar/Vocabulary

Name: _____ Class: _____ Date: _____ ___ /20

Grammar

A (5 points)
Complete these sentences with the verbs in the present continuous.

1 I _____ (study) for my driving exam.

2 My parents _____ (not work) at the moment.

3 Where _____ they _____ (go)?

4 She _____ (not wear) a coat because it's a sunny day.

5 _____ Sam _____ (sleep)?

B (2 points)
Complete the text with *is, isn't, are* or *aren't*.

Langley is a beautiful fishing village in Cornwall, in the south-west of England. There (1) _____ a lovely harbour with white houses. The village is very small. There (2) _____ a hotel and there (3) _____ any cinemas or discos but there are two parks where you can play football and roller skate. There (4) _____ great beaches for swimming and surfing and marvellous countryside.

C (5 points)
Complete the sentences with *some* or *any*.

1 He hasn't got _____ compact discs.
2 Have you got _____ sweets?
3 She is making _____ cakes.
4 They haven't got _____ cassettes.
5 I'd like _____ stamps, please.

Vocabulary

A (3 points)
Write these places.

1 You pay money to sleep here.

_____

2 You change money here.

_____

3 You catch a bus or train here.

_____

B (3 points)
Write these jobs.

1 You go to see him/her when you are ill.

_____

2 He/ She repairs cars.

_____

3 He/ She examines your teeth.

_____

C (2 points)
Complete the sentences with these verbs.

say / turn on / have / meet

When I get home I (1) _____ the TV and (2) _____ tea.
If you (3) _____ him, (4) _____ hello.

Name: _____ Class: _____ Date: _____ ____ /10

Dances With Wolves

John Dunbar was a soldier in the American army. John lived in a fort, but he was not happy because there were no other people there. He wanted to be with people. A wolf started to visit him and after a time the wolf was his friend.

Some Sioux Indians arrived. They lived near the fort. At first, John was frightened, but soon he and the Sioux were friends. One day, when the wolf arrived, John played with it. The Sioux watched him and called him 'Dances With Wolves'.

John visited the Sioux village. There was a European woman who lived with the Indians. John liked her and after some time John and the woman married. John liked the people and their way of life. He started to learn the Sioux language and he hunted buffaloes with them.

One day, American soldiers arrived at the fort. They killed John's horse and wanted to take him away. The wolf followed them and the soldiers killed it. John was very sad and angry. Then the Sioux attacked the soldiers and John escaped.

He returned and lived in the Sioux village, but now he wasn't happy. He didn't want the soldiers to attack the village. He and his wife decided to leave and their Sioux friends were very sad.

A (5 points)
Read the text and answer the questions.

1 Which animal was John's friend?

_____

2 What did the Sioux call John?

_____

3 Who did John marry?

_____

4 What did the soldiers kill?

_____

5 Why did John leave the village?

_____

B (5 points)
True or false?

1 There were lots of soldiers at the fort at first.

2 John wasn't happy in the fort.

3 John was frightened of the wolf.

4 John liked the Sioux way of life.

5 The Sioux Indians helped John escape.

Assessment

task 14 Writing

Name: _____ Class: _____ Date: _____ ___ /10

A

Read the information in the table.

Name	Nootka Indians
Location	north-west coast of America
Homes	villages / large wooden houses
Family life	men – hunt and fish / women – cook and make clothes
Transport	canoes / no horses
Food	fish, seals, whales, bears, goats
Education	no school / no books

B

Write about the Nootkah Indians (about 50 words).

_____

_____

_____

_____

_____

_____

_____

_____

_____

_____

_____

_____

Assessment

Name: _____ Class: _____ Date: _____ ____ /10

A (5 points)

Listen to the life story of Marco Polo and match the dates with the events.

a 1275   **b** 1292   **c** 1274   **d** 1324   **e** 1254

1 _____ – born in Venice.

2 _____ – arrived in China.

3 _____ – visited the emperor

4 _____ – left China

5 _____ – died

B (5 points)

Listen again and answer these questions.

1 How old was Marco when he left Venice?

_____

2 How did he travel to China?

_____

3 Who did he work for in China?

_____

4 How did he travel to India?

_____

5 Why did he leave China?

_____

Assessment

task 16 Grammar/Vocabulary

Name: _____ Class: _____ Date: _____ ___ /20

Grammar

A (10 points)
Complete the sentences with the verbs in the past simple.

1 Before Europeans _____ (arrive), the Plains Indians _____ (not have) horses.

2 _____ Native American children _____ (go) to school?

3 Billy the Kid _____ (kill) his first man when he _____ (be) twelve years old.

4 Where _____ (be) you at six o'clock?

5 I _____ (sleep) for an hour after lunch – I think I _____ (eat) too much.

6 The log cabin _____ (not be) very big and there _____ (not be) many things in the house.

7 _____ Gulliver _____ (swim) to the beach?

8 What _____ the little people _____ (do)?

9 Erik the Red _____ (leave) Iceland because he _____ (have) lots of enemies there.

10 Airships _____ (go) across the Atlantic faster than boats.

Vocabulary

B (5 points)
Write the plural of these nouns.

1 knife _____

2 person _____

3 child _____

4 baby _____

5 wolf _____

C (5 points)
Write the types of transport.

1 _____

3 _____

2 _____

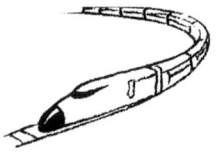

4 _____

5 _____

Assessment

Assessment tasks key

Task 1 Reading

A

mother: *Julia,* 40; father: *Craig,* 45; sons: *Charlie* and *Andy,* 12; daughter: *Kirsty,* 3 months

B

1 London
2 sociable; active; sporty
3 rugby; football
4 Andy
5 40; industrial engineer

Task 3 Listening

A

first drawing: Tom
second drawing: Sally
third drawing: Sam
fourth drawing: Liz

B

Tom: favourite animal:
  dog
Sally: favourite activity:
  grammar
  favourite animal:
  lion
  favourite colour:
  blue
Sam: favourite activity:
  speaking with his partner
  favourite colour:
  black

Task 4 Grammar/ Vocabulary

Grammar

A

2 has ('s)
3 are ('re)
4 have not (haven't)
5 is not (isn't)
6 can

B

2 Has she got a computer?
3 Where is Tim from?
4 How old are Brian and Jean?
5 Can they ride a bicycle?
6 Have you got dark hair?

Vocabulary

A

parts of the body:
  mouth; nose; eyebrows; eyes
animals:
  panther; tiger; lion
family:
  nephew; grandmother; daughter

B

2 good/bad
3 fat/thin
4 short/tall
5 true/false
6 big/small

Task 6 Reading

A

1 Australia; Kimberley in Tasmania
2 swimming; surfing
3 horse riding
4 canoeing
5 3 horses
6 model ships
7 25
8 simulation games
9 flying programme
10 with dad; people on the Internet

Task 7 Listening

A

Tina: London
Bobby: Manchester
Pam: Dublin (Ireland)

B

School clothes
Bobby: no uniform; jeans; shirts and jackets
Pam: a uniform; jacket; skirt

Party clothes
Tina: skirts and T-shirts
Bobby: fancy dress
Pam: long dresses and jackets

Summer clothes
Tina: trainers; jeans; t-shirts
Pam: trainers; t-shirts; jackets

Task 8 Grammar/ Vocabulary

Grammar

A

1 hate
2 does not (doesn't)
3 Does
4 our
5 him
6 do
7 do not (don't)

B

1 Do you like chess?
2 Does she collect badges?
3 Where does he live?

Vocabulary

A

1 d; 2 a; 3 f; 4 e; 5 c; 6 b

B

things people collect:
  badges; model planes; national dolls; coins
things people wear:
  t-shirts; trainers; jackets; shoes

Task 9 Reading

A

1 in the mountains
2 in the gardens in Rurt City
3 in the summer festival in Rurt City
4 in the forests
5 Lake Rurt

B

1 they can fly
2 eat/dance and listen to music
3 canoeing/swimming/ trekking/horse riding
4 a hat
5 Ruritanian piranhas

Task 11 Listening

A

church; castle; shop; hotel; restaurant; swimming pool; doctor's; factory

B

1 no
2 in the hotel
3 on Sundays
4 Dr Robert
5 the (furniture) factory
6 no

Task 12 Grammar/ Vocabulary

Grammar

A

1 am studying
2 aren't working
3 are (they) going
4 isn't wearing
5 Is (Sam) sleeping?

B

1 is   3 aren't
2 isn't   4 are

Assessment tasks key

C

1 any
2 any
3 some
4 any
5 some

Vocabulary

A

1 hotel
2 bank
3 station

B

1 doctor
2 mechanic
3 dentist

C

1 turn on
2 have
3 see
4 say

Task 13 Reading

A

1 a wolf
2 Dances With Wolves
3 a European woman
4 the wolf
5 he was sad

B

1 F   2 T   3 F   4 T   5 T

Task 14 Writing

B

Model Answer
The Nootka Indians lived on the north-west coast of America. They lived in villages. They didn't live in tepees. They lived in large wooden houses. The men hunted and fished. They hunted seals, whales, bears and goats. The women cooked and used animal skins to make clothes. They didn't have horses. They travelled on rivers and the sea in canoes. The Nootka children didn't go to school and they didn't have books.

Task 15 Listening

A

1 1254
2 1274
3 1275
4 1292
5 1324

B

1 17
2 on foot, by horse and camel
3 the emperor
4 by boat
5 he wanted to see his home again

Task 16 Grammar/ Vocabulary

Grammar
A

1 arrived/ didn't have
2 Did/ go
3 killed/ was
4 were
5 slept/ ate
6 wasn't/ weren't
7 Did/ swim
8 did/ do
9 left/ had
10 went

Vocabulary
B

1 knives
2 people
3 children
4 babies
5 wolves

C

1 aeroplane (or plane)
2 motorbike
3 boat (or ship)
4 train
5 bicycle (or bike)

ASSESSMENT TASK 3

Listen to the descriptions. Write the names of the students under the correct pictures.

I am a teacher and these are some of the people in my class. Liz is tall and she is thin. Her hair is long and blonde. Her eyes are blue and her nose is small. Her favourite activity in the class is listening to songs. Her favourite animal is the kangaroo and her favourite colour is yellow.

Tom is not very tall, he is not very thin. His hair is red and it is very short. His eyes are green and his nose is small. His favourite activity in the class is reading. His favourite animal is the dog and his favourite colour is red.

Sally is short and she is not very thin. Her hair is dark and it is very long. Her eyes are brown and her nose is small. Her favourite activity in class is grammar! Her favourite animal is the lion and her favourite colour is blue

Sam is tall and he is very thin. His hair is very short and it is brown. His eyes are blue and his nose is big. His favourite activity in class is speaking with his partner. His favourite animal is the piranha and his favourite colour is black.

ASSESSMENT TASK 7

Listen to the survey. Where are the people from?

Number one.

INTERVIEWER: Hi, can I ask you some questions, Tina?
TINA: Sure.
INTERVIEWER: Where are you from?
TINA: I'm from London.
INTERVIEWER: So, what kind of clothes do you wear at school?
TINA: Mmmm.... a brown skirt and a brown jacket– the uniform's horrible!
INTERVIEWER: And what about parties?
TINA: That's different.... I like short skirts and T-shirts...
INTERVIEWER: What about in the summer?
TINA: What summer? It's usually not very good in London. I wear trainers, jeans and T-shirts.
INTERVIEWER: Thanks very much Tina.

Number two.

INTERVIEWER: Hello Bobby, you're from Manchester aren't you?
BOBBY: That's right.
INTERVIEWER: What clothes do you wear at school?
BOBBY: Well, we haven't got a uniform– jeans and shirts and jackets.
INTERVIEWER: What about parties?
BOBBY: I really like fancy dress– Dracula, Frankenstein... that sort of thing.
INTERVIEWER: And in the summer?
BOBBY: We go to Spain in the summer – I always wear shorts and T-shirts.
INTERVIEWER: Thanks Bobby

Number three.

INTERVIEWER: Hi, Pam. What clothes do you wear at school?
PAM: A uniform– the usual thing–a jacket and skirt.
INTERVIEWER: And what about parties?
PAM: It depends... I like long dresses and jackets...
INTERVIEWER: And in the summer?
PAM: Well, I go to the coast – I'm from Dublin in Ireland you know – I wear trainers, T-shirts and sometimes a big jersey – it's quite cold!
INTERVIEWER: Thanks very much.

ASSESSMENT TASK 11

Listen to the description of Richard's Castle, a village in England. Which eight places from the list are in the village? Underline them.

My village is called Richard's Castle and it is very small. It has got a very old church and it is very beautiful. It has got an old castle, also called Richard's Castle. There's one shop in the village, the village shop. And there's a hotel – also called The Castle! It's quite small and old, but it's got a swimming pool. My friends and I go swimming there in the summer. The hotel has got a good restaurant. On Sundays I eat there with my mum and dad. What else is in the village? Er, there's a doctor, Dr Robert, and his surgery is just next to the church. And there's a small factory. It makes tables and chairs. My mum works there. My village is very beautiful, I suppose, but it's a bit boring! There isn't a sports centre and there aren't any cinemas or discos – we don't even have a village festival. When I leave school, I want to live in a city.

ASSESSMENT TASK 15

Listen to the life story of Marco Polo and match the dates with the events.

Marco Polo was born in 1254. His father and his uncle both travelled a lot. Marco wanted to go with them to China. In 1271, when Marco was seventeen, they all left for Venice. They travelled on foot and by horse. They crossed the deserts of Asia by camel. After three years, in 1274, they arrived in China. Then a year later, in 1275, Marco went to see the emperor, Kublai Khan. Marco lived in the emperor's palace, learned the language and started to work for the emperor. He travelled around China and also went to India by boat. He lived in China for eighteen years, but then decided to leave China because he wanted to see his home again. He left in 1292. When he arrived in Venice, he told everybody about his travels. He died in 1324.

Assessment

Oral Assessment

Introduction

To find practical ways of carrying out oral assessment is vital. Assessment gives very strong messages to students: if speaking is not assessed students assume it is not important and make little effort.

In the section on informal assessment on page 96 there are detailed instructions for assessing speaking throughout the year.

In the self-assessment activities throughout the book (especially the *Module Checks*) there are also activities which get students to reflect on their speaking. Particular emphasis is paid to attitude and participation. If students make an effort and have a go, half the battle has been won.

A useful rating scale with criteria is supplied below. This can be used for informal assessment and oral interviews.

Students will be interviewed in pairs. They will be marked on their ability to communicate as well as on accuracy. Try to speak as little as possible during the interview; the students should speak while you assess their work. However, help where necessary. Each assessment task has three parts:

Part 1: Information gap

First give each student one of the information gap sheets. The first question is easy. The other questions vary but all include areas that have been covered in the course.

Part 2: Describing a picture

You can either use one of the pictures provided or choose other photos or drawings with lots of things happening. Put one of the pictures on the table and give students about thirty seconds to look at it. Point out the prompts to them. Ask students to describe the picture in turn. You may prompt them by asking, 'Describe the place,' 'What is happening now?' etc.

Part 3: Role-play

Give out one part of the role-play (A or B) to each student. Give students time to look at the information and the instructions.

Oral Assessment Criteria

Fluency (maximum 5 points)

5 Tasks performed extremely well, little hesitation.

4 Tasks performed well, some hesitation.

3 Tasks performed adequately.

2 Tasks performed adequately, language sometimes disjointed or irrelevant.

1 Response totally inadequate.

Accuracy (maximum 5 points)

5 Correct use of a wide range of structures and texts. Good pronunciation.

4 Good range of grammatical structures and lexis with few serious inaccuracies.

3 Adequate range of grammatical structures and lexis. Inaccuracies not causing serious misunderstandings.

2 Only a small range of grammar and lexis. Inaccuracies hampering understanding.

1 Many serious inaccuracies of grammar, lexis and pronunciation.

Assessment

Sheet A

Ask questions to find out this information from your partner.

Information
Name
Age
Favourite colour
How he/she goes to school

Now answer your partner's questions.

Sheet B

Ask questions to find out this information from your partner.

Information
Name
Brothers or sisters
Favourite number
Hobbies

Now answer your partner's questions.

Sheet C

Ask questions to find out this information from your partner.

Information
Name
Date of birthday
Favourite activity in class
Sports (he/she likes)

Now answer your partner's questions.

Sheet D

Ask questions to find out this information from your partner.

Information
Name
Telephone number
Favourite music
What time he/she goes to bed

Now answer your partner's questions.

Assessment

Part 2: Describing a picture

Picture 1

Look at the picture and answer the questions.

- What places can you see?
- What are the people doing?
- Where is the place in the picture?
- Do you like the place?

Picture 2

Look at the picture and answer the questions.

- What things can you see in the classroom?
- What are the students and teacher doing?
- What can you see out of the window?
- Is your classroom similar or different?

Assessment

120

Role-play 1: Student A

Ask your partner questions about his/her free time activities. Then answer his/her questions.

- favourite hobbies
- favourite games
- favourite sports
- favourite activities in the summer

Role-play 1: Student B

Answer your partner's questions about the free time activities you like. Then ask his/her questions.

- favourite hobbies
- computer games
- favourite sports
- favourite activities in the winter

Role-play 2: Student A

Ask questions about your partner's friends and family. Then answer his/her questions.

- names of friends and family
- occupations of family
- physical descriptions (for example, Can you describe your sister/brother?)
- their favourite activities

Role-play 2: Student B

Answer questions about your friends and family. Then ask your partner.

- names of friends and family
- occupations of family
- physical descriptions (for example, Can you describe your mother/father?)
- where your family goes in the summer/what you do in the holidays

Assessment

121

Reinforcement

A

Complete these sentences with these words.

are / are / are / are / is / is / am / am

1 María and Dolores _____ twins.

2 _____ Jaime sporty?

3 I _____ very quiet.

4 My parents _____ from Zaragoza.

5 _____ I a good student? Of course!

6 _____ you sociable?

7 Orange _____ my favourite colour.

8 Elephants _____ big animals.

B

Complete the sentences with these words.

Where / Who / What / What / Where / How

1 _____ old are you? I'm twelve.

2 _____ colour are penguins? Black and white.

3 _____ is Nigeria? In Africa.

4 _____ are they? My parents.

5 _____ is your brother's name? Jordi.

6 _____ are your grandparents from? Teruel.

C

Make these sentences negative.

1 Jabu is three.

_____

2 Panthers are yellow and brown.

_____

3 My grandmother is tall.

_____

4 I am very silly.

_____

5 You are from China.

_____

6 Orange is my favourite colour.

_____

7 I am from England.

_____

8 My parents are strange.

_____

D

Give the matching word.

1 mother   _father_

2 husband   _____

3 son   _____

4 sister   _____

5 grandson   _____

6 niece   _____

7 aunt   _____

8 grandfather _____

Revision

A

Correct these sentences.

1 Pablo is very good student.
   *Pablo is **a** very good student.*

2 His father called Miguel.

3 Where are from?

4 He not sociable.

5 Is kangaroo a mammal?

6 I from Ávila.

7 How old you are?

8 I'm twelve years.

B

Circle the odd one out. Then add a word to the group.

1 aunt / sister / niece / uncle / daughter

2 brother / grandmother / grandson / nephew / son

3 elephant / lion / strange / parrot / tiger

4 basketball / maths / art / English / geography

Extension

A

Read the following text and answer the true or false questions.

Good parents in Antartica

Penguins live in Antartica. They live in large colonies of many animals and they are very active. All penguins are good parents and the male Emperor penguins are probably the best parents in the world! They put the eggs on their feet and keep them warm because if the eggs are cold, there are no babies. It is very cold and dark, and they are hungry. The females go away and forget the eggs but the males do not move. They are strange and wonderful birds!

1 Penguins are not very sociable.

2 Penguins are excellent parents.

3 The female keeps the eggs warm.

4 The males eat a lot when they look after the eggs.

B

Write the opposites.

1 small

2 bad

3 male

4 warm

5 remember

Language Work-out

Module 2

Reinforcement

A

Complete these descriptions with *have/has got* or the verb *to be*.

1 Dracula _____ a black cape. He _____ long teeth but he _____ a nice smile. His hair _____ black.

2 E.T. _____ a long neck. He _____ four eyes, he _____ two eyes. His arms _____ long and thin.

3 The Pink Panther _____ red, he's pink. He _____ a beautiful limousine and he _____ a top hat.

4 The Simpsons _____ yellow. They _____ funny hair.

   Lucy _____ a trombone but Bart _____ a dog.

B

Reorder the words to make questions.

1 Mandy / volleyball / well / can / play
   _____

2 say / can / the / alphabet / you
   _____

3 green / her / are / eyes
   _____

4 have / brown / you / hair / got
   _____

5 cartoons / draw / well / you / can
   _____

6 tarantulas / are / animals / strange
   _____

C

Answer these questions with short answers.

1 Can you swim? _____

2 Have you got a cat? _____

3 Is Bart Simpson blue? _____

4 Can parrots fly? _____

5 Is a dog intelligent? _____

6 Has E.T. got a hat? _____

7 Can you draw well? _____

8 Are your eyes pink? _____

D

Fill in the blanks with the following words:

fly / boring / cartoons / ride / chess / alligator / moustache / cook

1 I haven't got a _____!

2 I can _____ a bicycle.

3 My father can _____ very well.

4 Luis has got an _____ for a pet.

5 I think 'The Simpsons' is a very _____ cartoon.

6 Can you play _____?

7 Batman can't _____!

8 My favourite _____ are Garfield and Snoopy.

Revision

A

Match the words with the correct definition.

1 green
2 parrot

3 Internet
4 cartoon
5 elephant
6 piranha

7 aunt
8 Antartica

a a funny drawing
b a fish that can eat people and animals!
c a very big mammal
d a bird that can speak
e yellow + blue
f a communication system

g a very cold continent
h my mother's sister

B

Find these words in modules 1 and 2. Write the missing letters.

1 very, very good: f _ _ _ _ _ _ _ _

2 a boring colour: _ _ _ y

3 a cat: _ _ _ _ h _ _

4 a school subject: _ _ s _ _ _ _

5 a job in the country: _ _ _ _ e _

6 a person in the family: _ i _ _ _ _

7 a part of the face: _ o _ _ _

8 an activity in water: _ _ i _

Extension

A

Read the following text and answer the questions.

Asterix

Asterix is a famous cartoon character from France. He is a small soldier and he fights the Romans all the time. He is as strong as Superman because he drinks a magic potion before attacking his enemies. Then he can run very fast and jump very high. His friends Obelix and Getafix live in the same village. Obelix can hunt and cook; Getafix is a magician. Asterix has got a little dog called Dogmatix and together they have many adventures. The Romans are afraid of Asterix and Obelix.

1 Where is Asterix from?

_____

2 Who does he fight?

_____

3 What can he do after he drinks the magic potion?

_____

4 Who are his friends?

_____

5 What is his dog's name?

_____

6 Is Getafix a farmer?

_____

Language Work-out

Module 3

Reinforcement

A

Complete these sentences.

Hello! My name _____ (be) Teresa and I _____ (collect) posters. My brother Pavel _____ (make) model aeroplanes and _____ (fly) them in the garden. They often _____ (crash). The walls of my room _____ (be) full of posters and the garden _____ (be) full of broken aeroplanes!

B

Make these sentences negative.

1 Celia and Mary make model cars.

_____

2 Eduardo is a champion football player.

_____

3 His sister reads books in French.

_____

4 The students in my class play chess after school.

_____

5 Alligators are sinister pets.

_____

6 Gill goes horse riding in the winter.

_____

7 Peter collects badges and coins.

_____

8 The boys play tennis in the street.

_____

C

Match the questions and the short answers.

1 Can you play beach volleyball in the gym?

2 Is a tarantula an insect?

3 Does chess come from Persia?

4 Are computer games expensive?

5 Are panthers black?

6 Does 'numismatics' mean collecting badges?

7 Do you go sailing in the summer?

8 Is chess a difficult game?

a Yes, it does.

b Yes, they are.

c Yes, it is.

d No, it isn't.

e No, you can't.

f No, it doesn't.

g No, they aren't.

h Yes, we do.

D

Write these questions.

1 Where / you / live?

_____

2 Live / you / in a city?

_____

3 Play / he / volleyball?

_____

4 Where / they/ go swimming?

_____

5 What / Miriam / collect?

_____

6 Simon / sail / model ships?

_____

Language Work-out

Revision

Extension

A

Complete these sentences with the following words:

make / keep / give / buy / canoeing / guitar / coins / chess

1 I play the _____ very well.

2 My sister plays _____ with my father.

3 I don't collect _____ because I think it's boring.

4 I _____ interesting stamps for my friends.

5 We often go _____ in the summer.

6 My brothers _____ model submarines.

7 My parents _____ money for my birthday.

8 I can _____ new posters for my collection.

B

Reorder the syllables and write the adjectives.

1 pen / ex / sive   _____

2 lous / vel / mar   _____

3 i / rig / nal / o   _____

4 lis / tic / rea   _____

5 a /cre / tive   _____

6 ing / cit / ex   _____

7 in / ing / terest   _____

8 na / al / tion / ter / in _____

A

An interesting hobby

If you like insects, observing ants can be a very interesting hobby. You can buy a transparent plastic box and fill it with sand. Then you catch as many black or red ants as possible and put them in the box. The ants start digging tunnels and if you have a queen ant, they lay eggs in their tunnels. Red ants live for about a year and a half. They eat almost anything: flies, corn flakes, bits of meat and bread crumbs. They make very good pets because you don't have to worry about their food if you go away for a week. They stay in one place, and they only bite if you put your finger in their tunnels!

Read the text and answer the questions.

1 Where can you put your ants? _____

_____

2 What do the ants do in the box? _____

_____

3 What kind of ant do you need to have eggs? _____

_____

4 How long do red ants live? _____

_____

5 Why do they make good pets? _____

_____

6 When do they bite? _____

_____

Language Work-out

Reinforcement

A

Mark the things below that you like (✓) and those you dislike (✗).

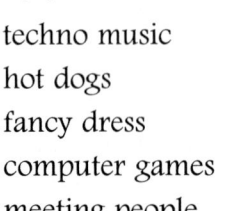

burgers

crisps

heavy metal

dancing

parties

techno music

hot dogs

fancy dress

computer games

meeting people

B

Replace the underlined words with pronouns:

him / we / it (x3) / she / them / us / they

1 <u>My parents</u> play tennis after work.

   They play tennis after work.

2 <u>The swimming pool</u> is in the park near our house.

   _____

3 <u>My sisters and I</u> often play with <u>our dogs</u>.

   _____

4 I'd like to dance with <u>Pablo</u>!

   _____

5 <u>Angeles</u> buys a new dress every week.

   _____

6 <u>The new dress</u> is usually very expensive.

   _____

7 Come to the party with <u>Montse and me</u>!

   _____

8 I love <u>this new music</u>.

   _____

C

Now write sentences using the words in A and the expression *I love, I don't mind* or *I hate.*

1 *I don't mind burgers.* _____

2 _____

3 _____

4 _____

5 _____

6 _____

7 _____

8 _____

9 _____

10 _____

D

Write short answers.

1 Do you study English? _____

2 Does a cowboy work with animals?

   _____

3 Does your teacher wear glasses?

   _____

4 Do nurses work inside? _____

5 Do you have spiky hair? _____

6 Does a pirate sail? _____

7 Does a dog sing?

   _____

8 Do alligators live in Spain? _____

Revision

A

Match the expressions.

Bad English	Good English
1 the sister of my mother	**a** my father's friends
2 the mother of my sister	**b** my friends' parents
3 the friends of my father	**c** my parents' friends
4 the father of my friends	**d** my mother's sister
5 the parents of my friends	**e** my friends' father
6 the friends of my parents	**f** my sister's mother

B

Complete the text with the following words.

music / fancy dress / ideal / dance / informal / have / hate / late

Our _____ party starts early and ends very _____ ! We play loud _____ and dance. We usually wear _____ clothes but during Carnival week we all wear _____ . We always _____ pizza and soft drinks. Our parents _____ heavy metal but they don't mind normal rock. Sometimes they even _____ with us!

Extension

A

Read the text and fill in the blanks.

Irish / colour / green / Ireland / food

♣ ♣ ♣ ♣ ♣ ♣ ♣ ♣ ♣ ♣ ♣ ♣ ♣ ♣ ♣ ♣ ♣ ♣ ♣ ♣
St. Patrick's Day

St. Patrick is the patron saint of _____ and March 17th is a national holiday in Ireland. In other countries it is also an important day for people of _____ origin. They wear the emblem of Ireland, the shamrock (a green leaf with three distinct parts) and in big cities like New York and Toronto, there are parades in the streets. All the Irish descendants wear something _____: a tie, a sweater, a dress, etc. Some people dye their hair green on that day! The beer in Irish pubs is green and sometimes the _____ is also green: green sandwiches, green mashed potatoes and even green eggs. Of course, green is the national _____ of Ireland, which is also called 'the Emerald Isle'.

♣ ♣ ♣ ♣ ♣ ♣ ♣ ♣ ♣ ♣ ♣ ♣ ♣ ♣ ♣ ♣ ♣ ♣ ♣ ♣

B

True or false? Say why.

1 The feast of St Patrick is celebrated in the summer. _____

_____

2 The shamrock is a plant. _____

_____

3 If you are Irish, your hair is green. _____

_____

4 Ireland is a part of North America. _____

_____

5 Ireland is an island. _____

Language Work-out

Reinforcement

A

Put each verb in the correct form and complete these sentences.

describe / carry / shake / wear / have / run / sit / give

1 Look! Luisa is _____ her new mini-skirt!

2 Pablo is _____ her a kiss.

3 Come in! We're _____ biscuits and lemonade.

4 The guide is _____ the city.

5 We're _____ in the garden and listening to the birds.

6 The mother monkey is _____ a baby.

7 She's _____ because she's afraid of the snake.

8 The match is over and the players are _____ hands.

B

Make the sentences in exercise A negative.

1 *Look! Luisa isn't wearing her new mini-skirt.*

2 _____

3 _____

4 _____

5 _____

6 _____

7 _____

8 _____

C

Write questions in the present continous.

1 you / eat / a hamburger?

_____

2 your teacher / smile?

_____

3 your classmates / write?

_____

4 you / listen / radio?

_____

5 your friend / talk / to you?

_____

6 I / wear / trainers?

_____

7 Ziggy / drink / petrol?

_____

8 Zed / fly / in a spaceship?

_____

D

Match the two parts of the sentences.

1 We've got   **a** television.

2 We sleep   **b** on Planet Earth.

3 We go   **c** eight hours a day.

4 We wear   **d** two arms and two legs.

5 We watch   **e** warm clothes in the winter.

6 We live   **f** to school during the week.

7 We sit   **g** hands.

8 We shake   **h** down quickly.

Revision

A

Write the advice for the Zorgons.

1 Zed is sitting on the TV.
   Don't sit on the TV.

2 Zag is kissing the dog.
   _____

3 Ziggy and Zog are eating the goldfish.
   _____

4 Zag is jumping on the sofa.
   _____

5 Zed isn't listening to you.
   _____

6 Ziggy and Zog aren't eating the icecream.
   _____

7 The Zorgons aren't speaking quietly.
   _____

8 The spaceship is going in three minutes.
   _____

B

Complete these questions.

1 _____ are you eating? A piece of cake.

2 _____ is he watching? A cartoon.

3 _____ are you talking to? My friend.

4 _____ is the alien laughing? Because humans look funny.

5 _____ are you going? To the cinema.

6 _____ are they going to the park? After school.

7 _____ are you running? Because I'm late.

8 _____ old are your parents? I don't know.

Extension

A

Read the text and fill in the blanks.

vegetables / cold / ice / moon / energy / water

Astronauts can live on the _____ if they have oxygen. Their special space suits protect them against the _____ and dangerous radiation. Of course, they also need food and water. Is there _____ on the moon? Scientists are investigating this. They think there may be water in the form of _____. If this is true, we can probably cultivate _____ on the moon with the help of solar _____.

B

Answer the questions.

1 What three things are necessary to survive on the moon?
   _____

2 What two dangers are there?
   _____

3 In what form is the water on the moon?
   _____

4 What energy can help astronauts?
   _____

Language Work-out

Module 6

Reinforcement

A

Complete these sentences about a place you know.

art gallery / bus station / church / cinema / disco / hotel / park / restaurant / school / sports centre / supermarket

1 There is a _____, but there aren't any _____

2 There _____ and there _____

3 Near the _____ there are _____ and there _____ also some _____

4 Are there _____? Yes, _____

5 It's an interesting place because _____

B

Complete these questions and write short answers about your town.

1 Is there _____cinema? _____

2 Are there _____ English banks? _____

3 Is there _____ public swimming pool? _____

4 Is there _____ bus station near your school? _____

5 Are there _____ hotels? _____

C

Complete these dialogues.

pounds / please / some / help / Thank you / much / like / Goodbye / sorry / any

1 A: Can I _____ you?

   B: Yes, I'd _____ some chocolate, please.

2 A: How _____ is that?

   B: That's three _____, please.

3 A: I'd like _____ crisps, _____.

   B: I'm _____. We haven't got _____.

4 A: Here you are.

   B: _____ very much. _____!

D

Make these sentences negative.

1 There is a big cinema here.

   _____

2 I have some ice-cream.

   _____

3 You are buying some crisps.

   _____

4 He can see some lions.

   _____

5 They are making a fire.

   _____

6 I have got some good books.

   _____

Revision

A

Write the correct form of the verb - is or are.

1 There _____ some beautiful parks in Madrid.

2 _____ there a hotel in your village?

3 There _____ many small villages in the mountains.

4 _____ there any good beaches here?

5 There _____ a police officer on the corner.

6 There _____ many famous castles in this area.

7 I think there _____ a good restaurant on this street.

8 _____ there any shops open on Sunday?

B

Underline the correct word.

1 Have you got (some / any) banana ice-cream?

2 I'd like (some / any) postcards, please.

3 We can't buy (some / any) cold lemonade here.

4 I want (some / any) sweets and a packet of crisps.

5 There are (some / any) very funny comics on that shelf.

6 Is there (some / any) coffee in the pot?

7 I can't see (some / any) CDs that I like.

8 Have they got (some / any) friends in the village?

Extension

A

Read the text and fill in the blanks.

children / rooms / hot / villages / outside / fish / tree / food

Small _____ in Venezuela are quite poor. There are always many _____ running around and playing. Pigs and chickens look for _____ in the streets. If the village is near the sea, they eat _____! The houses are made of adobe or cement blocks. There are usually two _____; the kitchen and the living-room. The bathroom is often under a _____! Families usually sleep _____ because it is very _____, even at night.

B

Answer the questions.

1 Are villages usually rich?

_____

2 What do the pigs and chickens sometimes eat?

_____

3 What are the houses made of?

_____

4 How many rooms are there usually in the houses?

_____

5 Are there bathrooms in the houses?

_____

6 Why do the people sleep outside?

_____

Language Work-out

Module 7

Reinforcement

A

Reorder the words to make sentences.

1 the / used / for / buffalo / clothes / skins / Indians

_____

_____

2 learned / horses / to / they / ride

_____

_____

3 Indians / were / parents / good / the

_____

_____

4 in / Billy the Kid / a man / a gunfight / killed

_____

_____

5 rocking / Laura's / in / was / her / chair / mother

_____

_____

6 Laura / in the / lived / Big Woods

_____

_____

B

Complete the text with these words and the past tense of the verbs.

dangerous / excellent / hunt / name / east / born

Buffalo Bill

Buffalo Bill's real ¹ _____ was William Cody. He was ² _____ in Iowa in 1846. When he was 14 years old, he ³ _____ (join) the Pony Express. He was an ⁴ _____ horse rider and he ⁵ _____ (cross) the country from

⁶ _____ to west with important letters and parcels. This was a very

⁷ _____ job because the Indians and the bandits ⁸ _____ (attack) the Pony Express riders. When he was about twenty years old, he

⁹ _____ (start) to ¹⁰ _____ buffaloes. He ¹¹ _____ (kill) more than 4,000 animals in sixteen months and this is why they

¹² _____ (call) him Buffalo Bill.

C

Make the sentences in exercise A negative.

1 _____

_____

2 _____

_____

3 _____

_____

4 _____

_____

5 _____

_____

6 _____

_____

Revision

A

Correct the mistakes in the sentences.

1 There was an Indian in the tepee?

_____

2 Butch Cassidy were a robber.

_____

3 The sheriffs wasn't in the prison.

_____

4 Annie Oakley's father died when she has nine.

_____

5 The Indians wasn't happy in the towns.

_____

6 There were any lights in Laura's house?

_____

B

Match a word from the first column with a word from the second one.

1 animal   a competition
2 log   b West
3 shooting   c chair
4 Wild   d stories
5 Native   e cabin
6 rocking   f skins
7 true   g Americans

Extension

A

Read the text and answer true or false. Say why.

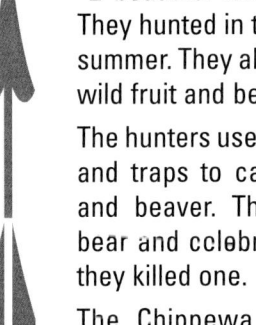

The Chippewa Indians lived in the beautiful forests of Ontario, in Canada. They hunted in the winter and fished in the summer. They also planted corn and picked wild fruit and berries.

The hunters used bows and arrows, spears and traps to catch deer, rabbits, caribou and beaver. They greatly respected the bear and celebrated a special feast when they killed one.

The Chippewa lived in oval huts with rounded roofs. These huts were called wigwams.

Fortunately, Europeans were not interested in forests and the Indians were able to stay on their ancestral lands, although their world changed after they obtained guns and alcohol from the white man.

1 The Chippewa were Plains Indians.

_____

2 They hunted and fished in the summer.

_____

_____

3 They cultivated corn. _____

4 The beaver was a special animal for them.

_____

5 They lived in huts called wigwams.

_____

6 The Europeans wanted the Chippewa

lands. _____

_____

Language Work-out

Module 8

Reinforcement

A

Put these verbs in the past simple tense.

1 Last year, my brother and I _____ (go) on a camping holiday.

2 We _____ (sleep) in a big, comfortable tent.

3 We _____ (eat) lots of bread and cheese.

4 We _____ (drink) water from the fountain.

5 In the afternoon, we _____ (swim) in the river.

6 We _____ (meet) lots of new friends from other countries.

7 In the evenings, we _____ (sit) around the campfire and _____ (sing) folk songs.

B

Write questions for the following answers.

1 We went to Germany for our holidays. (Where)

_____

2 We learned some German expressions. (What)

_____

3 We met young people from other countries. (Who)

_____

4 No, we didn't take any photos.

_____

5 We left Madrid on the 25th of July. (When)

_____

C

Look at the table. Write sentences about Arantxa in the affirmative (+) or the negative (-).

Last summer:

1 go to England on holiday (–)
2 learn some Italian with friends (+)
3 read lots of books and comics (+)
4 go sailing on the lake (–)
5 forget her sister's birthday (–)
6 meet nice people at the swimming pool (+)
7 eat too much ice cream (–)
8 have a big party at the end of the summer (+)

1 _Arantxa didn't go to England on holiday._

2 _____

3 _____

4 _____

5 _____

6 _____

7 _____

8 _____

Revision

A

Underline the correct word in these sentences.

1 How many people are there in *you/your* class?

2 Beatriz plays tennis with *her/his* brother.

3 Did you watch *our/we* video last night?

4 *Their/They* mum works in a shop.

5 *Our/Us* father is a dentist.

6 *My/I* teacher helped me to read.

7 Billy killed *she/his* girlfriend in a gunfight.

8 Does *he/his* brother collect stickers?

B

Match the questions and short answers.

1 Did Gulliver swim to England?   **a** Yes, it was.

2 Was he a Viking?   **b** No, they didn't.

3 Did the Vikings explore Iceland?   **c** Yes, he was.

4 Were the Vikings short and dark?   **d** Yes, they did.

5 Was Leif Erik's son?   **e** No, he wasn't.

6 Was the *Hindenburg* an airship?   **f** No, he didn't.

7 Did it arrive to the USA?   **g** No, they weren't.

8 Did the passengers return to Europe?   **h** Yes, it did.

Extension

A

Read the text. List the verbs in the past tense and write the infinitives.

Faith Annan escaped from Mozambique with her little son on a fishing boat in 1975. Her husband didn't escape. A rebel soldier shot him and he died in prison. Faith's journey was very difficult. First she wore clothes like an old woman from the country. She walked and travelled at night. She hid in the bushes and slept during the day. When she got near the coast she rode on an old bicycle that she found under a tree. She carried her son on her back all the way. When he cried she gave him little bits of bread and fruit to eat. She was very frightened. She didn't want him to cry and attract the attention of the soldiers on the road because she didn't have any travel documents. In the end she found a man who helped them. He hid Faith and her son in his car and drove them to the boat. Faith was sad to leave her country but she was happy to be alive.

_____

_____

_____

_____

B

Answer these questions.

1 Which country did Faith escape from?

_____

2 How did her husband die?

_____

3 How many different kinds of transport did she use in her escape?

_____

4 What did they eat?

_____

5 Why was she frightened of the soldiers?

_____

6 How did the man help them?

_____

Language Work-out

Language Work-out key

Language Work-out

Module 1

Reinforcement

A
1 are
2 Is
3 am
4 are
5 am
6 Are
7 is
8 are

B
1 How
2 What
3 Where
4 Who
5 What
6 Where

C
1 Jabu isn't three.
2 Panthers aren't yellow and brown.
3 My grandmother isn't tall.
4 I'm not very silly.
5 You aren't from China.
6 Orange isn't my favourite colour.
7 I'm not from England.
8 My parents aren't strange.

D
1 father
2 wife
3 daughter
4 brother
5 granddaughter
6 nephew
7 uncle
8 grandmother

Revision

A
2 His father is called Miguel.
3 Where are you from?
4 He's not sociable.
5 Is the kangaroo a mammal?
6 I'm from Ávila.
7 How old are you?
8 I'm twelve / I'm twelve years old.

B
1 uncle
2 grandmother
3 strange
4 basketball

Extension

A
1 F 2 T 3 F 4 F

B
1 large / big
2 good
3 female
4 cold
5 forget

Module 2

Reinforcement

A
1 has got/has got/hasn't got/is
2 has got/hasn't got/has got/are
3 is not/has got/has got
4 are/have/has got/has got

B
1 Can Mandy play volleyball well?
2 Can you say the alphabet?
3 Are her eyes green?
4 Have you got brown hair?
5 Can you draw cartoons well?
6 Are tarantulas strange animals?

C
3 No, he isn't.
4 Yes, they can.
5 Yes, it is.
6 No, he / it hasn't.
8 No, they aren't.

D
1 moustache
2 ride
3 cook
4 alligator
5 boring
6 chess
7 fly
8 cartoons

Revision

A
1 e 2 d 3 f 4 a 5 c
6 b 7 h 8 g

B
1 fantastic
2 grey
3 panther
4 history
5 farmer
6 sister
7 mouth
8 swim

Extension

A
1 France.
2 The Romans.
3 He can run very fast and jump very high.
4 Obelix and Getafix.
5 Dogmatix.
6 No, he's a magician.

Module 3

Reinforcement

A
is; collect; makes; flies; crash; are; is

B
1 Celia and Mary don't make model cars.
2 Eduardo isn't a champion football player.
3 His sister doesn't read books in French.
4 The students in my class don't play chess after school.
5 Alligators aren't sinister pets.
6 Gill doesn't go horse riding in the winter.
7 Peter doesn't collect badges and coins.
8 The boys don't play tennis in the street.

C
1 e 2 d 3 a 4 g 5 b
6 f 7 h 8 c

D
1 Where do you live?
2 Do you live in a city?
3 Does he play volleyball?
4 Where do they go swimming?
5 What does Miriam collect?
6 Does Simon sail model ships?

Revision

A
1 guitar
2 chess
3 coins
4 keep
5 canoeing
6 make
7 give
8 buy

B
1 expensive
2 marvellous
3 original
4 realistic

5 creative
6 exciting
7 interesting
8 international

Extension

A

1 In a transparent plastic box.
2 They dig tunnels.
3 Queens.
4 About a year and a half.
5 Because they don't need food every day.
6 When you put your fingers in the box.

Module 4

Reinforcement

B

2 It
3 We / them
4 him
5 She
6 It
7 us
8 it

D

1 Yes, I do.
2 Yes, he does.
3 Yes, he / she does. No, he / she doesn't.
4 Yes, they do.
5 No, I don't. Yes, I do.
6 Yes, he does.
7 No, it doesn't.
8 No, they don't.

Revision

A

2f 3a 4e 5b 6c

B

1 ideal
2 late
3 music
4 informal

5 fancy dress
6 have
7 hate
8 dance

Extension

A

Ireland; Irish; green; food; colour

B

1 False. It is celebrated in the spring.
2 True
3 False. You can if you want to.
4 False. It is a part of Europe.
5 True

Module 5

Reinforcement

A

1 wearing
2 giving
3 having
4 describing
5 sitting
6 carrying
7 running
8 shaking

B

2 Pablo isn't giving her a kiss.
3 We're not having biscuits and lemonade.
4 The guide isn't describing the city.
5 We aren't sitting in the garden.
6 The mother monkey isn't carrying a baby.
7 She's not running because she isn't afraid of the snake.
8. The match isn't over and the players aren't shaking hands.

C

1 Are you eating a hamburger?
2 Is your teacher smiling?
3 Are your classmates writing?
4 Are you listening to the radio?
5 Is your friend talking to you?
6 Am I wearing trainers?
7 Is Ziggy drinking petrol?
8 Is Zed flying in a spaceship?

D

1 d   2 c   3 f   4 e   5 a
6 b   7 h   8 g

Revision

A

2 Don't kiss the dog.
3 Don't eat the goldfish.
4 Don't jump on the sofa.
5 Listen to me.
6 Eat the ice-cream now.
7 Speak quietly.
8 Get into the spaceship.

B

1 What
2 What
3 Who
4 Why
5 Where
6 When
7 Why
8 How

Extension

A

moon; cold; water; ice; vegetables; energy

B

1 Oxygen, food and water.
2 The cold and the radiation.

3 In the form of ice.
4 Solar energy.

Module 6

Reinforcement

B

1 a
2 any
3 a
4 a
5 any

C

1 A help; B like
2 A much; B pounds
3 A some, please B sorry, any
4 B Thank you, Goodbye

D

1 There isn't a big cinema here.
2 I haven't got any ice-cream.
3 You aren't buying any crisps.
4 He can't see any lions.
5 They aren't making a fire.
6 I haven't got any good books.

Revision

A

1 are
2 Is
3 are
4 Are
5 is
6 are
7 is
8 Are

B

1 any
2 some
3 any
4 some
5 some
6 any

Language Work-out key

7 any
8 any

Extension

A

villages; children; food;
fish; rooms; tree; outside;
hot

B

1 No, they are usually
   poor.
2 Fish.
3 Adobe or cement
   blocks.
4 Two.
5 No, there aren't.
6 Because it is very hot.

Module 7

Reinforcement

A

1 The Indians used
   buffalo skins for
   clothes.
2 They learned to ride
   horses.
3 The Indians were good
   parents.
4 Billy the Kid killed a
   man in a gunfight.
5 Laura's mother was in
   her rocking chair.
6 Laura lived in the Big
   Woods.

B

1 name
2 born
3 joined
4 excellent
5 crossed
6 east
7 dangerous
8 attacked
9 started
10 hunt
11 killed
12 called

C

1 The Indians didn't use
   buffalo skins for
   clothes.
2 They didn't learn to
   ride horses.
3 The Indians weren't
   good parents.
4 Billy the Kid didn't kill
   a man in a gunfight.
5 Laura's mother wasn't
   in her rocking chair.
6 Laura didn't live in the
   Big Woods.

Revision

A

1 Was there an Indian
   in the tepee?
2 Butch Cassidy was a
   robber.
3 The sheriffs weren't in
   the prison.
4 Annie Oakley's father
   died when she was
   nine.
5 The Indians weren't
   happy in the towns.
6 Were there any lights
   in Laura's house?

B

1 f 2 e 3 a 4 b 5 g
6 c 7 d

Extension

A

1 False. They lived in
   forests.
2 False. They hunted in
   the winter and fished
   in the summer.
3 True
4 False. The bear was.
5 True
6 False. They were not
   interested in forests.

Module 8

Reinforcement

A

1 went
2 slept
3 ate
4 drank
5 swam
6 met
7 sat / sang

B

1 Where did you go for
   your holidays?
2 What did you learn?
3 Who did you meet?
4 Did you take any
   photos?
5 When did you leave
   Madrid?

C

2 She learned some
   Italian with friends.
3 She read lots of books
   and comics.
4 She didn't go sailing
   on the lake.
5 She didn't forget her
   sister's birthday.
6 She met nice people at
   the swimming pool.
7 She didn't eat too
   much ice cream
8 She had a big party at
   the end of the summer.

Revision

A

1 your
2 her
3 our
4 Their
5 Our
6 My
7 his
8 his

B

1 f 2 e 3 d 4 g 5 c
6 a 7 h 8 b

Extension

A

escaped/escape
shot/shoot
died/die
wore/wear
walked/walk
travelled/travel
hid/hide
slept/sleep
rode/ride
found/find
carried/carry
cried/cry
helped/help
drove/drive

B

1 Faith escaped from
   Mozambique
2 Her husband was shot
   by a rebel soldier.
3 She used four kinds of
   transport: she walked,
   rode on a bicycle,
   travelled by car and by
   boat.
4 They ate bread and
   fruit.
5 She was frightened
   because she didn't
   have any travel
   documents.
6 The man hid Faith and
   her son in his car and
   drove them to the boat.

1

1 is; 2 condition; 3 'm; 4 Is; 5 are; 6 old; 7 is

2

1 yes; 2 no; 3 Yes; 4 No, they're; 5 he is; 6 information;
7 sentence; 8 What; 9 is; 10 Africa; 11 old; 12 twelve

3

1 ability; 2 can; 3 can't; 4 Can; 5 Yes; 6 Batman

4

1 possession; 2 got; 3 haven't; 4 have; 5 you; 6 No

5

1 habitual; 2 singular; 3 don't; 4 doesn't; 5 s; 6 gives;
7 live; 8 doesn't; 9 don't

6

1 do; 2 does; 3 s; 4 comics; 5 Yes; 6 Do; 7 don't

7

1 like; 2 love; 3 mind; 4 OK; 5 don't like; 6 hate; 7 like;
8 my parents; 9 mind; 10 hates

8

1 nouns; 2 They; 3 She; 4 adjectives; 5 my; 6 Our;
7 possession; 8 before; 9 plural; 10 after; 11 cowboy's;
12 pirates'; 13 boy's

9

1 continuous; 2 present; 3 ing; 4 wearing; 5 aren't;
6 am

10

1 present; 2 now; 3 going; 4 Are; 5 aren't

11

1 present; 2 not; 3 isn't; 4 are; 5 Is; 6 aren't

12

1 a; 2 affirmative; 3 negative; 4 some; 5 any;
6 questions; 7 some; 8 any; 9 any

13

1 past; 2 Regular; 3 didn't; 4 loved; 5 hunted; 6 kill;
7 didn't

14

1 condition; 2 present; 3 where; 4 age; 5 were; 6 was;
7 was; 8 nine

15

1 questions; 2 did; 3 -d or -ed; 4 Did; 5 didn't; 6 swim

16

1 -d or -ed; 2 irregular; 3 didn't; 4 did; 5 made;
6 make; 7 Did

Grammar File

141

Your Own Notes